Boys and Girls at Play

EVELYN GOODENOUGH PITCHER
LYNN HICKEY SCHULTZ

BOYS
AND GIRLS
AT PLAY
the development
of sex roles

Bergin & Garvey Publishers, Inc.
Massachusetts

Photographs on pp. i, ii and iii courtesy of the Eliot-Pearson Children's School, Tufts University.

Library of Congress Cataloging in Publication Data

Pitcher, Evelyn Goodenough.
   Boys and girls at play.
   Bergin & Garvey Publishers, Inc.
   Bibliography: p.
   Includes index.
   1. Play.   2. Sex role.   3. Child psychology.
I. Schultz, Lynn.   II. Title.
HQ782.P513   1983   305.3   82-16579
ISBN 0-03-063203-X
ISBN 0-89789-055-8

All rights reserved
Bergin & Garvey Publishers, Inc.
670 Amherst Road
South Hadley, Massachusetts 01075

56789   056   987654321

Printed in the United States of America

Contents

List of Figures

List of Tables

Foreword

Boys and Girls at Play makes a very real contribution to the literature on sex role learning and behavior. This work makes it clear that boy-girl differences appear early and are reinforced by peer interactions and by same sex exclusivity. In addition the research is placed in a theoretical as well as a biological and social historical context that spells out the meaning and implications of these findings for parenting and for early childhood education.

Any solid piece of work, such as this one, speaks to many issues over and above those that were directly dealt with by the authors. It would be fascinating, for example, to see whether these observations on the "domestication of girls" and the "vying for power" among boys would be true in the commmunal child rearing settings of socialist countries such as Russia and China. One suspects that, despite the social system, the observations reported here would hold true, though perhaps in some muted form.

A more general issue and one that the data speaks to more directly derives from the work on the development of personality in general. On the one hand are those who argue that personality is a bundle of abiding traits whereas on the other are those who insist that personaliy is hardly more than a response to a series of transient situations. Put somewhat differently, the latter position would argue that boys and girls would behave in the same way in some situations (say at the dinner table) but not at others (say in the play situations described here). From this perspective boy-girl differences are evoked by some situations and not by others.

Another version of this argument is that boys and girls do not learn roles which are general and abstract, so much as they learn "frames" that are specific and concrete. Frames are repetitive social situations marked by their own rules, understandings and expectancies. "Going to bed" is a frame in the sense that it is a repetitive social situation with its own rules, expectancies and understandings. When told to go to bed the rule is that a little bit of protest is called for but not too much. One can also make demands (to be kissed, tucked in) that could not be made at other times.

The play activities that make up the setting for the observations reported here are clearly frames. Although the overall structure of the play frame and limits are set by the adults, what is fascinating here is that children are in a sense creating their own frame rules, they are dictating what expectancies, what understanding and what rules are to obtain in this repetitive social situation. Although children are heavily framed by adults, the observations provide evidence that children themselves can create frame rules that differ for the sexes.

In short these data speak for a personality or abiding concept of sex role learning rather than a transient one. This is true because it appears that even young children can create their own frames and that these are not necessarily learned from or instilled by parents or care takers. If children spontaneously construct frames that differ for boys and girls then it would seem that the traits determine the situation rather than the other way around. So the data provided here both raise and provide some additional evidence for the trait versus situation controversy regarding sex roles.

The last and most vexing issue is how much do young children really learn from their peers? Again, there are two polls of opinion. One group would argue that the effect of peers in early childhood is minimal. First because the primary attachment is to parents second, because cognitively children can't relate to the peer's perspective and, finally, because emotionally they are not sufficiently involved with other children to have much impact upon them. From this point of view, young children would have little impact on other children's learning.

On the other hand, the growing body of research in the response of even infants to peer groups, the group spirit displayed by children growing up in communal settings and data such as that presented in the present report speak for the importance of the peer group in the social learning of young children albeit in a different manner than say the impact of school age or adolescent peers.

That is to say, peer group learning in the early childhood years seems to one of enhancement and facilitation of spontaneously demonstrated propensities. Boys and girls come to a social setting with a certain "readiness" to learn sex related behaviors. The peer group activity seems to elicit this behavior and to support and reinforce it without being its primary instigator. Here again the study makes a most valuable contribution by demonstrating that peer group influences operate in different ways at different age levels but that they are not the less important therefore.

In short this impressive observational study speaks to many contemporary issues of social learning in addition to sex role learning. It will be of interest and of value to all those who study and work with young children.

David Elkind, Ph.D.
Professor and Chairman
Eliot-Pearson Dept. of Child Study
Tufts University
Medford, Massachusetts

Acknowledgments

The children observed in play were members of nursery school or kindergarten groups in the greater Boston area: Eliot-Pearson Children's School, Tufts Day Care Center, Clarendon Hill Nursery School, Radcliffe Day Care Center, Oxford Nursery School, Newtowne School, Plymouth Nursery School, and Gloucester Nursery School. We are grateful to these organizations for their cooperation in making the children available.

Play sessions were observed and recorded by the two authors, and by students in the Department of Child Study at Tufts University: Penelope Hauser Cram, Ellen Golding, Carol Baker, Pat Hartvigsen, Jan Emlen, Susan Perry, Sally Prescott, and Franklin Porter. Ms. Cram, Ms. Golding, and Ms. Baker also gave substantial help in establishing the validity of the coding procedures. In the pilot stage of the study Ms. Cram, a graduate student and research assistant in child study, worked with the senior author in formulating hypotheses, refining coding categories, and overall planning. Lynn Schultz, a graduate student who worked as a research assistant in 1977–1979, supported by federal funding, was responsible for the computer and statistical analyses of the data, and became co-author of this book. Rena Pine, another graduate student and research assistant, helped with the data analyses and literature review in 1978–1979.

David Lubin and Terrance Tivnan, faculty in the Tufts Department of Child Study, gave consulting services for statistical and design procedures. The authors would like to express gratitude to other faculty members, particularly Fred Rothbaum, for their reading of the manuscript. Lynn Schultz would also like to thank John Hancock Mutual Life Insurance Company for the use of their computing equipment to prepare the manuscript while she worked as a programmer.

The study received the support of H.E.W. grant no. 1 R03-MH-30987-01 in 1977–1978, supplemented in 1978–1979 by funds granted through the Faculty Awards Committee at Tufts University from H.E.W. grant no. 1-S07-RRO7179-01.

Chapter 1 Peers as Agents of Sex Role Development

INTRODUCTION

Men and women tend to differ in predictable ways in personality and the performance of social roles. A consistent finding, in a compiliation of previous studies of sex differences in human beings, is that males are more active and aggressive and females more passive, affiliative, and nurturant.[1] These are *aggregate* (not individual) differences that have been characteristic of interests and values in our societies. Men have tended to be more interested in scientific, mechanical, political, and physically strenuous activities. Women have tended to prefer sedentary activities, social services (including the role of housewife), and literary, musical, and artistic endeavors. Men are "adventuresome, have enquiring minds, are proud of achievement. Women prefer to stay at home, accept conditions and are sensitive to social relationships."[2] Compelling data in the socialization literature indicate that sex differences occur cross-culturally. A classic study found that for men there is a consistent emphasis on self-reliance and achievement, whereas for women there is a consistent emphasis on "ministering to the needs of others."[3]

These observed dichotomies in the interests and values of males and females prompted the senior author's initial research in sex differences over twenty years ago. Her interest was stimulated and fostered by the fact that she had a boy child and a girl child. Although these children had the same parents, and, so far as she mistakenly assumed, a similar environment, she was struck again and again by what seemed to be their differing orientations to the world. Toys that were available appealed to one and not to the other. Styles of play were different even with the same materials. The boy's drawings favored wars, actions, and catastrophes. The girl's drawings were

1

2 BOYS AND GIRLS AT PLAY

primarily of people involved in domestic activities. Relations with people suggested that the girl was more sophisticated about and interested in understanding social relationships. Observations of the author's own children extended to observations of other children who seemed to confirm in their behaviors such differences as have been noted. Two major studies substantiated her hypotheses.[4]

The findings of the first study were that (a) parents, through their verbalizations, indicate that they believe their boys and girls differ in their interest in persons; (b) the father tends more than the mother to delineate differences in sex roles; (c) girls from 2 to 5 years of age already show greater interest in people than do boys of the same age range; (d) boys define their own sex roles more sharply than do girls. In the second study, stories told by young children were collected and analyzed, and several chapters were devoted to an examination of sex differences. The freely fantastic content of the stories showed clearly not only age differences but also significant contrast between the sexes in themes of socialization and aggression. Girls told many more stories of personal relationships, especially of families. Boys' tales had more themes of violence and destruction involving objects or nonhuman forces. Subsequent studies by other scholars have supported the findings about sex differences documented by these studies.

Interest in sex differences in young children has recently rekindled as studies of psychological sex differences in general have proliferated. Parents and schools have increasingly attempted to negate sex role stereotyping. As evidence accumulated to show the sex stereotyping that is evident in textbooks and children's literature, teachers and parents began to read Zolotow's *William's Doll* to boys and Lasker's *Mothers Can Do Anything* to girls.[5] Boys are now being encouraged to be nurses and girls to be doctors in their dramatic play. Girls are urged to play with blocks and trucks. There are now many more male teachers in preschools and elementary schools than there used to be, although female teachers still predominate.

Other types of contradictory information came to the attention of the senior author, indicating that not all sectors of the population manifested a changed view of sex role stereotypes. Her daughter, an ardent feminist, reported with pride that after singing "Away in the Manger" to her then 3-year-old daughter, the child said, "Sing it again, Mommy, and make Jesus a girl." The child, although exposed at home and school to the best nonsexist environment, seemed highly "feminine" in her interests and behaviors compared with her brother. The senior author's women friends were fundamentally involved in domestic and personal interests, even when they had professional skills. A colleague produced a study of contemporary children's drawings showing that boys overwhelmingly engaged in the drawing of war pictures, whereas girls did not spontaneously draw pictures of war and physical conflict.[6]

Many parents are continuing in subtle ways to reinforce sex role stereotypes. An intriguing study of the bedrooms of first-born young children documents how upper-middle-class families reinforced sex differences in children from under 1 to 6 years of age.[7] The content of their rooms showed that boys had more variety of objects than girls did. Boys' rooms contained far more toy animals in barns or zoos and objects relating to space, energy, and time (magnets, puzzles, spaceships). The girls' rooms contained more dolls, floral designs in fabrics and wallpapers, and ruffles and lace. Even though boys' rooms contained some dolls (of cowboys, for instance), almost none represented females or babies.

A cartoon of *Doonesbury* by Trudeau captures the ambivalence of socialization agents in dealing with contemporary sex role issues and the persistently different interests of boys and girls.[8] A teacher urges a recalcitrant girl in a nursery school to join a group of boys playing with blocks. At length the girl complies, enters the block area, and rapidly builds a structure which is superior in size and complexity to that of the boys. "Aw, Ms. Caucus, this is boring! I wanna play with my doll," says the girl. "All right, dear, you did give it a fair chance," says the teacher.

A vast quantity of publications by women scholars, journalists, and novelists have suggested that major shifts are taking place in attitudes toward sex roles and power relations between the sexes. Currently popular books include a scholarly historical and social study documenting that males were rapists from the beginning of history. Brownmiller argues that men's control over women in marriage began because of the possibility of rape and the need for protecting women from it.[9] In another book, Millet attacks Freud's concepts, alleging that they have been used to justify higher status for men than for women. She asserts that the effect of Freud's work was "to rationalize the insidious relationship between the sexes, to ratify traditional roles, and to validate temperamental differences."[10] Millet contends that Freud fails to note the fact that "woman is born female in a masculine-dominated culture which is bent upon extending its values even to anatomy and is therefore capable of investing biological phenomena with symbolic force."[11] An amusing book that attempts to counteract traditional stereotypes describes women as capable of multiple orgasms, sexual fantasies, and aggression toward men.[12]

Bombarded with the many thoughts arising from such considerations and readings, the senior author was prompted to return to more extensive observations of children's play in nursery schools. She wondered if all the new and liberating forces in contemporary culture would transform the children of the seventies. Would the striking differences found in 1957, and again in 1963, be dissipated or less apparent after a fifteen- or twenty-year interval during which changing attitudes toward the sexes permeated the culture?

Certainly the children looked different. The long hair of the boys, the popularity of long pants for both boys and girls, and their sex-neutral names made it initially difficult to identify which sex was being observed in the nursery schools, although the children themselves could always set one straight. They knew their own sex and also the sex of their peers.

The present study began in pilot form in 1974 with some random observations of the play of 5-year-olds from middle-income families. The preliminary observations focused on house areas, which are standard in preschool classrooms. Girls were the primary occupants of this area. They were mothers, sisters, babies. An occasional boy was part of the domestic scene. He could be the father (but the father role was not well developed) or baby, and he was usually fed. Boys were mostly excluded, however, told by girls that they couldn't participate even if they were just passing by. Groups of boys in other areas engaged in more varied fantasy play.

The observations of 5-year-olds were followed by observations of 2-, 3-, and 4-year-old children. The pilot study led to more systematic, large-scale observations of children's play during 1975–1978, and during this time the junior author joined the study. These observations provided the data that we report in this book. They suggested that boys' and girls' behaviors differed at each of the ages we studied, not only in the roles they adopted, but in the types of behavior favored by one sex or the other. Girls, for example, tended to be nurturant, whereas boys favored rough-and-tumble play. The preference for same-sex playmates also seemed to be pervasive, yet there seemed to be developmental differences at each age level. Although cooperative play seemed to increase as children grew older, subtle differences were evident in the amount and quality of affiliative, cooperative play as contrasted with nonaffiliative, noncooperative play at the different ages as boys and girls engaged in social contacts. There also seemed to be age and sex differences in the numbers of same-sex and cross-sex alliances among the children we observed.

We focused our attention on the influence children have on one another in forming gender identities, and on what the developmental progression seems to be. We were prompted to more specific analyses of children's play and to a wide reading of the literature. Readings in the literature on peer relations stress two common themes: peer relations may be as important to social development as associations with adults,[13] and there is relatively little developmental research concerning peer relations[14] (which is still true in 1982).

METHOD OF STUDY

We collected narrative accounts of the free play of 255 ch
through 5 at nine preschools between 1975 and 1978. Th
located in the Boston metropolitan area, included traditional nursery
schools, day-care centers, and Headstart programs, with mixed racial and
socioeconomic populations, ranging from working class to professional
families. Two-year-olds were underrepresented in the sample because of
their relative scarcity in formal preschool programs. Table 1 presents the
distribution of children according to age and sex.

Table 1   Distribution of Subjects by Age and Sex

		Age			
Sex	2	3	4	5	Total
Boys	17	39	38	36	130
Girls	16	40	36	33	125
Total	33	79	74	69	255

The observations were recorded during free play periods either in a
classroom or on the playground. The observers were the authors and seven
students familiar with children. Each observer followed one subject at a
time, selected in random order, and described in running-record form all
the child's social activities with peers during thirty minutes of continuous
observation. Almost every child was observed in each participating classroom. Occasionally, when a child was absent or when the teacher felt that
for some reason his behavior would not be typical (e.g., if he was not feeling
well), the random order was not followed.

The presence of the observer did not seem to inhibit the children's play.
The observers probably affected the social behavior displayed by the boys
and girls to some extent, but the young ages of the subjects minimized these
effects. Such limitations in control were offset because our observational
technique provided access to a much wider range of behavior than would
have been possible otherwise.

A broad sampling of natural behavior was essential to achieve our primary aim of investigating the influence of peer interaction on young children's sex role development. To accomplish this, we chose a method of
study that took into account both the form of peer play (social interaction)
and its fantasied content (sex role adoption) in a real-life, natural setting. We

sought to explore how preschoolers' play was related to the sex role system in which they would eventually participate.

Two excerpts from our running records of play episodes follow. In the first observation two 5-year-old boys explore various possibilities for building: a supercave, a gas station, a house. The house becomes a blasting station for sending rockets to the moon. The boys' ideas are imaginative and expansive. There is a strong spirit of camaraderie coupled with a vying for property. Object-grabbing actions are controlled, but physical confrontations could easily develop. The boys' play focuses on issues outside the home. They are aggressive with each other, and are attracted by power, fantasy, property, and action.

*   *   *   *

Adam and John

Adam and John go to play with blocks. They hand each other blocks.

John: "I have a space monster in the house, and the rocket comes out of the door and flies up in the air."

Adam: "This is going down in the ocean because he's bad." (He has a rubber gorilla wrapped in a flag.)

John: "I'm gonna make a supercave."

John: "Hey, don't do that again, ever-ever," when Adam puts a block in the wrong place. Adam ignores John's reprimand.

John: "Hey, I got a good idea. I want a lotta blocks." They cooperate in a building. Teacher comes to look.

John: "Guess what I'm gonna build? A gas station over here. This is pepper gas that makes you sneeze."

Adam: "I'll show you where the pepper is."

John: "Hey, we can share the pepper together. These can be at my house in case someone steals it out of your house."

Adam: "Yeah, I don't need it at my house because you have it at your house."

John: "Mine is a better house because you didn't make a good house. I like this one, I like this one."

Adam: "I like mine the best because yours is different."

John: "Hey, don't take wood from my property."

Adam: "Well, we're sharing wood."

John: "No!"

Adam: "O.K." He gives it back and gets new wood.

John: "This costs a lot of dollars."

Adam: "This costs a lot too. No one can take our wood. We can kill the joker. We can use our sneezer gun to kill the bad guys. We're the good guys."

John: "Hey, I need some of your wood, please? I'll just take two."

Adam: "*Here friend.*" *Adam tosses some wood.*

John: "*Don't throw it, it hurts me, it's not funny.*"

Adam: "*Every time there's a lightning storm, supergun can throw the whole thing away.*"

John: "*My gun can break up the whole sun storm.*" *He sneezes.*

Adam: "*Don't sneeze the sun storm away.*" *John continues to sneeze. Adam ignores it and keeps on blasting. Puts toy gorilla wrapped in flag on rocket.* "*Now I'm gonna do wrecking.*" *Knocks his structure down.*

John: "*Now don't knock mine down. Next time try to be careful.*"

Adam: "*O.K., I'm gonna blast it—now here goes.*"

Adam continues alone. "*Now that's good—here goes a blast.*"

*   *   *   *

The second episode describes the play of two 5-year-old girls in the same block area. This time the house is a "home," and roles of mother and daughter are clearly defined. The mother kisses and grooms her daughter, and gives her numerous directives. The daughter is attentive to household chores. When she shops she frugally guards her purchases, since both mother and daughter are money-conscious. The girls' play, unlike that of the boys, is subdued, bound to the reality of everyday life, and involved in home issues and interpersonal relations. The girls are gentle with each other and attentive to each other's well-being, and they articulate guidelines for appropriate behaviors.

*   *   *   *

Wanda and Mom

Two girls in block area have arranged a "house." Two more girls are coloring in a corner of the same space.

Wanda to the other girl (who assumes the role of "Mom"): "*Mom, I'm going shopping.*"

Mom: "*O.K.*"

Wanda walks out of room. Returns. Says, "*Ma, I got some new paper and magic markers.*"

"*Ma*" *kisses her and says,* "*O.K., put them over there.*"

Wanda goes to other side of house. Mom says as she puts papers in slot, "*They're very expensive, so don't waste them.*"

Wanda spends a long time arranging papers and magic markers. Board in house falls. Mom says to Wanda, "*This house isn't sturdy at all.*"

Wanda: "*Yeah,*" *then goes back to Mom.* "*Would you please, Mummy, move out of the way.*"

Mom: "Go to the grocery store and get some colored paper. Go out the door and turn left."

Wanda goes out again. Returns with more paper and gives it to Mom, saying, "You could use that for wallpaper or writing paper."

Mom: "Will you give me a yellow magic marker, honey?"

Wanda gives her one and takes the rest. "The magic markers will be in this bowl, Ma," *says Wanda.*

"O.K., honey," *says Mom.*

A boy comes up and says, "Can I play?"

Wanda: "No, there's already too many people here."

A girl comes and asks, "Can I play?"

Wanda: "Yeah, you can be the dog."

Girl: "I wanna be the sister."

Wanda: "No, we already have enough sisters. Take your shoes off and put them there, but be careful of the baby." *Girl moves to where directed, but becomes distracted by other play. She leaves to join the two other girls who are coloring in another part of the "house."*

Wanda goes over to these girls, and says to one, "I tell you to use the back and front 'cause you're wasting paper." *Girl turns paper over and draws on other side.*

Wanda: "Hey, Mom, hang this up." *She gives Mom paper. Mom takes it and puts it away.*

Mom strokes Wanda's hair, saying, "We're gonna be rich." *Wanda goes over and gets a jar of paper coins from shelf and gives it to Mom, saying,* "Yeah."

"Rich," *says Wanda.*

"I know, dear," *says Mom.*

One girl in corner of house says, "Stacey always bugs us and we never have time to be alone. I don't like her."

Wanda: "Whoever likes Stacey raise your hand." *No one does. Stacey cries,* "I want my Mummy." *Teacher takes her from the room.*

Wanda: "You know, Ma, I'm already finished. Ma, can I go to the zoo? Ma, can I go to piano lessons?"

Mom: "Yeah, take turns, don't fight."

*   *   *   *

The striking sex differences manifested in these two play episodes are representative of all those we observed. Our inquiry into the nature and function of these sex differences in the preschool years centered on the following questions:

1.   What is the developmental progression of sex differences in the play of preschool children?
2.   What qualitative aspects of behavior differentiate the play of boys from that of girls?

3. What are the influences, particularly from peers, shaping sex differences in these behaviors?
4. Is it possible, and advisable, to intervene in early childhood to alter
   the nature and course of traditional sex role development?

We coded the running records of the play episodes we collected into a
series of peer "contacts." Social contacts with peers were defined as direct
physical or verbal communications in which the subject of an observation
either attempted to engage another child in social interaction or responded
to another's initiation. Each of the subject's contacts with another peer was
coded as an interaction followed by a response, the simplest meaningful
sequence in a social interchange. For example, one boy asks another for a
block (initiation), and the other refuses to give it to him (response). This
initiation–response sequence forms one peer contact. The behaviors of
both the subject and the other child in each peer contact were coded to
specify: 1. content (positive or negative); 2. dyad (same-sex or cross-sex);
and 3. sequence (initiation or response).

The affiliative quality of each peer contact we recorded was a major
variable in the study. Each valid peer contact was coded as "positive" or
"negative." We expected that positive behaviors with peers would increase
as children developed social skills, but that negative behaviors might persist
among the boys, who tend to be more aggressive than girls. The two main
categories of positive and negative contacts were each composed of seven
subcategories. The overall positive and negative categories are defined in
Chapter 2, and the subcategories are defined in Appendix A and illustrated
in Chapter 3.

The sex composition of the dyad, or interacting pair, who participated in
each peer contact was a second important variable in our study. The dyad is
the simplest unit of social interaction in any group, in this case a class of
preschool children at play. All the peer contacts we coded focused on a
dyad, or pair, which included the subject. We coded only those play
behaviors in which the subject child was interacting with another child.
Even when the subject played in groups of three or four, we analyzed just
his or her interchange with the single other child who was most directly
involved in that particular social contact.

The dyadic context of social interactions describes those aspects of the
relationship between the actor and target (e.g., older–younger, male–
female) which exert a powerful influence upon behavior. Because we were
studying interactions among children of the same age, the factor of age
could not exert its usually powerful effect, and the factor of sex was
especially influential in play patterns we observed. When observing boys
and girls at play, we focused on whether the interacting dyad was boy/boy,

girl/girl, or boy/girl, and coded the dyadic context of each peer social contact as either "same-sex" or "cross-sex."

Sears and his followers recognized that an individual's social actions are contingent upon those of the other actor in the interaction, and should be observed in the dyadic contexts in which they occur.[15] The responses of one individual in an exchange provide stimuli for the subsequent behavior of the other. This sequential property of social interaction, which dyadic variables address—i.e., the reciprocal controls which dyad members exert upon each other to facilitate, inhibit, or redirect the course of an interchange—is particularly essential in research on preschool social development. The preschool years mark the initial formation of peer relationships. Children's social actions become increasingly "dyad specific," with increasing awareness of the identity of the other child in an interaction. Not only do boys and girls learn to differentiate their reactions to specific individuals when friendships develop, their general initiations and responses become increasingly dependent upon the sex of the other child.

The data, coded into these simple components of social interchange, were analyzed both with quantitative, statistical measures and with more informal, qualitative evaluations in the following ways:

1. Statistical analyses were performed on peer social contacts coded as "positive" or "negative." The frequencies (rates per half-hour) of positive and negative contacts were evaluated separately for same-sex and cross-sex dyads as well as for initiations and responses.
2. A descriptive analysis was made of sex differences in the types of positive and negative behaviors that boys and girls displayed in their free play with same-sex and cross-sex peers.
3. The sex roles children adopted during episodes of dramatic play were examined in a second descriptive analysis.

The statistical analyses of our quantitative data, presented in Chapter 2, document a series of changes between ages 2 and 5 in the positive and negative interactions boys and girls have with their same-sex and cross-sex peers. The quantitative results were compared with relevant theories and related studies. A developmental perspective guided both our specific effort to document the process by which preschool peer relationships contribute to sexual stereotyping and our more general goal to determine whether or not there are conditions in the preschool period which would promote malleability and change in contemporary sex roles. Relevant research procedures and statistical results are reported in Chapter 2 and Appendices C and D.

The qualitative evaluation of young children's social contacts presented in Chapter 3 affords important and interesting new data reflecting subtle sex differences in children's play, which complement those we describe in the statistical data. The judgments involved in assembling these data were based on comparisons of behavior. Although our method of making comparisons did not permit experimental rigor and control, the information we gathered is compatible with our other findings and with findings reported by other researchers.

The coding of behaviors from the running records involved identifying specific actions or verbalizations which could be designated as "molest," "assault," "admire," or whatever. In our attempt to evaluate whether or not qualitative differences emerged for discrete categories, depending upon their coming from a boy or a girl, we listed for each age and for each sex those specific words or actions which were the bases for the coding of behaviors (excluding the large category of sharing, which contained few sex differences). Not every action or verbalization revealed a qualitative difference: in many instances there was more similarity than difference in what boys and girls said or did.

Some judgments about qualitative differences presented more problems than others. The nonaffiliative category of disagreement or reprimand, for example, included many behaviors that were quite neutral in tone (such as "No" or "I won't"), but also included a number of behaviors which, in our opinion, seemed qualitatively different. In this behavior, girls, like the well-known Lucy in the *Peanuts* comic strip, tended to be the guardians of propriety, order, and superior know-how. "Come here, don't act foolish; don't grab the food and spill it," says a typical girl. Boys, on the other hand, tended to invoke property rights and rules of prior possession. "Hey, get off my road; you can't be here—it's mine." Molesting acts were also different in orientation. Rough-and-tumble play and nurturance were expressed in different modalities.

We isolated, listed, and compared specific verbalizations and actions which were not neutral in the behavior categories we identified. Nuances in behaviors probably occur so naturally, and at such a low level of salience, that it is difficult to appreciate their differences most of the time in the case of individual children. It is rewarding, however, to look at subtle differences in the behaviors of children *in groups*. In so doing we are able to catch the nuances of expression, the verbal reinforcements, both positive and negative, which contribute to the social learning process. There is a persistency and consistency in the quality of what boys and girls say and do which undoubtedly influences children's learning about themselves and how they are different because they are a male or a female.

We are well aware that qualitative appraisals sometimes tend to tell more about the eyes of the beholder than about the reality that is observed. Hopefully the examples we provide will, in their totality, convey that there are indeed many differences in the *style* of behaviors which have identical labels depending upon whether they come from a boy or a girl, or whether they are expressed in a same-sex or cross-sex context. Sex roles develop with cognitive and social skills. The age of the child, as well as the sex, tends to color behaviors and verbalizations. The specific verbalizations of children underline the potentially crucial role of language in sex role acquisition. We look at provocatively different qualitative aspects of behaviors as they exist among children at 2, 3, 4, and 5 years of age.

SEX ROLES AND PEER PLAY

The processes by which male and female infants become boys and girls are complex; hypotheses seem to outstrip currently available evidence. The issue of how human beings acquire sex role identity has been addressed, clarified, and confused by various scholars. In part, the confusion stems from the considerable effort which has been devoted to establish explanations of sex role development focused on a single cause. Since there seemed to be no common agreement about which routes to knowledge are the more significant ones, our theoretical orientation became a multifaceted one, embracing ethological, psychological, and sociological understandings as they related to our interests.

Theories of sex role development have generally emphasized the role of parents more than that of peers in the child's socialization. Theories of parental identification assume that the young child will inevitably view parental figures of the same sex as powerful and worthy of emulation. Freud paved the way, postulating how, during the Oedipal stage, sexual rivalries forced the child to identify, in terms of sex role, with the parent of the same sex.[16] Bandura saw more than parent figures involved in sex role learning.[17] In his view young children acquire sex role behaviors through imitation, identification, and observation of parents, teachers, media personalities, and peers. They are expected to do so, and selectively reinforced in doing so. It is interesting, for example, that girls do not notice and retain the details of modelled aggression to the same extent that boys do. According to this view, masculinity and femininity reflect norms and values that are internalized by children through direct transmission.

Bandura's social-learning studies are criticized by those who favor a cognitive-developmental approach. Those following this point of view protested that children's imitations and identifications are dependent on their current level of cognitive functioning. Kohlberg emerged as a leading theorist who emphasized that children very early develop an understanding of whether they are boys or girls.[18] Like other major explanations of sex role development, the cognitive-developmental view postulates that masculine and feminine attitudes reflect a sex role "identification." However, the identification concept differs in important ways in each theory. Kohlberg's conception of the process of identification "rests somewhere midway between the social-learning treatment of identification as a situational modeling or imitation, and the psychoanalytic treatment of identification as a sudden, totalistic and permanent incorporation of parental images."[19]

Whereas the other theories postulate that sex role values are acquired by the internalization of external cultural values, Kohlberg, in the Piagetian tradition, argues that children construct their own sex role values within a sex-typed social order. These values begin to develop once children learn whether they are boys or girls. Children learn appropriate gender self-labeling at 2 to 3 years of age, and in the next two years learn to label others correctly. Imitation of adult male or female figures is believed to derive from a general sex-typing factor, rather than a specific father or mother identification. Children perceive their behavioral similarities to others of the same sex and model their behavior accordingly. They tend to be quite orthodox in their interpretations of what is or is not appropriate for boys and girls. An important stimulus for young children is the sex of a peer, and interest in the same-sex almost precludes interest in the opposite sex as children tend to "overlearn" their gender, somewhat as they tend to "over-apply" a rule in language acquisition. Gender identity, i.e., cognitive self-categorization as "boy" or "girl," is regarded by Kohlberg as the critical and basic organizer of sex role attitudes and the most stable of all social identities.

The cognitive emphasis, however, does not pay adequate heed to studies which point out strong, inherited, biologically determined influences on sex role behaviors. Animal research not only indicates that males play more with males and females with females but also that males display higher levels of aggression than females, and females display more affiliative behaviors, including grooming and other modes of social exploration.[20] Harlow's findings indicate that the appearance of gender-related behaviors (e.g., passivity, withdrawal, rigidity, play roles, and grooming) occurs even in the absence of an opportunity for learning.[21] Furthermore, girls whose prenatal masculinization of the genitals was corrected at birth have activities and interests more common to boys. They are not particularly interested in grooming or in feminine clothing or paraphernalia.[22]

An excellent summary of theoretical postulations of scholars who have contributed to studies in sex role development concludes that what is missing from other research that focuses on biological characteristics or perceived similarities to other individuals is an "effective coupling of positive or negative feelings with specific patterns of behavior and thought."[23] Gardner in his general analysis attempts to come to grips with understanding a phenomenon such as James Morris, whose sex was masculine but whose psychosocial identity was feminine. Morris underwent hormonal treatment and surgery to change his sex. Gardner uses Morris's case history to plead for a study of sex role identity that would consider not only biological and cultural factors but the emotions that provoke specific behaviors and thoughts. "Any consideration of the process by which sex role identity is finally achieved," writes Gardner, "must take into account initial appearance, interaction with others, others' reactions to oneself, changing conceptions of self, pivotal experiences, goals, and numerous other factors."[24] Maccoby speculates provocatively about transsexuals, noting that isolation from same-sex playmates seems to be a common feature of their early history. "Perhaps the fact that they are not subject to this highly potent source of sex-typing pressure is related to their failure to assume the prescribed sexual identity."[25]

In significant and purposeful ways, children from 2 to 5 years of age prefer to play with members of their own sex. We could, following the reasoning of Kohlberg, assume that such choices are prompted cognitively. The young child learns a gender label and prefers play with same-sex peers. Although this is undoubtedly true, we hesitate to put too much emphasis on cognition as the major explanation for these choices of same-sex peers. As already stated, we are mindful that the overwhelming proportion of social play in monkeys also occurs between members of the same sex, and we are reluctant to attribute this to cognitive gender labeling. We must also stretch our thinking beyond documented differences between the sexes in toy preferences.[26] We have observed that even when boys and girls play with the same toy or engage in what may be classified as the same activities, their investment of interest and their manipulation of materials is different.

A classic (but disputed) study by Erik Erikson reveals sex differences in block play: boys tend to build structures that are that are tall and formidable; girls tend to build structures that are lower and have enclosed spaces.[27] A psychoanalytic interpretation of such differences is that these differing behaviors are external assertions of what makes their bodies unique. Boys intrude, with something like a tool, and the intrusive nature of the male sex organ is presumed to correspond to an active, pragmatic orientation to the world. Girls have an "inner space" in which babies can grow, which supposedly predisposes the female to commit herself to the love of a man and the care of offspring.

We witnessed repeatedly in our school observations that boys and girls take a different interest in materials in the environment. Boys are primarily concerned with the doll as an object. They probe hair, body and leg motions, and methods of removing clothes (rarely methods of adornment). Occasionally there are self-identifications with dolls, particularly with one deserving punishment. Noticeably lacking in the male approach to dolls is nurturance. Our records show little incidence of boys' cuddling, comforting, or caring for dolls, and no sustained interest in providing a sequence of baby needs—feeding, diapering, rocking, dressing, burping, entertaining. Girls, on the other hand, spend much time in nurturing activities when they play with dolls. Middleton offers an amusing conjecture about how boys and girls would use play materials differently:

> If some mad sociologist should ever settle a thousand little boys in a compound and give them dolls to play with and give footballs to a thousand girls in another compound, I feel certain that within a few days a small minority of the girls would be kicking and throwing the footballs around, while the majority would be cuddling their footballs and scolding them for being naughty. And I'd bet . . . that 60% of the boys would have dismembered their dolls to use the limbs and torsos for batting the heads about the compound; and the 10% who went in for cuddling would have had their dolls stolen for dismemberment by the majority.[28]

A striking illustration of different uses of the same space and equipment is available from observations of play involving a wooden structure. Such structures, common equipment in nursery schools, are two-story edifices with semi-enclosed play spaces on the lower and upper levels. This particular structure was equipped with tables, telephones, carpentry tools, some dishes, large pieces of cardboard, and tinker toys. A heavy rope hung from the upper to the lower area.

First three boys came to play in the structure. One boy seized a hammer and began to attach pieces of cardboard to the rails, announcing, "I'm making a police station. I'm a construction worker." Another boy shouted, "Hey, it's the lunch break. I'm the boss. Don't forget I have machine guns." The boys moved rapidly to the tinker toys, put them together in long wands, and shot at one another; one boy announced, "We're in a space ship." Then another boy jumped to the lower level, and attached his tinker toy to the rope. The boys adopted deep, commanding voices as they organized the descent or ascent of the tinker toys. "O.K., pull 'er up." "O.K., throw it down."

Shortly after the boys departed, girls came to the same area. At first they spent considerable time arguing who would control the telephone. One girl finally got the phone and, with pauses apparently geared to accommodating the imagined party in the conversation, said, "My sister's gonna go to the school . . . She takes ballet lessons." The other two girls arranged dishes on the table, put tinker toys on the plates, and said, "We have chopsticks for our Chinese food." Then one girl left the table, went to the lower level, picked up the rope, and held it to her ear, as though listening to a telephone. "I'm cooking breakfast. See you later," she announced before she skipped away. The other two girls followed her to another area.

It is clear from this observation that boys and girls view and use the same spaces differently. Boys see more varied, active, and violent possibilities in the structure. They are construction workers, building a police station. One boy is the boss, with machine guns. Almost simultaneously, the boys are warriors. The structure is a space ship and they shoot one another. Girls, on the other hand, view the structure as a house, where they prepare food and care for children. The tinker toys become chopsticks and telephones.

Another instance of different play with the same space and materials involved activity in a structure where the upper area had the typical kitchen equipment: stove, table with dishes, refrigerator. Three boys came to the area, manipulated the dishes, and said they were going to cook. Each put a dish in the stove, then sat at the table. One went to the stove to retrieve his dish. "Hey, we're cooking fire!" he shouted. The others grabbed their dishes, pretended to eat the "fire," and laughed loudly, as over and over again, they engaged in pretend fire eating and falling down dead. Shortly thereafter two girls came to the same place. They stirred the pots and pans, named the pretend ingredients—sugar, flour, cinnamon. Refrigerator and stove doors were opened and shut, dishes were "washed." The girls assembled and prepared a "meal" that was put on the table. They then sat at the table, and each pretended to drink a cup of coffee.

The consistently dissimilar sex roles adopted by boys and girls led us to conjecture in the following chapters about the extent of sex differences in play experiences, how they may be invested with positive or negative feelings, how they are expressed at various ages, how they are influenced by the environment, and what their significance might be for adult gender identities. The research literature is careful to emphasize that sex differences found in psychological characteristics are only averages. There are wide variations within each sex and a great deal of overlap between the sexes.[29] Although the similarities between individual males and females are more marked than the differences, the group differences are still very influential in sex role learning. Biological sex translates into two distinct social classes. The innate differences that exist between boys and girls are amplified by the separation of children's peer groups into two same-sex camps.

Hartup describes how the segregation of play groups by sex affects the course of children's socialization by elaborating the sex-differentiated psychological and cultural environments which parent–child interactions initially create:

> Peer culture supports and extends the process of sex-typing beginning in the earliest preschool years. Sex is the overriding polarizer in peer group formation in all primate species from the point of earliest contact. . . . Sex

is a more powerful determinant of "who plays with whom" than age, race, social class, intelligence, or any other demographic factor with the possible exception of propinquity. And clearly, this sex cleavage is instrumental in transmitting normative sex role standards to the child.[30]

This book explores, through our studies and those of other researchers, the initial development of the sex cleavage through which boys and girls are socialized apart. The study contributes much needed empirical information about developmental changes in peer relations, which form an increasingly important arena in which aggressive boys and nurturant girls are socialized. Biological, cognitive, cultural, and affective forces contribute to a tapestry of sex role behaviors in young children. It is not our contention that such a tapestry is not, or cannot be, woven differently in later years. Clearly, conceptions of masculinity and femininity can undergo significant changes as cognitive and social development move beyond childhood understandings. Yet, a child's entrance into the peer group represents his entrance into society. Future functioning in society is influenced in profound ways by behavioral specializations that occur in early peer groups.

Chapter 2 The Formation of Same-Sex Relations

OBSERVATIONS OF CHILDREN PLAYING AT SCHOOL

Our observations of young children's play, along with our general reading about sex differences, led us to believe that in the preschool years social relations become increasingly same-sex; the peer group becomes segregated into a boys' group and a girls' group. This early preference for interaction with one's own sex is referred to as the "sex cleavage." The phenomenon is associated with an interesting pattern of sex differences in behavior among children 2 through 5 years of age as they develop sex roles in play with members of their own sex.

In order to further our understanding of preschool children's sex role development, we observed and recorded half-hour episodes of free play in nursery schools. We thus gathered narratives giving us information about the social interactions of boys and girls when adults were, for the most part, not directly involved. Each social interaction, or peer contact, we recorded represented an interchange of thoughts or objects, with word or deed or both, between two children. These observations of children's social contacts prompted us to formulate some assumptions, which we wanted to analyze. There are four such general ideas, or hypotheses, which we propose to clarify in this chapter.

First, children's peer contacts between ages 2 and 5 become progressively more positive or affiliative. We defined affiliative behaviors as facilitating, cooperative acts, which elicit approval and seem designed to attract or maintain contact with another child. Examples of such behaviors are acts or remarks intended to share ideas or materials, to express appreciation or admiration, to acknowledge friendship, or to offer a physical caress, comfort, sympathy, or care. We defined the composite of negative, nonaffiliative behaviors as occurring when a child acts (either physically or verbally or both) in a way that hurts or clearly conflicts with the interests of another child. Examples of negative acts are hitting, fighting, taking a toy, saying

18

"go away," blocking entrance to a place, calling derogatory names, and using bravado (asserting superior skill or know-how with the intent to deflate another's accomplishments).

In examining negative behaviors we were aware that the intent of a child's behavior is at times ambiguous. A child may bite another child because he is "playing lion" or because he is angry and intends to hurt. Although ambiguous contacts were few (less than 1%), we made every effort to identify these behaviors, and removed such data from the analyses.

Our first assumption may appear too obvious for special consideration, since it is usually taken for granted that as most human beings grow older they become, at least in terms of the behaviors they choose to show, more socialized. A commonly accepted mark of maturity involves behaviors that are more positive than negative, and children do indeed develop in this direction early in the preschool years. There is a corollary to our first point, however, which adds that the degree and timing of this social development differs for boys and girls. From our data we propose to offer specific information to support this very interesting sex difference.

A second general idea commanding our attention involves a striking difference between the development of same-sex and cross-sex peer contacts. We noted that same-sex peer contacts became increasingly numerous and positive, but cross-sex play did not seem to have a similar positive growth. This phenomenon becomes quite compelling to note when we ponder adult male–female attractions and antagonisms toward one another. We reflect on the love–hate dichotomies of adult sexual alliances and the remarkable prevalence of same-sex "best friends" among adults, as we seek to trace the origins of the "battle of the sexes."

The third area for investigation follows a similar line of thinking, namely, that boys and girls are involved in different amounts of same-sex and cross-sex peer contacts. We were interested to document how and when young children engaged in play with the opposite sex. Our data sheds light on *why* cross-sex play does not show a positive progression similar to that in same-sex play.

Our fourth hypothesis already has wide documentation from other scholars. We believe that boys experience more conflict than girls during the preschool years when same-sex alliances are initially forming. We wanted to demonstrate, however, that this higher degree of conflict predisposes boys at an early age to a fundamentally different type of socialization than that experienced by girls.

Development of the Sex Cleavage

We will now report major findings from our observations, which chart how boys and girls engage in contacts with each other in different ways at different ages. First we will identify our findings and describe their various relationships to one another, then speculate on their meanings and implications. Methods of analyzing our observations are reported in Appendix C.

Four of our findings achieved statistical significance, that is, they could not have occurred through the operations of chance. These four observed differences, between boys and girls (in the case of sex differences), and between 2-year-olds and 5-year-olds (in the case of age or developmental differences), signify that the groups are themselves really different.

First, there was a significant *age* difference in the rate of same-sex positive contacts: 5-year-olds had many more positive contacts with same-sex peers than did 2-year-olds. However, our data revealed a year's lag in the development of same-sex positive relations among the preschool boys, compared to the girls. In other words, girls as a group showed major clusterings of affiliative behavior a year earlier than did boys.

Secondly, a significant *sex* difference was found in same-sex negative contacts: there was a higher rate of same-sex negative contacts among the boys than among the girls. Boys after age 2 engaged in more contacts with one another that incorporated aspects of personal conflict.

Thirdly, all cross-sex contacts (except negative responses) showed a significant *interaction* effect, i.e., a sex difference present at one age was reversed at a later age. More frequently than was true at other ages, boys at age 3 tended to engage in contacts with girls, and girls at age 5 tended to engage in contacts with boys. These unusual increases in cross-sex contacts (positive and negative), which we found among 3-year-old boys and 5-year-old girls, are contrary to the general socialization trends toward same-sex and positive behavior.

Our fourth significant finding was a sex difference in cross-sex negative responses. Girls directed more negative responses toward boys than boys did toward girls at every age, even at age 3, when boys displayed more cross-sex behavior generally.

Figure 1 shows the enormous increase in children's affiliative interactions with same-sex peers between age 2 and age 5. The 2-year-old appears unsocialized in Figure 1: negative and cross-sex contacts are as prevalent as positive and same-sex contacts. At ages 3 and 4, same-sex positive contacts increase markedly when language and social skills, which faciliate peer interaction, develop. The rate of same-sex contacts *tripled* during the four preschool years we studied, from 3.5 per half-hour at age 2 to 10.5 per half-hour at age 5. In contrast, the number of cross-sex positive contacts observed per half-hour increased only slightly (from 2 per half-hour at age 2 to 3.5 per half-hour at age 5), and the rate of negative contacts did not increase at all. At age 5, same-sex play predominated: boys played with boys and girls played with girls for the most part. .

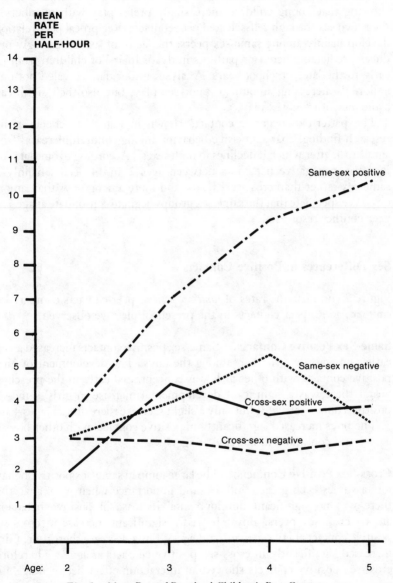

Fig. 1. Mean Rate of Preschool Children's Peer Contacts

Thus, our data chart the initial development of the sex cleavage during the preschool period. The findings support an abundance of other evidence showing that young children increasingly prefer play with members of their own sex through self-selected peer contacts. Reciprocal peer relations develop mainly among same-sex peers; the factor of sex increasingly produces predictable behavior patterns in dyads (pairs) of children from the early to the late preschool years. Analyses of our data revealed not only children's increasing amount of same-sex play, but also their significant avoidance of cross-sex play.

The pattern of negative contacts shown in Figure 1 reflects earlier research findings that aggressive behavior among children increases from ages 2 to 4, after which it declines in both sexes.[1] According to our data, the increase in negative behaviors between ages 2 and 4 occurs mainly in same-sex rather than cross-sex dyads, and more among boys than among girls. We speculate that the same-sex groups begin to consolidate at age 5, as peer conflict resolves.

Sex Differences in Positive Contacts

Figure 2 contrasts the rates of *same-sex positive* peer contacts compared to *cross-sex positive* peer contacts in the preschool play we observed.

Same-Sex Positive Contacts: Same-sex positive contacts increased a year earlier among the girls than among the boys. The development of girls' positive contacts with other girls was concentrated early in the preschool years: there was a significant developmental increase in girls' same-sex positive contacts at age 3, but only a slight increase thereafter, at ages 4 and 5. The boys increased significantly in positive contacts with other boys at age 4, and continued to increase at age 5.

Cross-Sex Positive Contacts: The large jump in same-sex positive behaviors assumes even greater interest and importance when we realize that there was no significant developmental increase in positive behaviors among cross-sex peers. Boys showed a significant increase in cross-sex positive contacts between age 2 and age 3, but a decrease thereafter. Girls increased significantly in cross-sex positive contacts at age 5. Therefore, cross-sex positive contacts showed an interaction effect between age and sex: 3-year-old boys tended to have more cross-sex positive contacts than 3-year-old girls, whereas 5-year-old girls had significantly more cross-sex positive contacts than 5-year-old boys.

Thus we found that at age 3 the girls had more same-sex positive contacts and the boys had more cross-sex positive contacts. At age 4, both sexes had

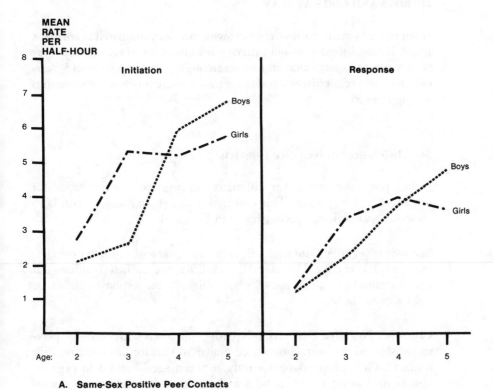

A. Same-Sex Positive Peer Contacts

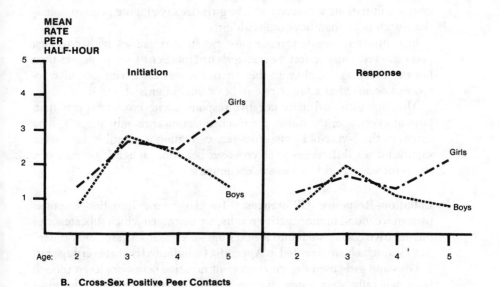

B. Cross-Sex Positive Peer Contacts

Fig. 2. Mean Rate of Preschool Boys' and Girls' Positive Peer Contacts

about twice as many positive contacts with same-sex compared to cross-sex peers. By age 5 the 3-year-old pattern was more or less reversed: same-sex positive contacts were more numerous among 5-year-old boys than 5-year-old girls, whereas cross-sex positive contacts were much more numerous among the girls.

Sex Differences in Negative Contacts

Unlike positive contacts, sex differences in negative contacts varied for initiations and responses. This occurred for negative contacts with both same-sex and cross-sex peers (shown in Figure 3).

Same-Sex Negative Contacts: Boys had more same-sex negative contacts than girls at every age. However, this sex difference reached significance at age 3 for *initiations* only, at age 4 for *both* initiations and responses, and at age 5 for *responses* only.

Cross-Sex Negative Contacts: Negative initiations with cross-sex playmates showed an interaction effect similar to that for cross-sex positive contacts. Girls dropped significantly between ages 2 and 3 in negative initiations, leaving 3-year-old boys with significantly more cross-sex negative initiations than 3-year-old girls. At age 5 the sex difference in cross-sex negative initiations was reversed: the girls displayed more negative initiations with boys than boys did with girls.

In contrast to negative initiations, negative responses with cross-sex peers showed a main effect for sex: girls had more cross-sex responses than boys at every age. Unlike all the other cross-sex categories, negative responses occurred at a lower rate in boys than in girls at age 3.

Although girls had more negative responses with cross-sex peers than boys at every age, the difference reached significance only at age 5. The extent of the 5-year-old girls' cross-sex orientation is notable: there were significant sex differences in all cross-sex behaviors at age 5, because of a sharp increase in girls' cross-sex encounters.

Initiation–Response Differences: To clarify the initiation–response pattern we found in the negative results, we examined which subcategories the negative contacts fell into for each age–sex group. These "rank-order" analyses, which are reported in Appendix C, indicated that at every age but 3, boys and girls used the same types of negative behaviors (even though boys generally were using more of them). At age 3, assault, the most

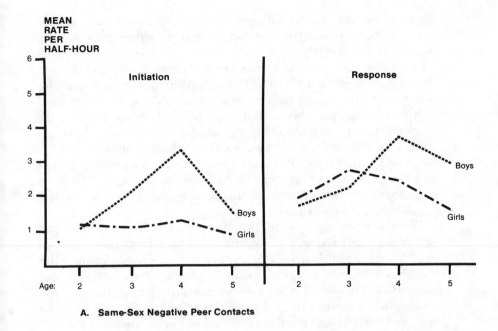

A. Same-Sex Negative Peer Contacts

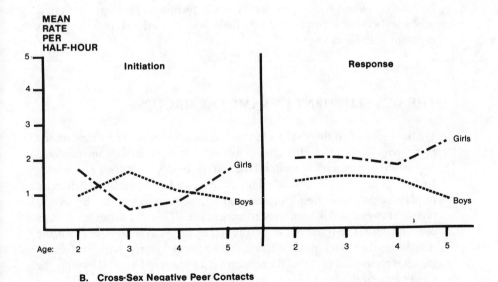

B. Cross-Sex Negative Peer Contacts

Fig. 3. Mean Rate of Preschool Boys' and Girls' Negative Peer Contacts

aggressive contact, was ranked significantly higher among the boys, and more passive forms of aggression—withdrawal and ignoring—were more popular among the girls.

Other noteworthy results emerged from the rank-ordering of the sub-categories of negative behavior. The most preferred form of hostility for both sexes was molesting (object-grabbing) at age 2 and disagreement at each succeeding age. This pattern suggests that language mediates the development of social skill and the large increase in positive social contacts observed in children at age 3. Also, boys and girls differed consistently on the second-ranked behavior at every age after 2: the boys tended to use a direct physical means of influencing their peers (molesting), whereas the girls used a more indirect means of influence (ignoring) as their most second frequent negative contact.

This sex difference in mode of conflict, with boys favoring direct and girls favoring indirect means of regulating their peer interactions, reflects a basic difference in male and female sex roles, and is a recurring theme of this book. Sex differences in negative social contacts during boys' and girls' play seem to be forerunners of basic dichotomies in their adult role behavior. We conjecture in Chapter 4 that the initiation–response differences found for negative behaviors are related to sex differences in dominance, with boys' negative initiations representing dominant strategies and girls' negative responses representing submissive behaviors. We believe that the negative initiations, or threats, are common among boys at ages 3 and 4 as they "vie for power" when their same-sex group is forming. This aggressiveness seems to become incorporated into male power relationships as same-sex relations stabilize at age 5.

THE DEVELOPMENT OF SAME-SEX GROUPS

We have identified three stages in the development of peer relations among preschool children that effect the transition from the relatively unsocialized 2-year-old just emerging from infancy to the highly sex-typed 5-year-old. In the first phase, evident in our data on 2-year-olds, there is little difference in play behaviors among same-sex and opposite-sex peers. In the second phase, at ages 3 and 4, same-sex alliances form. Then the same-sex groups consolidate in the third phase, beginning at age 5. We have specified the transitions that mark quite different types of peer contacts with the following descriptive labels: the domestication of the girls (age 3), vying for power among the boys (age 4), and the consolidation of same-sex alliances (age 5).

The Domestication of the Girls

An observer of 2-year-olds is initially impressed by the solitary or parallel play of the children. There are relatively few social encounters, and these include a high proportion of negative object-grabbing as children fight over toys. The general scene reflects a miniature society where activities seem directed by almost pure Freudian id or Piagetian assimilatory functioning. Wishes and wants prevail; the constraints on reality are typically overlooked. No statistically significant sex differences were found among 2-year-olds in our study. Boys and girls at 2 appeared relatively unsocialized. They directed many nonaffiliative and few affiliative behaviors to same-sex and cross-sex peers alike, although with same-sex peers, boys used more assaults and girls were more insulting.

Analysis of those social contacts that do occur, however, reveals that by age 3 the girls (in particular) manifest striking changes in social behavior. Girls seem to form same-sex alliances at 3. In our study, their positive contacts with other girls increased at 3 to the relatively high level which they maintained through age 5. This change was accompanied by dramatic drops in girls' negative initiations, both with same-sex and cross-sex peers. The negative behaviors that remained were concentrated in relatively passive response behaviors like ignoring and withdrawing. In contrast to the girls, 3-year-old boys increased in negative behaviors and failed to choose boys consistently over girls in their peer contacts. The shift we found toward same-sex positive behaviors and the decrease in negative initiations indicates the rapid "domestication" of the girls after age 2. "Domestication" refers to the socialization typical of girls in which they inhibit assertive impulses and develop nurturant ones.

The much greater number of same-sex positive contacts observed among 3-year-old girls compared to 3-year-old boys suggest that girls mature earlier than boys in acquiring social skills and establishing positive relationships. Boys' positive contacts at age 3 were altogether fewer in number, and were almost evenly divided between girls and other boys (with slightly more directed to girls than to other boys). We conjecture that the lack of differentiation between same-sex and cross-sex peers among 3-year-old boys indicates that boys have a greater initial difficulty than girls with gender identity, since the early nursery school years are spent in an environment that is created and maintained by females. Possibly in the school, as in the home, the female's gender identity and consequent ego control is stronger than that of the male. Closely identified with the nurturant and powerful mother figure, girls are relatively secure in initiating behaviors. The culture of the nursery school opposes negative encounters, and the message reaches the girls through the pervasive reinforcement of positive behavior by female–mother–teacher (male teachers are not common in nursery schools, although their numbers have increased recently). Abrasive contacts with boys, frequently characterized by prohibitions, snatching of possessions, and unsolicited interferences initially flourish among the girls, but are soon discouraged. Nursery school teachers intervene, and girls are rewarded for their more positive behaviors. These are especially common in their most favored same-sex play in the doll corner (house area), as they increasingly re-enact the mother–father–baby roles of the domestic scene.

A contrasting pattern is apparent among the young boys. The boy has a remarkably different initial preschool experience. Not only in our small sample, but in reports from other nursery groups, separation anxiety is more prevalent among boys than girls, and boys often cry for their mothers. It has been suggested that perhaps girls by this age become able to transfer dependency to teachers and other children, whereas boys have not yet developed this ability.[2]

The boys' contacts at age 3 show neither the "domestication" nor the same-sex shift that is evident among the girls. Indeed, during this period there was an increase in negative initiations with other boys (as well as with girls), particularly in behaviors we have labeled as assaulting and object-grabbing. It appears that boys during this time are involved in paying attention to girls, rather than allying with one another. The 3-year-old boys increased more in positive contacts with girls than they did with other boys. Their negative initiations with girls, like their negative initiations with other boys, increased when they were 3 years old, resulting in a sex difference in the number of negative contacts which 3-year-olds initiate with both same-sex and cross-sex peers.

The relative social "immaturity" of the social behavior of the 3-year-old boy has already been noted: he is described as engaging in less symbolic play, more "partial" use of play materials, and more solitary or parallel play than girls.[3] He is less inclined to initiate positive behaviors, possibly being less secure in gender identity and ego strength in what is for him a female-dominated world. Indeed, young boys have fewer negative responses, particularly in cross-sex encounters. They seem keyed to a subordinate role in relation to girls, not yet ready to seize the opportunity to explore and enrich their male identities in a plethora of encounters with other boys. The boys, unlike the girls, do not shift to a major same-sex alliance at age 3. Not yet emancipated from mother and female domination, boys at 3 still tend to be attracted to associations with girls.

The irregular nature of boys' social relationships at age 3 was confirmed by a study of middle-class black children, in which it was found that 3-year-old black males showed a higher level of social behavior in cross-sex dyads, whereas girls, at age 3 as well as at age 5, and 5-year-old boys showed higher levels in same-sex dyads.[4] The results of this study, which are confirmed in our data, demonstrate that the age of sex typing may be earlier among girls than among boys, since there are high levels of positive behavior among 3-year-old girls and older children of both sexes in same-sex social interaction.

Our observations of sex differences in the social behaviors of preschool children may shed some light on the "mystery" Carol Jacklin and Eleanor Maccoby identify in their study of 33-month-old same-sex and cross-sex dyads.[5] They found that social behavior of girls was reduced when playing with an opposite-sex partner; they became passive or sought proximity to the mother. Girls felt freer to show aggression or assertive behavior in same-sex dyads than in cross-sex dyads. The shift we have identified among 3-year-old girls—their dramatic movement toward positive initiatory behaviors, their early preference for same-sex dyads, their withdrawal from and ignoring of 3-year-old boys—helps our understanding of these phenomena. With same-sex partners, girls have apparently learned to expect positive behaviors at an early age. They also seem to feel freer to express negative response behaviors when these expectations are not met.

Jacklin and Maccoby's study presents additional data that is compatible with our findings on 3-year-olds. They report that girls paired with girls show less passivity than children in any other pairing. Our data reveal a marked increase in affiliative behaviors among girls at this age. We are also in agreement with their finding that boys seem not to engage in sustained episodes of same-sex play at the ages of 2 and 3, whereas girls are more likely to respond to one another, especially at age 3.

Among the 3-year-old girls, domestic role-playing flourishes, and boys gravitate to the familiar scene. Boys are invited to play the role of baby or father, to be the passive recipient of female nurturing. Still not fully free from domesticity (although they have begun to make a few excursions away from the home front in his fantasy play), boys are not yet equipped to hold a major role in play involving family functioning, as we will discuss in more detail in Chapter 3. So, while the boy obligingly engages in many cross-sex positive contacts, such experiences are not ultimately satisfying to his would-be mother or wife or to himself. He increasingly becomes aware that there is more fun, more excitement and power, elsewhere—namely in his contacts with other boys, to whom he will turn in the next year.

An interesting pattern concerning 3-year-old children emerged from our findings on negative peer contacts. In both same-sex and cross-sex contacts at age 3, the boys had more negative initiations than the girls, while the girls had more negative responses. The boys' negative initiations are not differentiated when they first increase; at age 3 their negative initiations are directed toward girls as well as other boys. Perhaps because of the nature of 3-year-old girls' responses to these overtures, however, the boys by age 4 withdraw their attention from the girls.

It seems that 3-year-old boys initiate aggressive contacts with peers of both sexes. However, whereas 3-year-old girls withdraw from or ignore these negative overtures from the boys, other boys respond with equally aggressive acts. This mutual aggression is the basis for a mutual attraction, and sets the stage for the same-sex alliances that begin to form among the boys during the next year. Not only are 3-year-old girls withdrawing from and ignoring the aggressive initiations from the boys, they also seem to be ignoring to some extent the more friendly initiations from other girls. This may contribute to the somewhat lower level of same-sex positive contacts we observed among the girls compared to the boys in the later preschool years.

Vying for Power among the Boys

After an initial tendency to ignore one another at 3 years of age, boys at 4 suddenly engaged in many same-sex encounters. Positive and negative contacts showed significant increases in boy/boy dyads. It appears that boys ally with other boys at age 4, after other boys have responded, whereas girls have failed to respond, to their many negative initiations. At the same time, cross-sex contacts decreased among the boys. By age 4, boys are no longer paying as much attention to girls, but are paying much more attention to one another. In other words, boy/boy relations are forming at the expense of boy/girl relations.

The boys' same-sex negative contacts peaked at age 4, in parallel with the marked rise in their same-sex positive contacts. (The girls had also increased in same-sex negative responses at the same age that their same-sex positive contacts increased sharply; 3-year-old girls showed an increase in same-sex negative responses that was uncharacteristic of the generally positive nature of their interactions.) We speculate that the initial stages of the formation of same-sex alliances at ages 3 and 4 demand a high proportion of negative contacts. Preschoolers' negative contacts—of a more direct nature among boys and a more indirect nature among girls—are numerous, as relative positions and hierarchies within the male and female peer groups are negotiated.

The formation of male friendships seems to be quite different from the growth of female friendships, which are generally more positive in nature. There is evidence of much more variety in boy/boy relations in this period when they first prefer association with other boys. The emergence of a high frequency of same-sex contacts among boys is marked by many negative behaviors, suggesting a high degree of conflict as they relate to one another. We labeled the preceding period among 3-year-old children when the girls' alliances emerged as the "domestication" of the girls. This second age period of 4-year-olds we call the "vying for power" of the boys. The boys are being socialized by influencing each other in a manner quite different from that of the girls: they fight out dominance issues with one another. Their same-sex contacts have more aggressive, nonaffiliative qualities than those of girls. Boys must explore new relationships without the benefit of an easily visible cultural model or ready access to a socialized identity figure, in contrast to the girls, who ally earlier, and with less conflict. In later chapters we will elaborate this contrast between masculine and feminine development, and its effects on adult relationships.

One way of viewing nonaffiliative behaviors among boys is to consider them under the rubric of aggression. A comprehensive review of recent studies of aggression by Maccoby and Jacklin presents compelling evidence that, in general, boys from various cultures at all ages have a sex-linked differential readiness for initiating and responding with what may be described as "aggressive" behavior.[6] The studies they review report another consistent result: girls and women are less often the object as well as the agent of aggressive actions. Boys are reported to fight primarily with each other, seldom with girls. They also tend to be more active, engaging in a larger number of interactions with their peers. (Although we did not find a significant sex difference in the total amount of peer contacts of boys and girls, by age 5 boys did tend to have more.)

The increased number of nonaffiliative contacts in same-sex male interactions may serve to heighten and prolong boys' interest in encounters with other boys. The varied and dynamic repertoire of male behaviors during this age range foster a continuing mutual involvement. Boys, with father roles still relatively undefined and unincorporated, have no immediately visible role models. This lack of specific male models is evident in their varied same-sex group and in the fantasy roles they re-enact with one another. We suggest in a later discussion of dominance hierarchies that boys are inevitably attracted to one another because of the potential they provide for role explorations and positions in power hierarchies. This functioning is less necessary for girls, who have had from the beginning a role model and gender identity readily available in the mother.

The Consolidation of Same-Sex Alliances

Peer contacts at age 5 are, in a sense, the most interesting to examine. The sex cleavage undergoes a qualitative change at about 5 years of age, when sex differences seem to become institutionalized in a peer group that is segregated into a boys' group and a girls' group. Different styles of conflict resolution (more direct behaviors like assault among boys, and more indirect behaviors like withdrawal and ignoring among girls) result in differ-

ent types of social interaction in the two groups, which become incorporated into sex role identities. Continuing the labeling system we adopted
earlier, we refer to the salient aspect of this period as the "consolidation of
same-sex alliances."

The change from 4 to 5 in same-sex relations was much more evident
among the boys than among the girls. Same-sex socialization continued to
develop among the boys as same-sex positive contacts increased, cross-sex
contacts decreased, and the rate of same-sex negative responses dropped
(but still remained higher than that of girls). The same-sex negative initiations of the 5-year-old boys, which had been high since 3, decreased
dramatically, almost to the girls' level. Boys seemed finally to learn what to
expect from one another, and relative power positions stabilized. Boys'
negative responses, mainly object-grabbing and reprimands, remained
high, however, as they protected their "territory."

Girls at age 5, in contrast to the boys, increased dramatically in cross-sex
contacts, resulting in large sex differences in every cross-sex category at this
age. Although the drop in same-sex negative contacts among the 5-year-old
girls suggests some adjustment in their same-sex relations, they showed no
increase in same-sex positive contacts, as the boys did. In the discussion of
the subcategories of positive and negative contacts to which we turn later,
we note that a large number of cross-sex contacts involve the girls' abortive
attempts to get into the exciting rough-and-tumble, teasing play of the
boys. These attempts also involve their highly successful maneuvering in
the use of the reprimand, or disagreement, as they endeavor to manipulate
their contacts with males through a type of dominance justified by rules of
appropriate behavior.

The finding that boys had significantly more same-sex negative contacts
than girls, while girls had more cross-sex negative responses than boys,
suggests that boys experience conflict within their own ranks during the
preschool years, while the smaller amount of conflict evident among the
girls was primarily directed toward the boys. It thus appears that male
conflict tends to be internal, and female conflict external, in relation to their
same-sex groups, when peer group alliances are developing. In later chapters we will explore various interpretations of the greater same-sex affilia-
tion among boys and the cross-sex orientation of girls when children are 5
years old. We speculate that the greater amount of conflict present among
the boys resolves into same-sex relations that are more highly developed
than those of girls. The cross-sex attentions of 5-year-old girls seem to
represent Oedipal (sexual) attractions to males and/or social subordination
to males in the larger social world beyond the family.

Negative behaviors in same-sex dyads decreased at age 5, as relatively
separate boys' and girls' groups seemed to evolve. We speculate that as the
boys' group becomes more united at age 5, conflict switches from initiation

to response, and they continue, although in a different manner, to regulate one another actively. Not only is the consolidated structure of the same-sex group apparently self-regulated among the boys, suggesting a hierarchy, the adjustment in same-sex interaction is consistently less among the girls, and concentrated at the beginning rather than the end of the preschool period, suggesting less group solidarity. Relations among the girls show neither as much conflict nor as dramatic a resolution; there is instead an initial sharp drop in negative social behaviors. At age 5 the girls emerge as more attracted by the opposite sex, as the boys had been at age 3. Cross-sex behaviors, negative as well as positive, rise among the 5-year-old girls as the same-sex groups stabilize and conflict. This marks the beginning of the "battle of the sexes," a term often applied to the relation between the two sides of the sex cleavage.

Why are same-sex relations so apparently satisfying? Why is there no similar increased development of positive behaviors in male–female interactions? Rubin, in his interesting book *Children's Friendships*, comments that the sex cleavage in children's groups appears to be universal, suggesting that the pattern may be influenced biologically.[7] He also suggests that there might be a greater compatibility of behavioral styles among children of the same sex, and that expressions of sexual antagonism may reflect cultural biases.

Early cross-sex antagonisms may be aspects of the process of learning gender whereby children exaggerate boy/girl similarities and differences in order to make them cognitively clear. Just as children can be uncompromisingly stereotypical about what is appropriate in same-sex behaviors, they seem to exaggerate antagonisms in cross-sex encounters. In learning gender children begin to guide their own behavior, incorporating attributes and skills similar to those observed in same-sex parents and peers. Children tend not to develop those behavior strategies that do not conform to their sex role; supported by the adult culture, girls learn to inhibit aggression, boys to avoid intimate attachments. Perceived similarities are accompanied by the salient perception of the differences of the other sex. Kohlberg emphasizes that children's perceived similarity to others of the same sex is a primary motivation in their gender role identification.[8] The issue of inclusion and exclusion is central to social life, and cuts across more than sexual lines, for children as well as adults. Even among toddlers in kibbutz groups, membership in the group is closely associated with the exclusion of nonmembers.[9] Faigin reports how very young children in a kibbutz express strong feelings of group belonging, shouting to the children in a different kibbutz, "We went for a walk and you didn't"; "We have a nice house and you don't."[10]

The sex cleavage intensifies in children's peer groups at the end of the preschool years; the sexes are relatively segregated during middle childhood as the child continuously processes and makes use of information regarding the relation of his or her own sex to the opposite sex. Gender provides a strong link between similarities and group membership. Young children may be prone to overemphasize in-group (same-sex) belonging, just as they overemphasize same-sex behavior identities. We believe, however, that cross-sex antagonisms may have more complex origins than the cognitive dilemma described here.

Chapter 3 Sex Differences in the Style of Boys' and Girls' Play

NURTURANT GIRLS AND ROWDY BOYS

While the strategy of examining grossly defined categories of positive and negative behaviors has yielded significant sex differences in the timing and sequence of social development in peer relations, this method masks subtleties in sex differences that are revealed when we examine specific, more narrowly defined, peer contacts. A consideration of the occurrence, timing, and quality of these contacts, which were sometimes too infrequent for statistical analysis, enriches our understanding of boys' and girls' social interaction. Table 2 in Appendix D indicates the proportions of contacts of children with one another in the various behaviors we have identified: assault, admiration, molesting, nurturing, etc. For a fuller description of the nature of these behaviors see Appendix A.

Only two positive categories of behavior, nurturance (representing 2% of all contacts) and teasing-rough-and-tumble play (5% of all contacts) emerge as significant in terms of sex differences. Note that we classify rough-and-tumble play as a *positive* behavior, since the style of children's contacts in this behavior appears, in our opinion, to be more positive than negative. In a sense these behaviors represent two different polarities of behavior especially characteristic of same-sex contacts at 5 years of age, when the cleavage between the sexes is most apparent. Nurturance is almost absent in boy/boy dyads, but progressively increases in girl/girl dyads. It is in full bloom in same-sex interactions of 5-year-old girls. The incidence of teasing-rough-and-tumble play reaches a peak among 5-year-old boys in interactions with other boys. Boys also engage in this behavior significantly more often than girls in same-sex interactions at 4 years of age. The behavior occurs minimally among girls before 5 and tends to increase among 5-year-old girls in cross-sex encounters. However, when it does occur, it seems a weak imitation of what goes on among boys, as we will describe later in this chapter. The female's proclivity toward nurturance and the male's proclivity toward rough-and-tumble play have been widely documented in previous studies.[1] It undoubtedly reflects the girls' developing identity with the nurturing mother and the female domestic provider of food, child care, and body care, and the boy's identity with a role of action and competition.

Three other positive behaviors represent a very small percentage of peer contacts: bonding of friendship (1%); admiration, compliment, and approval (.05%); and physical caress and awareness of human feelings (1%). These behaviors essentially occur in same-sex contacts and serve useful purposes in strengthening same-sex dyads.

Major Conflict in Boys' Socialization

Although as children grow older they become increasingly more positive in their same-sex social contacts, boys have altogether more negative contacts than girls in same-sex encounters. Negative contacts are actually or potentially aggressive in nature, and coupled with the quasi-agonistic contacts categorized as teasing-rough-and-tumble play (which, as already noted, we classified as a positive behavior), give a distinctively different flavor to what is typical in boys' peer relationships as contrasted with those of girls. Such a difference has also been widely documented in previous studies.[2]

In the nursery-school setting, the negative contacts categorized as assault (1.5% of all contacts) and molesting (9%) are usually carefully monitored by the teachers. Teachers repeatedly intervene to halt or redirect peer contacts where bodily hurt or misappropriation of property is involved. Other types of negative behaviors, such as disagreement (15% of all contacts), bravado (2%), insult (3%), ignoring (5%), and withdrawal (1%), are also monitored to some extent, but they are sometimes encouraged when individual rights are in question. These behaviors tend to depend on verbal rather than physical strategies, and are therefore "safer" and more favored by teachers and by girls.

Thus, these children in microcosm, and girls more than boys, move toward styles of interaction favored by our Western culture. Without benefit of United Nations monitoring, they increasingly eschew violent, physical encounters and attempt to manage their differences through verbal means, or through withdrawal from issues of conflict. Perhaps because of teacher vigilance, and because we studied predominantly middle-class children, assault is at a relatively low level across the board. Same-sex boy contacts account for the majority of this behavior, which peaks at 3 and decreases thereafter. All types of negative behaviors (except withdrawal) peak among boys when they are 4 years old, and drop to lower levels when boys are 5, as same-sex alliances consolidate and boys increasingly learn to curb overt hostile actions.

Negative behaviors among same-sex girls are altogether fewer in number. Assault is minimal. Molesting behavior reaches a high level among 2-year-olds, but drops to a low level thereafter. Bravado, insult, and disagreement or reprimand are highest among same-sex girls at 4 (although these behaviors occur less among girls than boys). The female is not as likely as the male to engage in "come-uppance" or contemptuous, denigrating behaviors with same-sex peers, suggesting that even in areas of verbal aggression the female is not as disposed as the male to fight for position or supremacy when interacting with others of the same sex.

Girls' same-sex cohesiveness, which begins to take hold at age 3, is not preceded by a period of major conflict. Boys' same-sex cohesiveness at ages 4 and 5 comes after an interval, from ages 3 to 5, when both assaultive and molesting behaviors are at a relatively high level. We have already speculated that the additional time of conflict among boys sets the stage for a different kind of peer relationship. These earlier experiences would prompt boys to regard other boys as potential adversaries in a manner different from girls, who move into same-sex choices without major episodes of conflict and vying for power. Boys thus develop skills for negotiating control that females are not prompted to develop in interaction with age-mates. Boys need to develop strategies for competition and probably learn to value these strategies more than girls do. We can speculate that such differences set the stage for the continuing trend among males for competition, group games, and even warfare.

By age 5, girls increase in negative behaviors toward boys; cross-sex disagreement or reprimand shows a significant sex difference. Girls apparently tend increasingly to use reprimand behavior as a culturally (teacher) sanctioned method of maneuvering for power over males. Because of their extensive use of the reprimand (often accompanied by "hands on hips" postures of righteous indignation), girls by age 5 have a distinctly "shrewish" flavor in their behavior toward boys in cross-sex encounters. "Now look how you've messed up this room"; "Do you *have* to make those yukky noises?"; "Beer! No beer served in *this* house"; "You have to shut your mouth when you eat," are typical of the remarks girls direct at boys. Girls also increase in insulting behaviors toward boys, and use bravado extensively.

Boys engage in bravado with girls primarily at age 3, but there is little evidence of it among the 5-year-old boys we observed. The drop in the incidence of 5-year-old boys' expressions of bravado with girls is perhaps suggestive of their attitude toward girls at this age. Possibly the 5-year-old boy is now more self-confident and more adjusted to his place in the social world, in contrast to his relatively subordinate position with girls when he was 3 years old (see Chapter 2). He appears to have less need to proclaim fictitious and extraordinary abilities or accomplishments in cross-sex contacts, unlike girls at age 5. Conceivably, as depicted in the cartoon *Dennis the Menace*, he acknowledges that the boy label is superior to the girl label, in the final analysis. In one episode, Dennis gets involved in an argument with "know-it-all" Margaret while playing marbles with his pal Joey. They begin trading insults—bonehead, dumbbell, addle-brained imbecile, dim-witted dolt. Margaret, of course, knows more (and bigger) words than Dennis. He does not allow her to have the last word, however, proclaiming, "Well, you're even worse than all those things you said I was!" "You're a . . . a. . . ." "You're a. . . a. . . *girl*!!" "Boy!" commends Joey. "You sure told HER!" Dennis replies, "Yeah. With all her big words she can't top that!"[3]

In cross-sex dyads, episodes of withdrawing and ignoring, are more common among girls than boys. Such strategies of negative response perhaps reflect a girl's realistic appraisal of potential vis-a-vis negative contacts with boys: her experience might inform her of the boys' greater expertise in negative behaviors that involve physical hurt or harm to property, and wisdom would suggest a strategy of withdrawal or ignoring in a situation in which it would be difficult to match behaviors in kind. Another interpretation is that in withdrawal and ignoring the girl utilizes a subtle power strategy in efforts to control the boy. The salience of negative initiations among the boys and negative responses among the girls suggests that, as same-sex relationships form, girls employ less direct means of influencing their peers.

Mine's the Best, a sex-stereotyped book for children, amusingly reflects aspects of male conflict, cross-sex estrangement, and bonding issues that were implicit in the foregoing descriptions of children's behaviors with one another. In this picture book two boys argue (with Freudian imagery) about their inflated rubber seals at the beach: "Mine is the best." "It is not, mine is." "Mine has more spots." "Mine is bigger." "Mine can stand up." "Mine can sit on my head." "Mine can sit on *my* head; I can ride mine." "I can ride mine better." The boys finally fight, pulling each other's clothing. Then a simpering girl comes by, carrying an identical blown-up balloon seal. "She thinks she's smart," say the boys. The girl sticks out her tongue. "I hate her," says one boy. They put their arms around each other and walk away, saying, "Ours was the best."[5]

DEVELOPMENTAL TRENDS IN NEGATIVE BEHAVIORS

Assault

Age Two: Only the vigilance of the teacher, or parents' prior socialization practices, can mitigate frequent minor and major incidents of personal attack among 2-year-olds. Contrary to patterns in subsequent ages, assault occurs not only among children of the same sex, but, even more frequently, in cross-sex encounters. The sexes are approximately equal in initiations and responses utilizing assault, and episodes of this behavior are equally violent in boys and in girls. When a boy tells a girl to stay out of his house area she hits him, but modifies her behavior when a teacher tells her she doesn't like her to hit. A girl playing tag yanks a boy down, whereupon he punches her and she kicks him. A girl "fireman" hits a boy with a firehose, and he kicks her. A boy pushes a girl; she smashes his train track when his track encroaches near where she is making a track. The behaviors are gutsy and immediate, like natural reflexes rather than premeditated acts.

Age Three: Among 3-year-olds, cross-sex assault diminishes, occurring mostly in unprovoked incidents initiated by boys. In general, attacks are mild, molesting rather than physically hurting. There seems to be no visible negative antecedent in the following instances: a boy hits a girl with a pipe when she comes to play near him at his water table; another hits a passing girl with a toy horse; one hits a girl during a story period, announcing, "You're a bad Rachel." Another smashes a girl's fire hydrant, as she is playing alone; another hits a girl when she identifies a cartoon on his shirt, and one pushes a passing girl who protests, "Gary, you almost knocked me down." Only a few girls engage in assault with boys, kicking or hitting after boys have pushed them or taken their toys. Apparently, by age 3 girls have fairly well assimilated the cultural taboo that they are not permitted to hurt boys; boys are just beginning to assimilate the converse taboo. A basic animosity, or a lack of sufficient socialization, seems still to be evident in their unprovoked attacks on girls.

There is also a great difference in same-sex encounters among 3-year-olds. Only a few girls ineffectively strike out at one another, hitting with blankets or straw candles. In contrast, there are numerous instances of boys attacking boys in quite violent ways. An assault prompts a counterassault. They hit, kick, punch, wrestle, destroy property, and hurl objects at one another.

Age Four: By 4 years of age cross-sex assaults virtually disappear and attacks are mild. The principal cause of trouble is property: a girl walks on a boy's boardwalk; he pushes her off so that she falls down and cries. Property rights also provoke her to attack. When he comes to a structure she occupies, she pushes him off, saying, "I was here first." When he takes her truck, she hits him. He hits her when she comes to take blocks from his area. There seems to be an implicit rule in such attacks, namely that assault is sanctioned in boy/girl relations providing there has been an infringement of property rights.

Same-sex assault patterns among 4-year-olds continue to show a major sex difference, with girls rarely attacking one another. The boys' encounters, however, are violent, often sustained, and generally reciprocal. They kick, pinch, shove, push, punch, and hit. They tackle, wrestle, jump on top of one another, hurl objects at one another, and attempt to destroy one another's property. Such episodes typically terminate when one boy withdraws, a teacher intervenes, or constructive play spontaneously resumes with apparent lack of animosity.

Age Five: By age 5, incidents of assault are at a very low level across the board; children have apparently incorporated the message that physical attack or destruction of property is not sanctioned in schools. Boys tend to hit girls who do not obey their commands. A few girls hit boys to protect their property. For the most part, girls do not hit back when boys attack—they cry, protest "He hit me," or utilize insult: "Go away, baby."

In the few instances when assault in same-sex encounters occurs, it is most often preceded by episodes of grabbing or physical attack. Possibly it seems to the child a logical punishment for the infringement of established property rights or the infliction of bodily hurt. Assault occurs slightly more often in same-sex male encounters than in those of same-sex females.

Molesting

Age Two: A predominant tone of 2-year-old interactions involves molesting, which also includes intruding, object-grabbing, and retention of property. Molesting behaviors seem to prevail indiscriminately among toddlers in same-sex and cross-sex interactions. When this behavior is initiated, it is usually responded to with an identical behavior, particularly when an object is involved; one child grabs and the other retains, and this is usually repeated in dyads over and again. At age 2, a negative response is likely to be preceded by a negative initiation and vice versa. In the narratives describing half-hour play periods, the words "grab" and "mine" appear with relentless regularity. Such behavior provokes constant teacher intervention—separating children, restricting property, providing another object, admonishing about taking turns. The behavior also elicits other nonaffiliative responses. Disagreement is among the most prominent, so that "no" is also frequent in the protocols, in addition to reports of whining or screaming. Parents and clinicians often describe the 2-year-old as oppositional and willful, using phrases such as "mind of his own" and "terrible twos."

Grabbing objects and retention of property seem to dominate the play of 2-year-olds. Catherine Garvey relates that she was once introduced to a 2-year-old and said, "Betsy, how are you?" "Mine," Betsy responded firmly, holding out a coloring book.[5] As children grab, push, tussle, and tug over spoons, cylinders, telephones, muffin tins, puzzles, straws, keyboards, play dough, juice, Legos, cars, dolls, and pacifiers, the object is the prime target of their attention. Other children, as such, seem only other objects who whine, protest, resist, ignore, or withdraw. In some cases, however, more socialized children seem to be quite aware of one another as persons, and molesting leads to assault as they poke at and crash into and step on one another.

Age Three: Among 3-year-olds, girl/girl molesting acts, which are fewer than those of males, seem to have the same quality as those of the 2-year-olds, except that there is not the same degree of mutuality in grabbing. When one grabs, the other often protests or occasionally reasons: "You have to share." "You can have my stapler, but give it back, O.K.?" Sometimes a girl anticipates the problem, saying to another girl, "Now, don't take this from Jessica. I'm going to give this to Jessica." Except for minor pushing, the molesting acts are primarily object oriented.

The boys engage in a fair share of grabbing objects from one another. The mutuality in grabbing persists and a large proportion of their molesting encounters verge toward personal, physical assault. A boy makes faces, and pushes his hands in another boy's face. Two boys hit each other with puppets, and one announces, "Bang. I put a gun in you, John." As boys tug for possession of a board, one yells, "I screamed at him!" Boys knock dishes on the table back and forth at one another; after a boy pushes some snow from another's structure, the boy warns, "I'm gonna hit you—I'm bigger." Then they both shoot snow at each other.

A scrutiny of cross-sex molesting encounters reveals that the boy is the initiator of the trouble in 75% of the incidents. These are primarily object-grabbing events—snatching a hammer, a saw, a blanket. Physical attacks are usually minor: throwing sand, pumpkin seeds, pushing a girl's hand away as she tries to go down a slide. The girl's response is generally withdrawal, whining or calling the teacher.

Age Four: At age 4, girls engage in relatively few molesting acts with other girls. Grabbing and countergrabbing exist only at minimal levels; the molesting girl is generally rebuked by the other, and does not continue. Physical molesting is relatively mild: poking with a pencil, hitting with a paper, throwing a piece of puzzle, flipping another's hair, and scribbling on another's paper suggest the quality of the attacks.

Appropriation and retention of property remain high among boys. Boys tug over cars, telescopes, hammers, chairs, shovels, keys, puzzles, and especially blocks. The wide variety of the objects over which they seek possession suggests the range of their activities. They assume and evaluate territorial possession: "I'm going to stand in this building—get off." "I only got a little—look at what he got." "You had too much than me." "These are my treasures—get away."

They run their trains against each other, and roll cars into each other's buildings. Physical molesting, again, verges on assault. They poke, bump, and take false swings at each other. They pretend to shoot. One marks another's shirt with a felt-tip marker and administers pretend karate chops at the neck.

Again, the boy is the principal initiator of molesting acts in cross-sex encounters and often they are unfriendly to girls. But the acts frequently take on more of a teasing aspect and some of the acts have sexual tones. A boy, although absorbed in painting a room, still flips his brush on a girl's hair as she passes. As girls play in water, a boy teasingly pokes his finger in the water and sprinkles them. Boys push girls' crayons off the table, poke at their books, touch a girl's head and say "tickle-tickle," sneak into a house area and teasingly grab a blanket, squirt water, try to pull a girl's pants down, poke a flower in her face. There is apparent satisfaction in girls' shrieks, protests, or summoning of the teacher. The pleasurable aspect of the molesting is clear: boys pretend to shoot at girls, who scream and giggle and then run after the boys. "Let's get those bionic sharks," shouts a girl to others as they pursue in high spirits and laughter. In this and a number of other instances, the game is one where boys ostensibly chase, but girls actually do.

Age Five: At age 5, girls seldom engage in grabbing from one another, and express little feeling when they molest. Often they prompt each other to share, or remind the other of prior possession. Same-sex boy encounters are slightly more numerous than those of girls, but less frequent than in the younger ages. Control of property is still a major issue, but a new dimension, which emerged among 4-year-olds, especially characterizes the encounters in this category. The 5-year-old boy emerges as a skilled tease. He does this frequently with other males, splashing them, slyly dumping what others have gathered, ramming cars into another's construction, engaging in taunting games with pretend shooting. One boy verbalizes his intent, "You better be careful 'cause I'm gonna bother you guys."

The boy's talent as tease is utilized again and again in cross-sex encounters. At 5, most of the molesting contacts initiated by the boys have a teasing quality. The girls tend to scream or shriek in response, but the protests have a somewhat faked quality in that they are often accompanied by a smile or giggle. Boys jump in and out of house areas or throw small objects into house areas, flip doll clothes around, pull down dolls' pants, screaming, "I see her tush," pull girls' pigtails, throw pillows at girls, squirt water at them, and pretend to shoot them with crayons or to bite them with toy animals. They snatch property from girls that they themselves don't really want: mops, pocketbooks, dolls, dustpans, gloves. As boys saunter across a room exploring activities, they dart in to kick a girl's puzzle, grab a girl's stapler to hide it, or deliberately step on a girl's drawing. Girls do not often similarly initiate teasing acts with boys or with other girls.

Disagreement or Reprimand

Age Two: Disagreement is among the most prominent of the nonaffiliative behaviors of 2-year-olds; "no" is one of their most frequent words. The disagreement prompted by molesting acts sometimes goes beyond a simple negative assertion. In these instances we can observe that some children are becoming aware that they are indeed coping with other people, as they suggest strategies, priorities, and proper adjustments. Sometimes the 2-year-old gains success when he announces, "It's my turn." The fact of prior use is invoked to secure an object—"I was driving that first"—as are squatters' rights. "You took some of my sand," a girl complains.

Children recognize the need of others primarily when the need is like their own. Boys grab the same pegboard piece from one another, and one boy suggests, "Get one over there." But his adversary refuses. A boy grabs a girl's cup; she grabs it back, protesting. "It's mine," she says, and takes a different cup. Then both say about the cup they possess, "This is mine. This is mine."

In the following incident, 2-year-olds resist attempts by a teacher to generate rules during a tug over possession. Sara watches as Adam pours water into a water wheel. "I want this," she says as she grabs the water wheel. "No, mine," Adam whines as he grabs back. The teacher lifts the water wheel from the two of them and places it in the middle. "Now you can both use it," she says. Sara grabs it and pulls it back toward her. Adam counters: "No, that's far away. Everybody can use it." The teacher takes the water wheel and returns it to the middle of the table. "It needs to be in the middle so everybody can reach," she explains again. Sara stands silently watching as Adam moves to the middle and begins to use the wheel again. "Why don't you move over by Adam so you can reach better," the teacher suggests. "O.K.," Sara agrees, as she scampers over to stand next to Adam. Sara begins to use a spoon to put water into the water wheel. Adam reaches over and takes the cup that Sara has been using previously. "Can I have my cup back?" Sara asks. Adam makes no response. Sara grabs the cup from Adam. Adam makes no response. The teacher reaches over and gives each of them a bottle. They pour for a few seconds, then Adam leaves.

Age Three: Among 3-year-olds, most disagreements continue to be simple assertions of "no" or "mine," but increasingly reasons for disagreement become verbalized, and rules or precedents are mentioned. A scrutiny of these disagreements or reprimands, which are numerous, reveals a pervasive qualitative difference in the sexes. Girls, in such episodes, tend to be the guardians of domestic order, propriety, and allegedly superior know-how in both same-sex and cross-sex encounters. Pronouncements from one girl are usually uncontested by the other girl: "Come, sister, you have to go to school." "Go to sleep, and don't laugh while you're sleeping." "Now, Momma, stop breaking the cradle." "Don't say 'you can be the father and I can be the father'—we're one family and we can't have two fathers." "Don't tell me to get your earrings; can't you see I'm cleaning up this mess!"

Boys' more extensively verbalized directives and refusals with one another have a different quality in that they more frequently invoke property rights, or contest one another's right to power, possessions, or opinions: "You ain't taking my blocks." "Yes, I am." "You can't park your car here; I'm building here." "Don't get in my house." "Don't ride your truck here." When a boy steps on another's block structure, the other replies, "Get off, you stupid." A boy pushes a car at another's car. The first boy says, "Stop it. I've got armor so you can't get me!"

When propriety is invoked, it tends to be more global than specific: A boy squirts water on the walls. "You're gonna get into trouble," the other warns. A boy reminds another he should share. He rejoins, "I don't have to share any more." "Well, some people do and some people don't," is the sage reply. In one instance the rebuttal is humorous: "Missed me, missed me, now you gotta kiss me."

Girls in cross-sex contacts use this behavior extensively. Reprimands directed toward boys convey a veneer of superiority. The boy counters primarily by denial, although he often accepts or ignores reprimands without rebuttal. In this behavior the girl adopts an extraordinary identification with the female adult. The following incidents reveal the sharp contrast in boy and girl behaviors. A girl holds up an accusing finger and scolds a boy about the noise he is making. A girl is condescending about an obstreperous boy: "John's into everything!" Another is self-righteous when a boy throws seeds: "You're making it go all over the floor." A boy asks for some candy. "Just one!" the girl monitors. A boy applies glue in big blobs on his paper, and the girl moves in to instruct, "You have to do it like this, you have to smear." A boy refuses to eat pretend food put before him, saying, "It's hot." "No it's not, Gary," the girl corrects. "It's cooled down now. We can eat it any way we want."

Sometimes girls are not as successful in enforcing their edicts as the adult females they model: "Time to clean up," a girl announces. "I'm not gonna clean up," the boy says to her (although he does so at the teacher's request).

"Don't do that, Tom," she commands. "I can do it if I want," he defies. "You're the baby," she announces to a boy in the house area. "No I'm not; I'm the superman getting away from you, witch." And, to a girl who tries to induce him to put on a dress, a boy protests, "No, no. Only girls wear these."

Age Four: Sex differences are also abundant in the focus and quality of the numerous contacts involving disagreement and reprimands among 4-year-olds. Many of the same-sex girl disagreements or reprimands are similar to those among 3-year-olds, as girls refer to "appropriate" behavior sanctioned by social roles, or assume a superior knowledge of social conventions.

"Could I have half your life saver?" "No, it's in my mouth and I have germs."
"You marked on the table!"
To a girl who was peeking during a game that required her to cover her eyes: "Why do I have to tell you tons and tons of times? Stop it or I won't be your friend."
"I took your clay 'cause you weren't minding them."
"Sit up straight in your chair when you're coloring."
"Can I buy dancing shoes?" "No, I'm talking to her; wait your turn."
"I bought some earrings and they hurt me, so can I have my dollar?" "No." "Well, that's what real stores do!"
"Come up here; don't act foolish, I want you right away."
To a girl who put on some beads belonging to the school: "Well, when you go home you'll have to put them back."
A "mother" directs her children: "If you're not good, you can't stir. Now when I bring the plate in, don't grab plates."
A "nurse" is adamant that her patient (who has just had a baby) cannot leave the hospital. "You can't take her home, you can't. It's too early. You gotta wait eight days."
"You know how many chldren I'm gonna have? Six minus two twins plus two children. 2 + 2 + 2 = 6. Can you count to seven backwards?" "7, 6, 5, 2, 1."
"Oh, you didn't do it right. You left out 4 and 3."

The boy/boy disagreements and reprimands again tend to focus on intrusion, territorial and property rights, and details of work procedures:

"You stepped on my car!"
"Hey, you got more puzzle pieces than me."
"Hey, you're wrecking my house."
A boy walks on another's blocks. "Get off. It's not a street."
"You're stacking those chairs the wrong way."

> *"Stop breaking David's sand."*
> *"Stop raking my property."*
> *"Hey, you can't be here. I'm working here."*
> *"Make your own road." "You have to fix the road." "If you wreck it, you're fixing it."*
> *"You had too much than me." "I only had a little. Look how much you got."*
> *"Get out of here 'cause I'm not playing."*
> *"And if you do that again, I'll do what I did before, hit you."*
> *A boy draws on another's shirt. "Hey, don't do that. This is my nice shirt. My mommy will be mad."*
> *"Can I play?" "No, I'm too busy with my work."*

Numerous other disagreements involve arguments over possession of clay, boards, cookie cutters, etc., or procedural matters, such as building a structure or painting a room.

The girl, much more frequently than the boy, tends to invoke propriety or rules; she displays the "Ann Landers phenomenon" in cross-sex disagreements:

> *A boy grabs a girl's blocks, and she counters: "I don't like that. I'm leaving."*
> *A boy starts to get juice. "No, no, let the teacher do it."*
> *A boy wants to play a card game. "No, you're too little. You don't know how to play 'fish.' "*
> *To a molesting boy, "Don't be mean. You'll get in trouble." And to another, "Adam, will you take it easy if you come in here?" "No." "Well, you can't be rough in here: you'll have to get out."*
> *A boy wants to buy a necklace in a store. "No, that's for girls. Get yourself some sneakers."*
> *A boy buys some eggs in the store. "Be sure to bring that carton back when you're through with the eggs."*
> *To a boy at the easel, "Hey, what are you doing mixing all those colors up?"*
> *To a boy who is painting, "It's got four eyes and two legs. It's in the wrong place. That's not right."*
> *A girl asks a boy if he can marry her when he's a prince. "No," he says, "I'm gonna marry my school." The girl says, "Well, a man's gotta marry a woman and a woman's gotta marry a man."*
> *A boy apparently uses the wrong word and a girl corrects him: "You shouldn't say 'sour' [about his lunch]. Say 'tart.' "*

Boys' cross-sex disagreements, on the other hand, tend mostly to be outright refusals or general judgments about a girl's behavior. "No, that's not right." "You should share." When a girl knocks a structure down a boy says, "That wasn't nice." "Well, it was my building," says the girl. When a girl complains about a boy grabbing her glue, he says, "You're not using it." In several instances, boys object to girls' amusement at what they are doing: "Don't laugh, it's not funny."

Age Five: Among 5-year-olds, disagreements and reprimands continue to flourish at approximately the same high level as was true with 4-year-olds in same-sex encounters, although they are somewhat more numerous among same-sex males. Again, among girls, approved social behavior or correct household management is often invoked. With what might be described as a "goody-two-shoes" mentality, girls issue a lot of warnings:

> *"You're wasting paper; take turns, don't fight; you have to look where you're going."*
> *"It's not polite to watch people eat; don't put it in the refrigerator, it will be soggy."*
> *"They're expensive, so don't waste them."*
> *"Why don't you go and be calm."*
> *"Now, sister, do you have to keep on doing this?"*
> *"Don't touch the dough; we don't want it to get dirty."*
> *"Don't eat the dough, it will make you sick."*
> *"You have to put on your shoes. I'm going to tell the teacher."*
> *"You hit me, so you're not going to have my candy."*
> *"Take your shoes off and be careful of the baby."*
> *"Now look at the spilled water! I have to clean up the whole table."*
> *"Don't put Scotch tape on the stove. It will melt the burner."*
> *"You gotta eat your supper first."*
> *"You don't need to mop the whole floor, just where he sprayed."*
> *"Why do you have to talk?" (during a story).*

There are disagreements about role assignments or faulty knowledge or procedures:

> *"I'm not Mom. I'm sister. Mother isn't home so I'll have to tell you what to do."*
> *"Can I be the sister?" "No, we already have enough sisters."*
> *"I must milk the cow." "You mean cream the cow."*
> *"They're coming." "No, the next time they're coming."*
> *A girl gives directions for playing a game. The other advises, "No, since it's your game, why don't you do it first?"*
> *"It's a big piece of white." "It's not a big piece of white, it's just the size of me!"*
> *Girls argue about the proper position of their male patient. "No, he has to put his feet here so the medicine won't run down, just stay in his mouth."*

They argue about the cause of measles. "Measles has nothing to do with the looks of you. It has something to do with something else."

The same-sex reprimands or disagreements of *boys* continue to reflect dissension over property or territory:

"Can this be my house?" "No, this is only my house."
"Don't dig here."
"I don't need water. Don't pour it here."
"You're wrecking my castle." "No, I'm not. I'm fixing it."
"Get out of my fire engine." "I want to be the driver." "I was here first."
"Wait, this is not a jumping thing; it's a train." "I don't have to get off, 'cause I made it."
"Hey, if you want to paint, you can't, 'cause the job's closed up."
"Hey, don't do that again ever. You put the blocks in my place."
"You took a dozen of those raisins." "I did not, just four."
"Don't take wood from my property." "Don't take all my things. All I have is two."
"Don't knock mine down. Next time try to be careful."
"You shouldn't explode the moon up."
"I can fly with you." "No, I want to do it myself."
"I went to change my pants, and you took my glasses. Give me my glasses. Next time I'm gonna hit you."
"You're not helping, so you're not gonna be in it."
"Hey, you're wasting my blocks. Don't put them crooked."
"Hey, you stealed all of them."
"No, I'm not giving you this, whether you like it or not."
"He had them for ten minutes. It's not fair."

Boys tend to argue over their rights and facts, rather than etiquette. "You can't be a guard 'cause you don't have a guard hat." "He thinks this is a snake. No, it's a caterpillar." "Here's Allosaurus." "No, he's not, he Tyrannosaurus."

More frequently than girls, boys reject directives from other boys. In contrast, girls tend to meet directives from other girls with compliance or a neutral response. In general, boys are not *givers* of socially approved directives. They are, in fact, often ostracized for taking that role. "Come play with the water." "No, I'm gonna play with the corncobs." "Here's your parachute." "I don't need one." "Here's how you get on a ship." "No, this is how you get on a ship."

In cross-sex encounters the girls very often refuse to comply with male directives and frequently reprimand boys' molesting acts. Girls seem self-righteous and assured as they display social expertise. To a boy who touches an electric plug a girl says warningly, "You'll get burned." When a boy asks to be served beer in the house area, she rebukes, "This is not a restaurant." "But we always have beer on a ship," he replies.

There is a subtle difference in boys' and girls' directives. When a boy issues directives, they tend not to be "approved," in the sense of being socially desirable, or in the sense of emanating from the teacher. Girls, however, display implicit adverse criticism of boys' behaviors with directives of this type.

'You have to clean up all those staplers."

"Don't talk with your mouth full."

"That guy needs to be punished. You're punished for the rest of the day."

"Don't push things off the table."

A boy pretends to use scissors on his hair, and a girl screams, "Don't do that. I'll tell the teacher you're cutting."

When a boy inadvertently knocks a table over, a girl exclaims, "Now look at that! I told you it would happen."

"You're dropping clothes on the floor."

When a boy says, "You can't have that roller, 'cause it's Matthew's," a girl reminds him, "It's everybody's."

When a boy asks for some of her play dough, she uses an approved teacher directive, "Use some at the other end of the table."

When a boy suggests, "Pretend I'm the little boy and I'm fishing," a girl anticipates deviant behavior. "O.K., but be sure you be the little boy."

At 5, boys assume attitudes of power and authority, and their inferences about "dumb girls" are apparent: "Don't take this one; take that one." "Clean that stuff out." "This is the stove, that's the ladder. Can't you see?" "Put that in my coffee." "Don't put too much water here." "You don't *pull* it out; *turn* the key!" They often correct the girls' faulty knowledge: "It's a houseboat," the girl says. "No, it's a water boat." A girl advises, "Put heat in the car," and the scornful boy corrects her: "Oh, you mean *gas*." "Your name is Andy." "No, my name is fireman." "It's not a castle, it's a house." "Fire her. She's making bubbles instead of paper." A girl suggests, "Get in the wheelchair," and the boy replies, "It doesn't have wheels!" When a girl says, "It's seven o'clock," the boy replies, "I'm afraid you're wrong. It's five o'clock."

Disagreements can imply the male's superior authority or rank: "You're not flying faster than me. I'm Superman, you have to follow." "You're not driving this car, I am." Boys can protect themselves by referring to an ultimate authority. One boy calls a color navy blue; when a girl corrects him, "It's not navy blue," he replies, "My daddy told me." Boys can say, "Time out!" when they are overwhelmed with female directions, or they can resort to a superior reasoning, as one did when a girl told him to leave an area where she was playing. "I need to be here so we can be together. Together is better than alone."

Insult

Age Two: Insult and bravado, behaviors dependent on verbal skills and sophisticated social understandings, are nonaffiliative behaviors that were not available to 2-year-olds we observed.

Age Three: At age 3, insulting behavior occurs infrequently in girl/girl contacts, and is likely to be quite mild, such as a refusal of proffered friendship, or a denigrating remark, such as, "You don't even know how to write your own name." "Stupid" is the only word used in name calling between girls.

Insult is more prevalent in boy/boy contacts. Boys push other boys away from preempted territories. Reason and rule are called upon to keep another away: "There's no room up here; that sign says 'no.' " Name calling is more common in boy/boy encounters; liar, stupid, jerk, dummy, and bad boy are in the repertoire and are used in defense of property or territory. "You're going to knock it over, dummy." "Get off that board, you big stupid."

Although two girls seldom use insults with each other, they are talented in addressing insulting remarks to boys.

"You cucumber, you cucumber," a girl shouts to a bewildered boy.
"What a dum dum," another girl says to a boy who is building a house.
"Marty, Marty, you're a farty; four, four, you're a bore," she chants.
A girl refuses to allow a boy to look at things on her table. He says, "Then I won't be your friend any more." She replies, "You're not my friend anyway."
A girl announces another girl to be her friend, but advises a boy, "You can't be her friend."

Verbal attacks are initiated and responded to almost equally by the sexes; boys also insult girls. Boys order girls away from their territories without reason. One boy calls a girl "cuckoo." When a girl tells a boy, "I'm going to a party today," he replies, "I don't care." One boy tells a girl, "You're a fuckin'," whereupon she reports to the teacher, "He says I'm a fuckin'!"

Age Four: At 4 years of age, girls' insults to one another are infrequent and minor. A girl makes a face at another who tells her she marked on the table. A girl criticizes another's drawing: "The sun is dumb." A girl gives a shiny button to another, who tosses it away, saying, "I don't like this ugly one." They announce withdrawal of friendship or personal dislike of one another.

Boy/boy insults, however, are numerous and tough. Again and again, boys eject one another from their play. They are forthright in expressing their dislike: "Get out of here. I don't like you." "I hate you." "If he's not my friend, I'll step on his building." There is a wide range of insulting words: stupid, dum-dum, idiot, dumbbell, big fat mouth, baby. They frequently shout, "shut up," and often accompany the remark with a push.

The girls' repertoire of insults, at a low level in same-sex contacts, expands in cross-sex encounters. "You don't know how to play so good; you're too little," or "I don't like your painting. Mine is pretty." The girl uses denigrating words with boys: "Shut your mouth up, stupid." "You're not playing house with us, you old fatso." Boys are called bad boy, silly, and rough. One girl spits at a boy. Two girls sitting at a table share their opinions: "Can you hear that noise outside? Boys are chasing." "Yeah— yukky." Girls push boys away from areas they occupy, saying, "Oh, you allergies—go away." They also threaten disaster: "A real Spiderman will come and kill you." A boy tries to deliver some mail to a girl, who says, "I don't want any. I'm talking to Sara." When he persists, she knocks the mail from his hand.

Boys also reject girls. "You girls can't play with this puzzle." "You can't come up here." "Get out of here." "We don't want your skinny blocks." Yet their epithets to girls are relatively mild, such as, scaredy-cat and copycat. "Oh, bump your bum," a boy says to a girl who calls him a bad boy.

Age Five: Among 5-year-olds, girls' insults to other girls tend to be relatively mild, withdrawing or rejecting friendships, or denigrating another's productions. Insulting remarks are not strong; "shut up" is a typical one. Boys, on the other hand, engage in more frequent insulting remarks toward other boys. Epithets are more gutsy: idiot, dum-dum, stupid sucker, cry baby, dope. They offer unflattering judgments, "You're mean, you're disgusting, I don't like you." They also threaten withdrawal of friendship: "You do that once more and I won't be your friend," and threaten violence, too: "If you don't let me I'll bust your head."

Insults occur in almost equal distribution in cross-sex incidents. With girls, the major type of insult is to order a boy away. This is frequently accompanied with a belittling remark:

> *"Get out of here, you numbskull."*
> *"You thief, I hate you."*
> *"Very bad one."*
> *"You poo-poo, ka-ka."*
> *"Go away, baby."*
> *"He's cuckoo."*
> *"Out, you are an idiot."*
> *"Get lost."*
> *"I'll call the police."*
> *"You're a very bad father."*

One insult prompts another: A girl calls a boy stupid, and he responds in kind. A boy disagrees with a girl, "No she's not, dummy." Girl: "We're not dummies." Boy: "Yes you are." Girl: "Teacher isn't here, dummy." Boy: "Yes she is, silly." They make faces and stick out tongues at each other. Boys also (but less frequently) chase girls away: "Stephanie, can't you hear? You're fired. Go away. Go take a rest. Get out of here. Now you stay in jail till I tell you to get out. Stay in jail," says a boy. The girl replies, "Get out. You're a peanut head."

Both sexes make belittling remarks about the other's productions:

> *A boy looks at a girl's painting and says, "Yuk."*
> *A boy holds up a product to be admired, and a girl pushes it away.*
> *A boy says he has drawn a boat. "That's no boat, so we might as well cross that off, professor," a girl says.*
> *When a boy says he has made a train, a girl replies, "Well, it doesn't look like a train to me."*
> *"It's a flying shark, but never, never, never a flying fish."*
> *A boy looks at some girls who are painting. "What are you guys, stupids?"*
> *A boy pauses to look at a girl who is reading, and announces, "It doesn't spell anything."*

Bravado

Bravado is an early expression of competition in children. This is especially remarkable since a commonly held view is that competition between children does not occur until they are considerably older.

AgeTwo: There is no incident of this type of behavior among the 2-year-olds we studied.

Age Three: Three-year-old girls seldom use bravado with one another. Its primary function is an assertion of a potentially superior product or authority. "I can make a bigger cake than you," or "I can mess the room; I'm the mother." Instances of bravado among boys are more numerous and potentially more violent than those in girl/girl contacts. Again, assertion of control over property is a common message. The messages are taunting and challenging:

> *"Ha, ha, I got the string and you can't get it."*
> *"I got a padlock and key, you're not having it."*
> *"Ha, ha, I sat in your place."*
> *One boy grabs a toy from another, who says, "I don't care, I got two toys."*
> *"I got a ramp." "I got two ramps," says the other. "Well I got three ramps," rejoins the first.*
> *A potentially superior clay production is announced: "Ha, ha, I'm making a worm." "Ha, ha, I'm making a merry-go-round."*

Toughness and size are sources of strength among 3-year-old boys: "I'm gonna hit you." "I'm bigger." The other stands beside him, disagreeing, "*I'm* bigger." Scary threats probe another's weakness:

> *First boy: "One spider will scare you."*
> *Second boy: "No it won't."*
> *First boy: "I'm higher than you, father. I'll get three or four spiders and they'll throw it in your mouth. I'll get mad and throw it in your face."*
> *Second boy: "I like spiders."*

The minor use of bravado among girls in same-sex encounters is no indication that the 3-year-old girl is not skilled in its use. Cross-sex encounters flourish when boys and girls tend to refer to size or age as potential ego builders. A girl says to a boy: "I'm bigger, bigger, bigger; you're little, little, little, little," to which he shouts, "No!" Another boy screams, "No," when a girl announces, "My feet are bigger than yours." Strength as well as size is an issue. "I'm bigger than little people. I'm stronger than other people," a girl announces to an unresponsive group of boys. When a boy says, "I'm the biggest," a girl says, "I'm the toughest." However, on another occasion a boy announces to a girl, "I'm the toughest," and his assertion is uncontested. Competitive remarks about age are a sure winner. "After I get my birthday, I'm gonna be five," says the 3-year-old girl. "I'm gonna be five," the boy matches. She retorts, "I'm gonna be 5, 7, 8, 15, 16, and all those numbers." He leaves. Superior knowledge can be ego deflating also: "I know where I go swimming," says a girl. "You don't know the name of our swimming club," says the boy. "I'm going to call your mother," says a boy as he dials a telephone. "You don't even know her number," says the girl. Statements of accomplishment are received by both sexes with belittling remarks of one-upmanship such as "so what" or "big deal."

Age Four: Bravado occurs in the same-sex encounters of girls at age 4 more than at age 3. Bravado among girls has qualities similar to the previously discussed nonaffiliative contacts. Behaviors tend to focus on superior knowledge, superior age, or superior experiences or possessions:

"I know how to play cards, 'cause I go to my friend's house and she taught me."
"I know how to play better, 'cause my brother has a little pack."
"My bed is bigger than this table."
"Yesterday I went to gymnastics, and you didn't."
"I found a diamond." "I found a beautier."
"You don't know how old I am."
"You don't know my mother's name."
"You don't know what color my dress is." "So, I got my dress on, so!"
"My birthday is Christmas." "So what! I'm going to the Easter Bunny."
"I'm four." "No." "Yes, I am." "No." "Yes, my mommy said."
"Next time you can't come to my party."

Same-sex boy contacts involving bravado are more numerous than those of girls, and again focus primarily on property: "I have two cars." "So what—see what I got." "I got the cutter!" "Well, I wasn't using it anyway." "He's not my friend." "Well, I already have a friend." "Look at my Batmobile." "Look at mine; it's better." "Ha, ha, you don't got some coffee."
Strength or power is often mentioned:

A boy hits another on the head and he asserts, "That doesn't hurt."
"When I was chasing you around, I wouldn't get you. But if I want to get you, I will." "I could take you! I'm five; you're four, ha, ha."
"I'll break this whole room." "I'll break it first, ha, ha."
"I had the idea." "I had the next idea."
"I'm a tiger." "I'm a wolf and a tiger."

In addition, there are many assertions and counterassertions about size, and remarks of "I don't care" and "so what."

In cross-sex encounters both boys and girls tend to refer to numbers and size to gain superiority:

> *When a boy says he has on a jersey, shirt and vest, a girl says she has on a jersey, shirt, vest, and sweater.*
>
> *A boy tells a girl that he went to two or three fairs; she replies that she has gone to four fairs.*
>
> *A boy says he's making a pile; a girl says her pile is bigger.*
>
> *On another occasion a boy and girl discuss a cake. "This is the biggest cake," says the girl. The boy says, "I'm making mine bigger!" to which she replies, "I'm making mine bigger." The boy has the last word, "I'm making mine up to the sky."*
>
> *When a boy announces he is the biggest, a girl has the last word: "I'm biggest cause I'm fatter than you."*

Often they dismiss one another's protestations with the "sour grapes" phenomenon: "I don't care" or "so what," which has been mentioned as characteristic of same-sex contacts among boys as well.

Age Five: Bravado is utilized less frequently at age 5, with approximately the same degree of incidence in same-sex male and female encounters. Girls' rallies with one another don't tend to come off very well: "You can't use it [the speaker's doll] any more." "Well, you won't be able to use my View Master." They try come-uppance over a rubber band: "I almost took it. But it broke." "If I found another, I won't let you have it." "If you have a broken one, you can't put it in your hair." Aside from the forthright boast of one girl to another, "I can handle boys, right?" bravado among girls tends to be weak "so what" remarks.

Same-sex male bravado continues in the same spirit that characterized the 4-year-old boys: assertion of superior size, product, or ability:

> *"It's hard building this city—I built most of it." "Well, I started it."*
>
> *"My tunnel is longer than yours." "No, mine is."*
>
> *"I have a better shirt."*
>
> *"We're making greater things than you guys."*
>
> *"Mine is a better house 'cause you didn't make a good house." "I like mine best 'cause yours is different."*
>
> *"Look what I got." "Look what I got. The priest gave it to me. They were having a parade at the church and the priest gave it to me." "So what."*

Boys do not initiate much cross-sex bravado at 5, but girls use it frequently in cross-sex encounters, especially in responses:

> When a boy tells a girl, "My friend's car goes any kind of speed," she replies, "Mine can go twenty-one seventeen thousands."
>
> "I can fly even better," a girl asserts to a boy who brags of his flying. "You can't go faster than me. I'm real speedy."
>
> A boy says he can reach across the table (which he cannot do). "I can reach all across here," says a girl, waving her arms vaguely. "Me too," says the boy. She retorts with wider gestures, "I can reach all over here."

The boy asserts superior strength: "I can take you." "So," a girl retorts. The girl asserts superior privilege: "I'm gonna go to a dance and you're not gonna come." Age continues as a source of bravado: "Baby, baby, come uptown with me," says a girl to a boy. "Yeah, I'm gonna be ten," retorts the 5-year-old "baby." She counters, "I'm five and a half." "Ha, ha, I'm six," he says. "So—I'm seven," she concludes.

Summary

Assaultive and molesting behaviors are higher among same-sex boys than among same-sex girls. Among girls, hitting, grabbing, and pushing are relatively mild and infrequent. The boy tends to be the chief initiator of these behaviors toward girls. When boys are 4 and 5 years old, their molesting acts toward girls take on both teasing and sexual tones, and girls tend to respond with shrieks of protest and excited giggles. There is a tendency among girls to instruct males to curb this behavior.

Among boys, assaulting and molesting behaviors often involve appropriation or retention of property; this is also true in boys' disagreeing with or reprimanding one another. They are concerned about other boys' infringements on territorial or property rights: their house, their car, their garage. They are attentive to equitable divisions of property: "You have too much more than me." They argue over such matters as methods of building, differences of opinion, and issues of control—who will be first, who will be the driver. Directives refer to rights and rules, not to what is socially desirable. Possessions are a major issue, and there is a pervasive concern that other boys will destroy or steal possessions. They infer that work entitles one to property: "Whoever helps build this building, it's gonna be theirs"; "I don't have to get off this train 'cause I made it." It is the work world, the "thing" world, not the world of convention and etiquette, that is reflected in the boys' disagreeing and reprimanding behaviors as they are busy with cars, houses, trucks, blocks, fire engines, and castles; as they fix, build, wreck, paint, drive, fly, and explode.

Whereas boys tend to use rules or reprimands instrumentally for their own purposes, girls seem more interested in the larger issue of preserving social order for its own sake. Girls, more than boys, assume a role of guardian of domestic morality; they formulate judgments about social misbehavior and mete out verbal punishments for what is considered inappropriate.

Although girls' cross-sex behaviors tend to be similar to those they use with other girls, it is notable that boys' cross-sex disagreements or reprimands, before they are 5, have a "feminine" quality; with girls, they are more likely to invoke social regulations than they are with other boys. By age 5, however, boys' disagreements or directives begin to have a "macho" flavor. Many of their remarks seem calculated to "put down" the girl, to ascribe to her a fundamental stupidity vis-a-vis males' overall superiority. Boys tend to assume a superior knowledge of the world and its functioning as they deal with girls in a supercilious manner, often addressing them with contempt.

Insulting behaviors are consistently infrequent and mild among same-sex girls at 3, 4, and 5 years of age. Boys insult one another frequently and intensely; they engage in a wide variety of name calling at every age. In cross-sex encounters, however, girls are in command of a wide repertoire of insulting behaviors toward boys. The "battle of the sexes" is apparent at every age (but particularly at age 5), as both boys and girls belittle one another.

Bravado, although not used much by girls in same-sex contacts at 3 years of age, is used frequently at 4, and somewhat less frequently at 5. Girls' expressions of bravado with other girls tend to refer to personal things (age, clothes, skills, social events). Boy/boy bravado, which flourishes among 3- and 4-year-olds but diminishes among 5-year-olds, focuses on property, strength, and ability. Bravado is useful in cross-sex encounters at all three ages. Girls tend to assert superior strength, ability, and size, as well as their more favorable personal attributes, when they cope with males.

Beginning with 3-year-olds, the major nonaffiliative target areas identified in this study show a higher proportion of incidence in boys than in girls. By 3 years of age, girls have made a major shift to positive same-sex behaviors, which we have labeled their "domestication." Boys increasingly move toward a "discovery" of one another, and a major shift occurs toward same-sex contacts among 4-year-old boys, an age when negative behaviors flourish. We can speculate on the potential impact of this increasingly aggressive behavior among boys on the girls who are their peers and playmates. While a cognitive awareness of sex differences is questionable, or at best variable, among 2-year-olds, by age 3 children are generally aware of, and generally identify with, their gender.[6] Thus girls in their association with boys have a multitude of experiences to instruct them that boys are not generally cooperative in play, that they are more aggressive in their interactions with one another, and that they tend to initiate molesting and abusive encounters with one another and with girls.

In looking at expressions of the various nonaffiliative behaviors at each age, we note that the forces of socialization have operated so that not only is the overall behavior of older children more affiliative, but such children tend to utilize indirect, verbal aggressions rather than direct, physical aggressions. Girls, however, use verbal aggressions with boys more than they use such behaviors with one another, and the style of these behaviors with boys is more forthright and intense than similar behaviors with other girls. Girls' verbalized negative behaviors toward boys, which begin at 3, reach a peak at 5. Boys' negative behaviors toward girls, however, are increasingly lessened and modified, taking on a teasing (and often sexualized) quality. By the time boys are 5, negative behaviors toward girls take on a new supercilious, arrogant tone, implying that the female is lacking in both knowledge and judgment.

DEVELOPMENTAL TRENDS IN POSITIVE BEHAVIOR

Cooperation or Sharing

This category, as we have already mentioned, constitutes the greatest number of peer contacts; 48% of the children's play was spent in their manipulating and sharing ideas and materials. We have deliberately omitted a qualitative analysis of this category from this presentation, finding the material both cumbersome and repetitious. A pilot effort indicated that qualitative analyses of the numerous contacts involving sharing ideas and materials yielded information that was often "bare-bones," lacking qualitative distinctions. It was also repetitious information, which we could present more vividly in analyses of the smaller categories.

Teasing–Rough-and-Tumble Play

Age Two: Among 2-year-olds, after sharing ideas and materials, rough-and-tumble play prompts the greatest number of contacts that we classify as positive. However, some behaviors included in this category (which, in our classification, also includes teasing and foolish word-play) have an aggressive quality that may be termed quasi-agonistic.

Cross-sex encounters are most numerous. Boys and girls laugh and shriek together as they stomp on bubbles, jump on mattresses, playfully crash into one another on bikes, bang on the table with spoons, and randomly kiss one another. There are only two incidents of boy/boy rough-and-tumble play: boys scream silly words to telephone and tape recorder, push over blocks, and make foolish noises. And only one pair of girls engages in this play, chanting "fuckaship," and laughing wildly at their wicked word.

Age Three: Among 3-year-olds, although rough-and-tumble play, foolish word-play, and teasing have approximately the same incidence in both girl/girl and boy/boy contacts, an apparent difference is that boys' interactions in this category involve much more direct *physical* contact and activity: they often wrestle, playfully shoot water at one another, shove cars at one another as they chant, squeal, or laugh wildly. Girls are not as likely as boys to engage in physical encounters. They engage in minor jostling as they playfully spill small objects; they gently poke at one another as they jump on mattresses or hand little pieces of paper back and forth; they chant foolish words as they giggle and squeal.

There are almost twice as many cross-sex as same-sex episodes, and these do not involve the sort of physical contact apparent in boy/boy play. Boys and girls run and giggle, chasing one another as they make animal noises. They hit playfully with gloves, pretend to throw balls of clay as they poke at one another, play peek-a-boo, stuff their mouths with peanut butter and make foolish faces. They chant foolish words—"strawberry, strawberry," "ya, ya, ya," "dummy-dum-dum." The high cross-sex incidence of teasing and foolish word-play and its "gentle" quality is interesting; perhaps this behavior is the forerunner of seductiveness between the sexes.

Age Four: Among 4-year-olds, boys have a boisterous heyday in their numerous same-sex contacts in rough-and-tumble play, positive teasing, and foolish word-play. They wrestle, bump into, and fall on one another. One child pushes another back and forth in playful tussles, shouting, "You're my brother." They make machine-gun sounds, and chase one another around with space guns and spray bottles. They are convulsed with laughter as they pretend to make toy horses sneeze and fall down. Boys put clay in one another's hair, play puppet fighting, tickle and pretend to shoot one another, fall dead and roll on the floor. They slide from piles of blocks, fall over chairs, pretend to drink and eat fire.

Boys are distinctly different from girls in their direct alliance of sex and humor. Poking a toy lizard through a hole over and over a group of boys laughs uproariously when the lizard comes through. In falsetto tones they chant silly words and make rhymes: "Me ear, see ear, key ear, pee ear." A group of boys, laughing wildly at the play-dough table, moves into full-fledged, raucous bathroom humor:

"Silly putty is nutty."
"Silly putty!"
"How about pa?"
"Here, Dean, piss in it."
"Look at my strawberries."
"It goes piss in it."
"I took it out."
"It's piss in it."
"Dog mess in this."
"Ugh!"
"I put this right there."
"See that spot right there?"
"It's piss."
"Eat this piss."
"Eat this ka-ka."

Girls enjoy a muted form of teasing and rough-and-tumble play. Games of poking, peek-a-boo, and shut-eye bring laughter. They run in circles, giggle, and dance around chanting, "da, da, dum-dum-dum, yuk, yuk." They jump up and down and make up words: "Jackel, Wackel, Succo, Wonkel, Lacco." They chant things that aren't so: "Michelle has a mustache, a green black mouth, ha, ha, la, la, la." Or they yell, "King Kong" or "Jamie Sommers" as they run around. They tap one another on the head with crayons, and they flirt with bathroom play. "We can see Tara's underpants," they say as they giggle, lie on the floor, and kick their feet.

Proportionately, there is less cross-sex rough-and-tumble play among 4-year-olds than there is among 3-year-olds. But the incidents that occur, like those among 3-year-olds, are fairly restrained. Boys and girls playfully hit one another with pieces of rubber, poke one another with blocks and laugh. They gently push and shove, chant such benign remarks as "pink face, pink face." There is brief pretend shooting by girls of boy "bionic sharks," with much giggling. A girl throws pretend cake to a boy horse who makes foolish noises and faces as he eats. Again, this cross-sex play has a seductive quality.

Age Five: Rough-and-tumble play, silliness, and teasing reach their zenith among boys, and descend to their lowest level among girls, in same-sex contacts at age 5. Boys engage in the usual wrestling, poking, shooting, punching, and tossing of objects. Their silly word-play has a wide variety: Smacky-Wacky; pow-pow, boo-boo; the last strawberry; Davy Crockett, Joey Crockett; bee-bite bissy-bite, bitty-bite; Billy-Billy Boolat; a man named Grunk-Grunk; baloney head; fat chicken; Byron Ryron; David the Joker. More frequently than girls, boys take delight in perceived novelty. Unexpected experiences can send them into gales of laughter, as when they see a toy hippopotamus "too fat to drown." They love humor. One tries a joke which doesn't come off, but which provokes wild laughter in both. "What did Tessen say when he saw an elephant with glasses on?" "I don't know." "He said, 'I didn't recognize them.'" More often, however, seemingly sexual humor (similar to that reported among 4-year-old boys) flourishes. Boys repeatedly touch the long nose of a clay product; they squeeze one another's toes between blocks and roar with laughter.

A reference to romance can prompt them to bodily contact. "Tommy loves Cheryl," says one, which provokes poking, wrestling, and giggling. Even at age 5, there exists a close relationship between sex and romance among boys. During the dramatization of *Sleeping Beauty*, a boy acquiesced to putting on a dress. "Ha, ha, this is what you're gonna get," said his friend wickedly, as he rushed up and kissed him mischievously. With that, the boy snatched off the dress, attached a raccoon tail so that it dangled at his rear, and the two hopped around gleefully.

Most sustained and frequent, however, is the foolish word-play involving bathroom or sexual humor. "Bum-bum" (referring to rear-end) is a favored word. "Happy birthday, bum-bum," "I felt your bum-bum." They bend over to show one another their underwear, shout "tinkle-pinkle" and "wee-wee." When girls hear such words they either giggle or report the misdemeanor.

One episode involving four boys playing with liquid corn starch lasted for almost the entire half-hour observation. As they let the liquid drop into one another's hands, the boys chant, laugh, and comment:

"Here's my stinky ka-ka. Here's my stinky ka-ka."
"Hey, you have a ding-a-ling, right?"
"Kiss my booby. Kiss my bum."
"I'm sitting on the toilet."
"You make poo."
"Kiss my ding-a-ling."
"Why don't you poop in the house and put out the fire with your bum-bum?"
"Hee, hee! Bum, bum, bum."
"Look at all this stuff coming out of my shower."
"Out of my ding-a-ling."
"You know what you can make pee out of?"

"What?" Boy points to penis. Both laugh.
"Anyone wanna kiss my pink-dink?"
"Ah, you made ka-ka on me."
"Ah, you made poo on me."

As we mentioned earlier, rough-and-tumble play (apart from teasing and foolish word-play) did not occur among the girls we observed in their play with other girls. The few contacts in this category among 5-year-old girls are interactions involving playful teasing, with minimum bodily contact, such as their giggling and hitting one another with celery stalks as they pretend to cook. It is noteworthy, however, that girls, more than boys, engage in cross-sex foolish word-play. These cross-sex contacts are both relatively minimal and distinctly "feminine" in quality. It is interesting to speculate about why cross-sex contacts, although latently sexual, do not assume the robust sexual humor characteristic of same-sex male contacts. Possibly young children recognize that the blatantly sexual content of boys' teasing of other boys may be too risque in cross-sex play. Girls may be attracted to the arena, but once there may show a restraint or a style characteristic of their adult female counterpart: sex is attractive, but sex play invites censure or secretive behavior.

Boys and girls say "woof-woof" and jab one another with clay, poke one another gently and squeal, hit with brushes and chant "bad-bad," peek, laugh, and chant "Hooray for the Hippo," "Kirk, funny money." Occasionally a boy tries to be funny with "I see your underpants" or "Can I have some wee-wee?" but girls do not join the potential frolic the boy would like to create. On one occasion a boy put balls under his shirt and a girl remarked, "You look like you have boobs." He jumped up and down and laughed hysterically, but she did not prolong his merriment, as another boy might have done.

Nurturance

Age Two: Although 2-year-olds, especially girls, spent time in the house areas, their play tended to be solitary. Only occasionally did the girls' manipulation of pots and pans prompt them to offer food or drink to another.

Age Three: By 3, however, girls show much more nurturing behavior than boys. The many incidents of nurturance among girls are accountable mainly because of the large amount of time girls spend in the house area or in mother roles, dispensing coffee, tea, dessert, vegetables, and baked goods to one another. Boys are sometimes recipients of the food but rarely the providers. Although boys sometimes manipulate pots and pans at the stove, it is the mechanics of cooking and stirring that occupies them, not serving food to others. In addition to serving food, girls protect babies, "water" (bathe) and diaper them, and care for their injuries and illnesses. There are many instances of kissing, hugging, patting, stroking, and endearing remarks with other girls who assume "baby" roles. "How are you doing, sister?" says one girl to another as she pats her head. "I'll hold your hand so you won't fall," says a protective mother. "Come, honey, let's go to the house to eat your cake" is a typical invitation.

One unusual episode merits special attention in that the recorder happened to know the working parents of the two children involved. The parents of the children were unusually concerned about sex role stereotyping; in both families the father spent time at home while the mother either worked or went to school. It is interesting that although the girl has the model of the father staying at home, at play she elects to have both parents work, and the boy seems to agree. Yet finally they adopt traditional roles in their play—she stays at home to care for the baby and cook, and he goes out to work digging.

Age Four: At 4 years of age, girls continue to spend much of their play in preparing and serving food. Although they primarily cook for one another, they also serve boys. Boys in our study do not cook for girls in the house area. Only one boy prepares tea for another boy, and it is only at a barbecue of hot dogs and marshmallows that the boys serve the girls. Girls help boys put on painting smocks and coats; they comb a boy's hair. They also care for the welfare of other girls: "Heidi, I'll hang your picture so it won't get lost." "Mom, I'll put your coat in your cubby."

Age Five: At 5, girls' same-sex contacts reach a high level of nurturance and grooming. The variety of their cooking endeavors in restaurants and homes is enormous. Their helping behavior branches out into many areas. They help one another adjust aprons, put on beads, and arrange veils, dresses, and hats. They involve themselves in many aspects of baby care. Putting water at the foot of the bed, a girl announces, "This is in case they want some later," and, returning for a check before leaving the house, "I have to see if baby's settled." They coo special words of comfort: "You're all right, little baby, gonna put you in a safe place." They are particularly attentive to the sick or wounded. They cut gauze, bandage legs, provide medicine, and arrange for hospitals and operations. Sometimes their fascination with the props for sickness intrudes into domestic chores: "I'm putting pills in this cake. A good kind of cake that makes you sick."

Same-sex boys' contacts reveal no such involvement in providing food and care. The incidents are also few in cross-sex contacts. Here again, the girl is in the lead, more often offering food, drink, or clothing to males. Boys' involvement with food and drink is likely to be silly or inappropriate: "Hey, give me a little beer to drink," or "I'd like some Bingo juice—some wee-wee in my cup." They are the jovial recipients as they grab plastic food, then giggle and throw it around.

Admiration, Compliment, Physical Caress

Age Two: Two-year-old girls have slightly more contacts than boys in one affiliative category—admiration, physical caress, and endearing epithet. In most cases, the girl initiates an affectionate overture to a boy, hugging, kissing, stroking him, taking him on her lap, calling him "honey" and "darling." In all instances he either pulls away or apparently ignores. In the few instances where he initiates kissing or stroking, the girl responds in kind or with a greeting. Girls kiss and stroke one another; only one boy hugs another boy, who is unresponsive to his initiative.

Age Three: At 3, admiration among girls is confined to expressions of liking: "I like you very much." There are no expressions of admiration among boys, however. There is evidence of only two cross-sex compliments, both from girls to boys: "Thank you, Adam, you're a nice boy," and "Bruce, you have a nice horse on your sweatshirt."

Age Four: At 4, girls' contacts with one another involving admiration, caress, or endearing epithet are more personal than those among same-sex boys. Girls express approval of one another's clothing or jewelry. They hug and kiss one another, hold hands, say "I love you," and call one another "honey" and "dear." Boys tend to admire other boys' productions or another boy's prowess. A boy cheers another who is hitting: "Go Ricky, go Ricky. Do it again." Endearing epithets are not used among boys, and approving remarks tend to reflect the wider range of boys' fantasy play. "He's a good shark," says one boy to another, as he puts his arm around him. The girl is the initiator of admiration in cross-sex encounters. "You have a nice pin on," she says to a boy, whereupon he tugs at his sweater so that they can both touch the pin. She admires a boy's clay product: "Put it in the oven. It looks great."

Age Five: At 5, girls continue to address other girls with endearing epithets: "I'm going out, honey, to eat. I want you to be a good honey." "Here's your pillow, darling." They stroke hair, kiss, and pat. The cultural taboo against affectionate overtures between males has apparently taken hold, since there is an absence of such words or overtures in same-sex contacts among the boys in our sample.

In girls' same-sex contacts, the expressed admiration is, for the most part, directed to clothing, jewelry, or paintings: "That's pretty." "That's a beautiful color." "How do you like my ring?" "Pretty slippers; I have some, too." "You wear this today. Let me see how you look. You look so pretty. Tomorrow we wear this, 'cause you look so pretty."

The quality of same-sex male contacts continues to be admiration of products rather than of persons. "Wow, that's good," a boy says, admiring another's building. "Here's my nice house. Like it?" "Yeah, it's good," the other boy replies. They admire skill. One boy applauds another's feat of jumping over boards. When one boy dramatically "kills" a pretend shark, the other acclaims, "Yay! The championist of the day!" A boy approves of another's suggestion—"After I paint this, I'll put it in the water—nice and juicy"—with the remark, "Good idea."

Cross-sex examples involving admiration are still small in number, with girls admiring boys slightly more than boys admire girls. A fascinating aspect of this cross-sex admiration is that girls give boys the kind of flattery boys like (i.e., product-oriented) rather than the kind girls are accustomed to giving and getting. Boys, on the other hand, give girls what they want: person-oriented flattery. A girl admires a boy's product, "That's a very good ship you made." Another girl flatters his potential, "Michael, any picture you make, I'll like." When a boy remarks, "There's a sun that shines in the sky, and there's a boy son," a girl admires his ingenuity, saying, "That's a good idea."

Boy's cross-sex compliments sometimes have ulterior motives. A boy compliments two overtures from the same girl. When she cuts out a picture of a stuffed Yogi Bear to give him, he kisses it and laughs. She is encouraged to bring him another. "Oh, boy, balls, basketballs! Just what I wanted," he says. Another boy also pays a double compliment to a girl: "Wow, you're getting dressed up pretty," says a boy as a girl puts on a scarf. He adds, "Now look at her!" when he adds a necklace.

Awareness of Feelings

Age Two: There is no incident of this type of behavior among the 2-year-olds we studied.

Age Three: Awareness of feelings emerges in girls' same-sex contacts at 3, primarily in conventionalized expressions such as "I'm sorry." The girl shows a more individualized awareness with a boy, "I'm sorry, Monster. I won't do it again. And you won't scare me, O.K.?" The boy, briefly, puts his arm around the girl, in what may be an acknowledgment of her feelings and a gesture of comfort.

Age Four: Very few children at age 4 expressed an awareness of human feelings in their contacts. Girls sympathize with other girls who lose toys or miss their mothers; boys express concern when another has an accident or shows his "boo-boo." In one instance boys shared their negative feelings as they retreated to a table after active play with a group. "I'm upset," said one. "I'm really upset," said the other. Unfortunately the observer could not determine the reason, if any, for their being upset. Perhaps they were exploring "upsetness" without their really *being* upset; they may have been merely pretending to be upset.

In cross-sex episodes, boys and girls are similar in commenting about one another's feelings: feeling fine, being mad, getting hurt. In a few distinctive examples, the girls appear somewhat more conciliatory. When a boy insults another, a girl combines reprimand with sympathy: "Don't say that to Charlie; he's just a little boy." And when a boy's building falls down, another girl is comforting: "That's all right, Michael." Boys can be potentially protective: "Call me if you need me," says one to a girl who has been expressing dismay at her tangled fishing lines. An interesting male–female contrast in these examples points to the male's emerging image as the protector of girls.

Age Five: At 5, awareness of feeling in same-sex contacts is infrequent among both boys and girls. Five-year-old girls, like girls at 4, try to make amends when they realize they have hurt another: "I'm sorry I stepped on your foot." "You can wear one of my scarfs. Don't cry." Girls at age 5 can anticipate feelings: "Don't be angry, Mom," one girl remarks to another girl who is crying because she was hit. A new quality also emerges, which develops later as "cattiness." A girl perceives another girls' interest in a boy and tries to probe its dimensions: "Don't you like Matthew?" "A little." "I do, too." A girl comments about the objectionable behavior of another girl: "Stacey bugs us. I don't like her. Whoever likes Stacey, raise your hand."

Boys are involved in the feelings of other boys at 5. When a block thrown by one boy lands on another's foot, the first rushes over and asks solicitously, "Did that hurt?" Then he rubs the other's foot, and asks his companion as they build together again, "Batman, you all right?" And, as at 4, one boy identifies with negative feelings in another in a spirit of comradeship. "I'm getting bored. Let's go someplace else." The other replies, "You're right, I'm bored. Let's go." There is no incidence of awareness of feelings in cross-sex interaction at age 5.

Bonding of Friendship

Age Two: Compliments, expressions of admiration, and the sharing of feeling all contribute to bondings of friendship, which flourish primarily in same-sex dyads. This begins as early as 2 when one girl asks another, "Are you my friend anymore?" and receives an affirmative reply.

Age Three: At 3, bonding of friendship in same-sex contacts does not advance much beyond the announcement or questioning of friendship. Two girls explore a unity of relationship because of their similar appearance. "Hey, we have pigtails," says one. "Yes, we have the same as mine," says the other, and they touch each other's hair. On one occasion a girl announces another to be her friend but advises a boy of his exclusion: "You can't be her friend."

Discussion and bonding of friendship occurs most frequently in same-sex girl contacts. Sharing possessions, recognizing similar clothing, telling a secret are avenues to friendship. "I'm glad you're wearing pants, 'cause I am." "We both got the same barrettes." "I'm telling you a secret. Can't tell anyone else." "If you let me color in yours, I'll let you use mine when I bring it."

Announcements of friendship are common: "Now don't hurt my friend." "From now on I'm playing with you, my friend." "Let's be friends, Juliet." "Can I help color? I'll be your best friend." "Do you like me? Remember when I gave you a gumball?"

Sometimes the ramifications of friendship are too complicated to cope with, and too many friends can be troublesome: Jenny tells Meredith she will share her skates with her. Suddenly another girl comes and says, "Didn't I say I'd be friends with you?" Jenny says, "O.K., I'll be friends with you; I forgot." Meredith reminds her, "You were my friend today." Jenny concludes, "I forgot. We can still share roller skates."

And on another occasion, three becomes a crowd. Jessica and Joan are painting together when another girl enters the area. Jessica says, "I'm only playing with Joan." Joan tries to be the peacemaker, "Yeah, but we could all play together." The intruder bows out and adopts a face-saving strategy: "I don't want to play anyway." Jessica is pleased: "It'll be more fun ourselves."

Three-year-old boys did not develop friendship contacts with similar intimacy or intricacy. The friendship contacts we noted were, for the most part, just announcements of the fact of friendship.

Age Four: Friendships among boys tend to be utilitarian, a means to an end, and groups or gangs begin to form among 4-year-olds. The concept of friendship can mend wounds: "Are you my friend?" a boy asks of another whom he has just hit. "Be my friend," says a boy to another who controls a favored truck, but there is no response. "Are you my friend?" a boy asks. "Yes, but I don't want to wreck it [a structure]," the other boy replies.

Among boys, friends can form power coalitions. Two boys in the block area have been warding off other boys who smash blocks, saying, "We can have this all by ourselves. We got it, then we'll fight them, huh?" They cement their union: "Me and you got a big one; we don't like him. Huh, pal, huh?" On another occasion a boy is invited to join forces. "Want to be in our gang?" Another boy says about nearby boys with trucks, "These guys can be part of the farm."

The qualitative nature of girls' same-sex contacts at age 4 matches those of the 3-year-olds, primarily reflecting mutual possessions, experiences, or appearances. Cross-sex friendship contacts are virtually nonexistent; only one incidence occurs. A boy says that a girl cannot play with them. She cajoles, "I'll be your friend," but is ignored.

Age Five: A new trend emerges in the 5-year-olds in the bonding of friendship in that the quality of boys' same-sex contacts assumes a variety and richness not found among those of girls. Girls with other girls tend primarily to assert or question friendship: "Are you my friend?" Friendship continues to be linked with experience or appearance. "You and me is friends, 'cause we both have red on." It is also associated with gifts. "You let me use yours, and I'll be your friend," and "Thank you [for a bowl]. You're my best friend."

Boys, on the other hand, continue to develop themes of partnership and group cohesiveness: "We're building blocks together, right?" asks a boy as he gives a pat of camaraderie. "You're Batman, and I'm Superman, and we're friends, right?" Boys argue over who made a train of blocks. "We all made it; we're friends," says one. A boy seeks entrance to another's "house." "How do I get in?" he asks. "Give the password," the other boy commands.

Two boys build together and share wood: "Here friend!" says one as he passes the blocks. "Hey, we can share the pepper together. These can be at my house in case someone steals it out of your house." "We can use our sneezer to kill the bad guys." "We're the good guys."

Two other boys change their names: "Today you're Chris; I'm Emmett." "Tell your mother today you're Emmett." "You can share my tunnel. Pretend my sign says, 'No one can come in but Emmett.' " This example shows boys' relationships going beyond physical sharing: they are engaging in, and learning, social exchange.

Cross-sex episodes are at the same low level as at 4, with simple assertions or questioning of friendship. "You wanna be our friend next door," a girl asks two boys. "No, we wanna be our own friends," is the prophetic reply.

Summary

Girls' positive or affiliative contacts tend to involve less bodily contact, to be more gentle (in the case of rough-and-tumble play), and to be more personal (in the other categories). The positive behaviors of girls seem to reflect the socially oriented, domestic, nurturing mother. Boys' positive behaviors are more active, physical, and sexual. Whereas girls find it more appropriate to express approval of personal accoutrements, such as clothes or jewelry, boys find it generally more appropriate to express approval of productions, work, and prowess. Increasingly, boys avoid the boring company of girls, and girls criticize the boorish company of boys.

Teasing and rough-and-tumble play with its sexual innuendo, which shows one of the strongest sex differences, persists in later years as a style of play characteristic of males. Same-sex touching, which is strictly forbidden among men, flourishes among preschool boys in rough-and-tumble play. Udry sees this behavior carried on in adolescents in " 'horseplay,' 'horsing around,' a kind of fake aggression such as bopping, tripping, wrestling, and other minor physical abuses."[7] Adult males compete with one another in a verbal manifestation of the same type of behavior, as they often engage in an intimate exchange of friendly insults.

Humor (equated with laughter and teasing) also continues to be more powerful among males than females. In the spoken language of 4-, 8-, and 12-year-old boys and girls, who talked together in same-sex and cross-sex dyads of peers, girls laughed the most when paired with a boy, and only half as much when paired with a girl. Boys, on the other hand, laughed almost twice as much among themselves compared to their frequency of laughter when they were with girls. Boys seemed to be the initiators of humor, and girls, the recipients.[8]

The sexual innuendo in this behavior also continues in male peer groups; the male peer group becomes the prime reinforcer of women as sexual objects. Male bonding continues to involve "forbidden" sexual language, jokes, and information, which become increasingly geared to denigrating and dominating women. "To get 'fucked,' 'screwed,' 'reamed,' or 'had' (among the slang words used widely among males to describe sexual intercourse) implies that one has been victimized."[9] Almost all pornography, which circulates widely in male groups, is directed specifically to arousing sexual fantasy in *males*.

The differences in their styles of affiliative behaviors suggest basic differences in what attracts peers to boys and to girls. The differential attractions also suggest the forthcoming dyad and group coalitions in the latency and adolescent years.

SEX ROLE PLAYING

The masculine or feminine roles that boys and girls adopt in their play reveal developmental and stylistic differences. A study by Esther Grief suggested a model for identifying all incidents of sex role playing or preparation for sex role playing in our observations.[10] We designated episodes of sex role playing as being either brief (no longer than one minute) or long (more than a minute). Our data of brief and long episodes from a random sample of our half-hour observations of preschoolers' play showed the following distribution:

Table 2. Distribution of Brief and Long Episodes of Preschool Sex Role Playing

| | Same-Sex | | | | Cross-Sex | |
| | Males | | Females | | | |
	Brief	Long	Brief	Long	Brief	Long
2-Year-Olds	4	0	2	3	1	4
3-Year-Olds	3	2	3	5	3	7
4-Year-Olds	5	8	5	5	8	5
5-Year-Olds	3	10	3	10	11	8
Totals	15	20	13	23	23	23

The table reveals that approximately equal numbers of boys and girls engage in sex role play. Those at the older ages do so more frequently than the younger children. Boys begin sex role playing with other boys relatively later than girls, but role playing among 4- and 5-year-olds tends to be almost equal for boys and girls. The high incidence of cross-sex role playing among 5-year-olds may seem an anomaly until we consider the qualitative nature of such play, for sex role playing in cross-sex pairs becomes, among 5-year-olds, a veritable arena for the battle of the sexes.

The following play episode of 4-year-old children involves a boy and girl "playing house." The episode is appropriate to consider here, for it incorporates a number of stereotypes about mother and father roles, which are further elaborated in the play of other children. In this episode, the mother is the dominant care giver. Her comments reveal the extent of her responsibilities: she is responsible for her children's warm clothing, worried by a sick child who won't eat, and harrassed by her children's bad behavior (which includes their breaking a sweeper). At the same time, the girl, Michelle, is protective of her husband, concerned lest the children awaken him before he is ready, and tolerant of a life style that sends him repeatedly outside the house "to work." The boy's role is implicitly dominant: child behaviors are reported to him, and children are rewarded by sleeping in his bed. Derrick gives the ultimate directions about family outings, controls the keys to the house, and has the money to pay the babysitter. He is woefully inadequate about techniques of child care, however, so that when he puts the baby in the bureau drawer, the mother intervenes to protect it.

*   *   *   *

Derrick and Michelle

Derrick and Michelle are in the house area. Michelle has the baby in a cradle, wraps it up, says it's sick. Derrick, in another area, puts on a hat, picks up a toy tiger.
Derrick: *"Goodbye, Mommy, I'm going for a walk." He comes back, saying, "I'm home."*
Michelle: *"I'm glad, these babies are being bad for me."*
Derrick lies in bed with his toy animal.
Michelle: *"Give the kids a kiss first," but Derrick doesn't. Derrick lies on bed near the babies holding the tiger for about five minutes. Michelle washes dishes.*
Derrick: *"Honey, it's light out."*
Michelle: *"Oh, honey, did the kids wake you up?"*
Derrick puts on his hat, runs out of the house again with the tiger. He sits on a bench a few seconds, then runs back saying, again, "I'm home."
Michelle coos to baby: *"You can sleep with daddy in tiger's bed, O.K.? Here, Daddy's home."*
Derrick shouts: *"I have to go to work." He goes out again with hat and tiger and sits on the bench for a considerable time. He then returns and says, "Honey, I'm home from work." He puts away his hat, still holding the animal.*
Michelle reports to Daddy (Derrick), *"He was being the best boy; he was being good."*
Another girl comes in. Mother gives her dishes and admonishes, "Be sure you don't cut yourself."
Michelle to Derrick: *"Look what the kids did to my sweeper." She holds it up and shows its broken bottom. Derrick does not react.*
Michelle: *"This kid's sick and won't eat." Derrick picks up the baby and looks.*
Derrick: *"I'm ready, honey."*
Michelle: *"I know, we're going to the wedding."*
Derrick: *"We're ready for the wedding." He arranges the clock to a certain time.*
Michelle: *"No, it's not time. Baby has to have a sweater and a hat."*
Derrick: *"The baby can't come to the wedding."*

Michelle: "I know. She'll mind the baby." (She is referring to the other girl, who is still at the table.)
Michelle to girl: "Your father will have the keys, and don't let robbers come in and steal the babies and the animals."
Michelle, with veil on, to Derrick: "Can we have three cents?" Derrick gives her something (pretend money). Michelle takes off her veil and puts it into a drawer.
Derrick shifts to putting the baby in the refrigerator, and says, "Happy dreams." He then picks up another baby and puts it in a drawer.
Michelle: "Don't put baby in the drawer—it smothers."
Derrick: "Goodbye, honey; I'm going to work." He goes off again with hat and tiger.
Michelle: "Come back."

$$*\quad*\quad*\quad*$$

This is one of the few episodes in which a child—boy or girl—sustains a father's role throughout a half-hour period. The sex role playing among 2-, 3-, 4-, and 5-year-olds substantiates the elusive quality of the father figure and reveals the other masculine roles with which boys instead tend to identify. There are significant differences in the types of roles boys and girls adopt, which are, perhaps, predictive of the parents they will become.

Two-Year-Olds

Episodes of girls engaging in role playing with other girls, although nearly the same in number as those of boys, are longer and more elaborate. Two such episodes document the domestic scene as girls set the table, eat, sing to the baby, put it to bed, and care for its sickness. In one episode, a girl adopts the masculine role of fireman and even entertains the fancy that she is a monster. She fire-fights and crashes into blocks with great excitement. In an episode of cross-sex play, boys and girls play roles of firemen, but one boy does not like it when a girl controls the hoses.

There is an episode of a boy assuming the role of a parent. Holding a doll, he chants, "Baby, baby, baby." Then he hits it, shakes it, and tosses it to the floor, saying, "No biting." More typical domestic play involves the girl's being a controlling, frustrated mother. Although she initially considers the boy a potential father, she does not entertain the idea for long. When he assumes the role of a baby, he is fed, cajoled, warmed, directed, and reminded of the girl's ultimate authority, "Darling, better stop fighting 'cause Mommy says 'No.' "

The examples of sex role play among 2-year-olds are different from the play in older children in that a few males, at 2, assume child-care roles with babies, although their nurturing is fleeting. In general, boys engage in only brief episodes of sex role play. Episodes of feminine role play last longer, and are harbingers of things to come. The girl is more likely to adopt both masculine and feminine roles. She already moves into the house-caring, baby-tending scene with considerable assurance and specific knowledge of work to be done.

Three-Year-Olds

With the single exception of an ambiguous sex-typing of "baby," boys assume roles primarily associated with the masculine sex: fireman, fire chief, gas pump attendant, Darth Vader, good guy, bad guy, doctor, monster, Superman, and father. Although the father role is adopted frequently, the specifics of the role lack definition. Among boys, there is a greater variety of roles, but they tend to be stereotyped, lacking between-child variation, creativity, or embellishment. They are global rather than specific, and they frequently depend upon props (more so than among girls), such as the fireman's hat or the doctor's stethoscope.

Girls are willing to assume masculine roles: doctor, fireman, driver of the fire truck, father. Boys, when it is called to their attention, do not go along with inappropriate sex role play in either sex. When a girl suggests that she be doctor, a boy will set her straight. Another girl advises that boys be witches; they ignore her suggestion and make her the witch. A boy refuses to wear dresses, presumably suitable only for girls. Another boy, addressed as "Mom," at once says that he is the daddy (although he does not develop the role). Girls, like boys, do not go beyond a nominal adoption of their masculine roles. Roles of baby, sister, and mother are most popular, and that of mother is the favorite. This role is extraordinarily well embellished in terms of activities and style. Mothers wear earrings. They feed, clothe, nurture, and protect baby. Girls telephone, cook, and serve specific foods. They shop, go to restaurants, visit friends and relatives, and have house guests. Mother is perceived as an authoritative and powerful person who orders children to bed and school, and can even mess up a house with impunity. She is the ultimate arbiter of appropriate behavior.

Although there are a number of long episodes (each lasting more than a minute) in which the two sexes play together in differing roles, there is little development of roles in these situations. Boys do not like to be assigned roles, and girls tend to be frustrated by their lack of compliance. Girls often ignore or admonish boys, or assign them to insignificant roles. The most varied and creative, and presumably most satisfying, sex role play seems to take place when children of the same sex are involved.

But clearly, at this youngest age where sex role playing flourishes, the girls have a lead over boys. Although the domestic household scene has been equally visible to both, the specifics of the father role have escaped both. The female, knowing that she is a girl and a potential mother, has a highly visible and potent model. The boy seeks the specifics of his identification in a variety of models, none of which he knows about, all possibly attractive in terms of power.

Four-Year-Olds

At 4 years of age, boys continue to assume roles primarily associated with the masculine sex: bad guys, good guys, hunters of sharks, brother warriors, mailmen, house painters, fire chiefs, plumbers, and fathers. They are attracted by the grandiose, fantastic and warlike: Mickey Mouse, Superman, Batman, and monsters. Roles continue to be global. None of the domestic roles is perceived in full dimension. Baby and mother roles are seen as nominal only (babies are really unpopular), and a girl who is invited, by a boy, to be a mother soon loses her position and is requested to hold the fire hose until a boy wants it. One of the few sustained examples of the father role depicts a figure always off to an undefined work, whose life at home is spent mostly in bed. His managerial wife looks after his creature comforts but does not invite his participation in domestic activities. In another play episode, a boy refuses to assume the role of a girl whose house is on fire. He also protects himself from female dominance, refusing to be the child sent for the mail, whose mother puts his coat on. He avoids incipient romantic overtures, and he is not lured by the invitation that he be a prince to marry a princess, withdrawing in disgust from a kiss. The boys' cooking lacks qualities of nurturance and detail. They cook marshmallows, hot dogs, and stew on grills in a restaurant. When they cook bread in an oven at "home," the bread is filled with fire, and the fire-bread kills them all.

In a few instances, girls adopt masculine roles: fireman, brother, and father. They are also alert to inappropriate sex role behavior in boys — a boy cannot buy jewelry. Girls are only briefly attracted by the fantastic (and, more to the point, fantastic power), such as King Kong. Even when they more fully explore the role of witch, and engage in a kind of domestic cooking of deadly potions, they cannot divest themselves of mundane household chores. Marriage and romantic relations engage their attention. They refer to husbands, discuss kissing, talk about getting married. Domestic activities continue to be most popular, particularly cooking, baby care, and household care. They continue to move, in imagination, out of (but not far from) the house, often equipped with purses. They go to the bookstore, shopping, out to supper, to a picnic, and to the beach. They are cognizant of the childbirth drama, although in their play they suggest that the mother might give birth to a kitten as well as a child. As mothers, they continue to be authoritarian, demanding obedience and propriety. Although they sometimes invite a boy to the domestic scene, he is usually regarded with suspicion. Girls will view a boy as convenient if he plays a prescribed role, but he is primarily there to be manipulated or ignored.

The battle of the sexes emerges full fledged in cross-sex play. Boys are obstreperous and molesting; they tease and destroy. Girls regard them as "crazy," "fatso," "mean," and potentially scary. Boys are advised to "take it easy" when they enter a girl-dominated territory. Boys tend to be the intruders, either chased away by girls or causing girls to leave when they enter the girls' territory. Even boys who are initially conciliatory reject girls. At age 4, the girls' group is consolidated as a domestic "in" group, and boys do not fit in well in domestic play.

Five-Year-Olds

The masculine nature of the boys' roles continues: good guys and bad guys, builder, guard, Batman, Superman, doctor, fireman, father, little boy, Steve Austin, Cato, Green Hornet, Captain Kirk, and the Lone Ranger provide models for identification. Boys explore the building of friendship in roles of "brother" and by assuming one another's identity and protection. The doctor role takes on a new dimension: the scientist doctor examines blood vessels and evaluates temperatures. Boys muster forces to protect against danger, and they enjoy the equipment and activity of warfare. They revel in death and destruction.

Although most of the boys' roles are characterized by vitality, they are still largely global, and domestic roles continue to be elusive. A boy baby cannot maintain the essential characteristics of a baby. One father dresses and goes to work. A fireman husband demands coffee from his wife, then throws the empty cup at her. Another father, in his "cabin," manages one household chore (ironing), but then examines all the equipment in the house as though it were unfamiliar and is active in chasing away robbers. When one boy asks to play house, he is rejected; when girls invite another to be father, he ignores them. A boy is not even interested in being a girl's friend next door. When hospital play emerges, a boy assumes the brief and sometimes reluctant role of patient with girl nurses. In fleeting fantasy play involving a Wonder Girl and Superman, the boy establishes his leadership by driving vehicles.

Girls tend to be unsatisfactory when assuming masculine fantasy roles. In "no way" (quote from a girl) will one girl assume the role of killer. Even as passenger, a girl rejects the opportunity to go to England, preferring to go to a candy store. Another refers to the need for "heat" in an engine, rather than gas. Although a boy is momentarily ensnared to play the part of a prince with a princess, he cannot be lured to pursue the romantic role beyond adopting the cape and crown of prince. Boys' latent hostilities are often expressed. "Stay in jail till I tell you to get out," one boy shouts to unsuspecting girls who are off to the "hospital" with their babies. "Get out, get out, peanut head," another boy screams at a girl intruder.

Girls are contemptuous about boys' domestic play, but girl/girl role play flourishes. The mother in the domestic scene is most popular, and the helping nurse in the home or hospital is a close second in popularity. It is interesting that in but a single brief incident, girls announced a mutual exchange of names and roles, but this was not developed in the protective bonding manner that was true in a similar exchange of identities between two boys. A policewoman is named, but the role is not developed. There are brief allusions in our records of girls assuming a father role; the most memorable is that of the gift-giving daddy who reads books and buys treats for his daughter after school. Older sisters, often seen as teenagers, and mothers dominate the household, and the mother role is even more fully documented than it was among the 4-year-olds. Mothers grant permissions and provide advice about good behavior: "Take turns and don't fight"; "Be calm"; "Don't you ever use a saucer?"; "It's not polite to watch people eat." They commend a baby who "eats herself, no spilling," and chide a "naughty baby who spills." They are alert to the drama of a child who does not come home on time, and they cannot tolerate a contradiction of what they say. Mother is the ultimate authority: "I'm the mother; you shouldn't tell me what to do." Dominant behavior extends to nursing roles, with boys as patients. The girls' dominance suffers in briefly assumed power roles such as Wonder Girl, driver, or witch, when boys tend to assert their leadership, after which the play deteriorates.

Mothers, sisters, and nurses are also very nurturant and hard working. They kiss their children, use endearing epithets, caress the sick. Their primary work is cooking, but they also engage in all aspects of baby care. They wash clothes and dishes, sweep and mop the floor, answer the telephone, care for the sick. They are concerned about money and sometimes see their chores as overwhelming. "I haven't swept for the past four days, I've been so sick. We have to work hard because we are so poor," remarks one girl. They enjoy their pocketbooks, dressing up in high heels, long skirts, blouses, hats, and ballet costumes. They adorn themselves with beads, shawls, pins, and veils. They shave their legs, and even their faces, and look at themselves in the mirror. They also cultivate a social life, serving one another tea, going "out of town," and attending a dance, a ballet, and a wedding. It is interesting to note how romance and the wedding theme continue to be fostered among girls, but not among boys. It is the girl who introduces the theme of prince and princess. She anticipates marriage and realizes that the ceremony can bring special helping favors: "I'd like you to clean up the table, 'cause I have to get married."

The battle of the sexes among 5-year-olds is rampant. Girls increasingly initiate combats in boy-dominated areas, and boys teasingly intrude into girl-dominated areas, from which they are cast out before any role can be assigned or developed. In cross-sex play, the boys reject the girls, not really allowing them to develop any role in their territory. Boys frequently treat girls as subservient. When some girls in the house area go to an adjacent block area, they are evicted with, "Get out of here." Returning to their "house," one girl finds a block on the floor. She picks it up as though it were contaminated, throws it into the block area. "Who put this block in here?" she asks accusingly. In another situation, two boys come to the house area where girls are playing and open bureau drawers. One mutters, "You two ladies get out of here." They are ignored and soon leave. A single girl in the house area is teased by a boy who rushes in, picks up some plastic gloves, and shakes them in her face. She leaves.

In role-playing episodes, the ejection of boys from girls' areas seems to occur quite frequently. Boys delight in a new talent, that of provocative tease, molester, or intruder. They storm into house areas and grab, destroy, or defile property; they tease with behavior carrying sexual innuendo (forerunners of "panty raids"). Girls retort by calling for teacher's help or screaming insulting remarks. The following are examples of these stereotyped behaviors:

Boys are invited to come to a house for tea. They initially just look things over, then run away, squealing loudly. They soon return, sit down at the table to be served, but the table collapses.

"Now look at that. I told you that would happen," a girl admonishes, and then dismisses the boys.

A boy pauses to observe girls giving one another shots for their illnesses. "Give me your arm," the girl says, and applies her food baster to his arm as though giving him a shot. "That will teach him a lesson; he's cuckoo," gloats the girl as he runs away. But the boy returns to squirt water on the floor of their house. "I hate you," says the girl.

A boy dashes into the house area, grabs a hat and pocketbook, then runs away. "Get out, you numbskull," says the girl.

A boy enters the house area and announces, "I'm gonna grab it and crumble it up." "Get lost," retorts the girl.

As girls are discussing marriage a passing boy says teasingly, "I know who you're gonna marry—Chris." "Go away," the girl replies.

A boy comes to the house area and grabs some dolls. The girls scream, and the teacher intervenes, telling the boy not to bother them.

Girls are cooking in the house area. A boy comes from the nearby block area, which had been identified as a ship. He asks for a bottle of beer, but is refused. "This is not a restaurant," the girl says. He goes away, then comes back with water, which he spills on the floor, and girls rush to mop it up. He returns with two other boys, and they shout their requests for "Bingo juice" and "a bottle of wee-wee." They are told to go away, but one boy throws a fire hat into the area, and another throws a wooden cylinder, saying, "It's dynamite, and I'm going to explode this whole restaurant."

A boy comes to the house area and flings doll clothes around. Girls call to the teacher, who takes him away.

A boy comes, picks up a doll, and starts taking off the doll's clothes. The girl warns, "I'll call the police." He persists, pulls down the baby's pants and yells wickedly, "I see her tush; I see her tush." The teacher is called to remove him.

A boy throws water on the floor, hits a girl with a cloth, and pulls her pigtail. She summons the teacher.

A boy pokes at a baby's cradle, and tells the girl who is playing with the baby that it isn't hers and that she didn't bring it from home (which she did). The girl cries and the teacher dismisses him.

Girls immediately push a boy out of the house area he has just entered, with the remark, "You idiot."

A boy who picks up a telephone and pretends to call is told at once by girls to leave. He does.

The foregoing episodes reveal that boys are more aggressive and more prone to use bathroom talk than girls, that girls put down boys' intelligence and knowledge, and that teachers are summoned as advocates and protectors of girls. By age 5, boys, who have never really developed a congenial or suitable role in domestic play, increasingly cast themselves in oppositional roles in the "home." They seem to expect to be rejected and to enjoy the turmoil they can arouse. Attacked with verbal insults, they threaten devastating punishment. The girl, locked in domestic chores, finds solace in clothes, outings, and vague dreams of a romantic marriage with a nebulous father–prince. The boys meanwhile carry on exciting, satisfying play with other boys. Alternating as friends and foes of one another, they explore fantastic and varied sex roles of protective fellowship, power, and leadership.

Summary

Sex role playing represents only a minor part of the total play of the children in this study. With only a few exceptions, the play took place in block or house areas. Except for 5-year-olds, whose role playing was frequent in all play groups, most of the sex role play reported here occurred in day-care and community nursery-school settings where the ratio of teachers to children was not high and where there was not a wealth of curriculum materials. The laboratory nursery school, with a high teacher–child ratio (one teacher for four or five children), apparently was not as conducive to role play among 2- and 3-year-old children. It is possible that young children do not readily engage in fantasy play (and peer interaction in general) when there is a great deal of adult surveillance, that they may be more inhibited with playing a part when an adult is watching or interfering. Adults may also be potentially more attractive than other children. Children often vie for their attention and companionship. The laboratory school, with its wealth of materials, unquestionably tends to attract young children to the exploration of these materials rather than to role playing.

The overall power of the data documenting sex role play comes from its consistency. Ten different persons observed and recorded the play of children in nine different schools. Yet the descriptive analysis of the sex role play of children at 2, 3, 4, and 5 years reveals noticeable and consistent differences, which highlight those features of role identification salient to these children.

Boys play more varied and global roles that are more characterized by fantasy and power. Boys' sex roles tend to be functional, defined by action plans. Characters are usually stereotyped and flat with habitual attitudes and personality features (cowboy, foreman, Batman, Superman). Girls prefer family roles, especially the more traditional roles of daughter and mother. Even at the youngest age, girls are quite knowledgeable about the details and subtleties in these roles. Their family roles attest to their abilities to manipulate personalities and to their skill in inferring others' reactions. From a very early age girls conceive of the family as a system of relationships and as a complex of reciprocal actions and attitudes.

Neither sex is able to develop the role of father adequately, although both are aware that a father belongs in the home. Bruno Bettelheim comments on this phenomenon:

> The reason children do not have, and hence do not act out, the parallel fantasy about father staying home all day—irrespective of whether a child's father actually spends more time with his child there than does his wife—is that the mother is just so much more important as the source of physical and emotional security. Though he is not consciously aware of it, the child has an intense unconscious perception of who succors and nurtures him because it was his mother's womb he lived in for nine months; because it was she who predominantly nurses him; because his receiving the life-giving nutriments is, in his conscious and unconscious mind, deeply connected to nursing from the mother's breast, regardless of who gave him the bottle if he was bottle fed.[11]

We have witnessed that despite the allegedly greater importance of the mother for both sexes, male children tend not to play the role of the mother.

Boys, with a positional rather than a personal identification with their father, have a need to break away from their mothers. They need to discover and affirm a still tenuous masculine identity in a patriarchal world. The male child must overcome the power of the mother and increasingly protect himself from female dominance within the haven of the male peer group.

From the outset, girls favor domestic play and increasingly realize that boys are inadequate as fathers, and noncompliant in the domestic scene. By 5, boys are clearly regarded as a nuisance in the house and are subjected to many reprimands. Our data did not reveal that in sex role play boys are as frequently or openly rejecting of girls as girls are of boys. Perhaps they really don't need· to be, for the data suggest that the boys are getting increasing satisfaction from association with other boys. They indicate that girls are fun to tease and molest but have no fundamental place in the carrying out of popular masculine role playing.

Previous studies, as well as this one, document that girls are less rigidly sex typed, whereas, ironically, it is boys who have no clear-cut role to model.[12] From the earliest ages, the girl's interest in males prompts her to draw his image in her drawings of persons. She freely plays with traditionally masculine toys, such as moving vehicles and blocks, wears masculine clothes, and assumes masculine names. When she role plays, she is comfortable assuming the role of father, doctor, brother, or fireman, whereas the boy is not comfortable being mother, nurse, or sister. The father is a natural and ever-present, although illusive, image in the domestic play girls love, and girls care for boy babies as well as girl babies. Marriage and the glamor of weddings and potential romance preoccupy young girls (and the vision presumably includes a male), but boys are not similarly attracted.

The different type of boys' sex role play does not need a female for its fulfillment. War, work, and grandiose fantasy are not dependent on feminine participation or identifications. Thus the socialization of the boy appears to be going on apart from, and apparently with increasing resistance to, feminine influence. And girls, although paying more attention to males, seem to disapprove of, and even have contempt for, the opposite sex. On the one hand, boys narrow their interests by eschewing feminine roles, dress, and domestic interests. On the other hand, the domestic scene so overwhelmingly dominates girls' interest that it preempts their explorations of wider horizons. In a sense, boys define themselves by what they are not, girls by what they are.

This descriptive data on sex role playing show that young children increasingly learn and adopt traditional parental roles. We see antagonisms between the sexes flourish in house areas, which reflect neat microcosms of the problems in our society. The female likes to order and reprimand the male, and the male likes to tease and disrupt the female. As the sex cleavage develops, the implication for both sexes is, "If you can't join them, disrupt them."

Equal parenting, advocated widely by those who deplore our division of the social world into unequally valued domestic and public spheres, each the province of a different gender,[13] is far removed from the vision of the 5-year-old children we observed. Foundations for the sex role behavior we described in children's play begin in infancy, when the phenomenon of parenting involves a man and a woman. The woman is a mother involved from the beginning in childbearing and child care. The man is a father involved in work outside the home. "Why can't a woman be more like a man?" asks Professor Higgins in the popular song from *My Fair Lady*. This question, and its converse, is central to any study of sex role development.

Chapter 4 Theoretical Perspectives on Sex Roles and Peer Relations

TRANSMISSION OF SEX ROLES THROUGH PEERS

Our observations suggest that children in their earliest years move into same-sex alliances with their peers. Boys and girls at play develop different styles of social interaction and learn different social and cognitive skills within their same-sex groups. We turn our attention to selected studies and theoretical explanations of sex role development, and interpret our results in light of this evidence. We examine ideas about the influence of gender on social development from three broad areas: ethological, psychological, and sociological perspectives. These various disciplines serve to enrich our understanding of the sex cleavage that begins in preschool children's peer groups, and the legacy of sex differences that is substantially carried on in middle childhood, adolescence, and the adult years. In choosing same-sex peers, boys and girls reinforce qualitatively different types of play behaviors and power relationships. Adult sex roles, as well as early peer relations, are characterized by sex differences in social interaction.

A model of social analysis developed by Hinde provides a frame of reference for interpretation of the age and sex differences that we found among young boys and girls at play.[1] The model identifies four levels of social behavior description: individual action, dyadic exchange, dyadic relationships, and group structure. Each successive and more complex level describes consistent patterns of behavior present in the preceding level. For example, the structure of children's peer groups reflects general patterns of dyadic relationships, or friendships, within the groups; namely, that the majority of friendships form between same-sex peers, dividing the peer group into same-sex groups with differing friendship patterns.

The data in our study describe children's social behavior only on the first two levels of Hinde's model—individual behavior and dyadic exchange. However, using social and psychological theory and research relevant to the development of sex roles through peer relations, we have interpreted our dyadic data in light of what is known about the more complex levels of social life—peer relationships and group social structure. We infer the formation of same-sex relationships, but our research was not designed to confirm what is, nevertheless, strongly suggested by our data and corroborated by other researchers. Our conclusions about the structure of boys' and girls' groups are also speculative, but are consistent with ethological studies of children's peer groups and with sociological evidence.

Parents, who are probably the most crucial mediators between the natural and cultural forces in children's social development, are particularly influential in sex role socialization. Parents play a fundamental role in the complex, multifaceted social system that contributes to children's sex-typed experiences. They set the stage for the processes of learning gender identities and roles that young boys and girls soon express in their associations with other children. Parents impute meaning to their children's gender in the twenty-fourth hour after birth, when information about the infant's individuality is minimal. Female infants are noted by their parents as significantly softer, finer featured, smaller, and more inattentive than male infants.[2] Both mothers and fathers use significantly more affective terms in reference to their female infants and seem to show greater investment in the social behavior of their daughters than of their sons.[3] In their second year of life, infants are given more encouragement by adults for activity and choice of male sex-typed toys if they are boys, and more interpersonal stimulation and nurturance play if they are girls. In one study, the emotional response of 18- to 25-month-old infants to surprising stimuli is labeled "anger" if the attributed sex of the infant is male, and "fear" if the attributed sex is female.[4]

In infancy and later, parents contribute to the establishment and maintenance of sex-typed play activities in young children. Parents try to engage boys more than girls in physical, rough-and-tumble play. They also communicate differing social standards about what the child is expected to like and which activities are more appropriate.[5] Mothers place greater demands on their daughters than on their sons to become involved in conversational exchanges, asking more questions, repeating their children's utterances, and engaging in longer utterances themselves.[6] These studies and many others show that there is different treatment of the sexes by care givers. Such differential treatments stimulate processes that pose a chicken-and-egg problem, whereby the biological sex of the child sets the stage for a self-fulfilling prophecy: girls are reinforced in feminine behaviors; boys, in masculine behaviors.

Although parents' contribution to their children's sex role development is considerable, contemporary evidence indicates that peer relations have a unique and significant role to play in sex role learning and are not a simple extension of adult–child relations.[7] Play emerges almost completely within the context of peer interaction, which increases in the third and fourth years. There is an unequal, subordinate status inherent in dependent relationships with adults that inhibits independent sex role behaviors. The unique value of peer interaction derives from "the egalitarian features existing in the interaction between individuals whose behavioral adaptations exemplify equivalent complexity" and from "the lack of constraints, imposed by both attachments and hierarchization that mark the child's relations with adults."[8] Eisenstadt finds that the relations between different age groups are necessarily assymetrical in terms of authority, respect, and initiation. He argues that cooperative patterns of behavior are developed mainly with age-mates, where no severely authoritarian element exists in the definition of the situation.[9]

Interaction among peers particularly influences the socialization of aggressive behavior. Aggression has become central to sex role definitions;[10] masculinity and feminity are closely identified with its presence or absence. Hartup asserts that children master their aggressive impulses within the context of peer culture rather than within the family.[11] A repertoire of aggressive behaviors is particularly adaptive for children when interacting with peers, since leader–follower status and power relations among peers are based on individual strengths. Peer interaction represents an opportunity for asserting power as an individual in the first social role of potential equality. Unlike interactions with either older or younger partners, peers negotiate status relationships as their group forms and becomes hierarchized. Sex differences in dominance and aggression are amplified as status is negotiated in separate boys' and girls' groups.

In addition to egalitarianism, peer relations are particularly characterized by reciprocity. Suomi notes the prevalence of peer interactions among monkeys and argues that peer relationships are the bridge between infant and adult roles, providing an important means by which adult-level social competence is developed.[12] Not only do young monkeys interact more with peers than with anyone else, the patterns of response that characterize their activities are similar to those shown between adults. He observes that the sequence of exchanges, particularly in play activities, is an important characteristic of peer relationships. The behaviors that are displayed most frequently when infants play "are the very patterns most likely to be reciprocated by a peer partner, while those displayed infrequently are almost always ignored or actively rejected by a peer infant."[13] Suomi emphasizes that young monkeys do *not* interact with adults according to this format. Instead, the levels of behaviors of mothers with their infants, and infants with their mothers, are often independent of the other's pattern of responses. Interactions with adult males are unlike those with either peers or mothers, "characterized by both reciprocating and rejecting responses to high-frequency behavioral initiates."[14]

This reciprocity in peer interaction helps explain the development of the sex cleavage. Children who behave in a certain way toward their companions are likely to be treated in kind. An individual is most likely to reinforce another person for behaviors that are relatively high in strength in his own repertoire, and the sex of the other person becomes a clearly identified discriminative stimulus for reinforcing behaviors.[15] A study supporting this thesis reports a positive relationship between the seeking and the giving of nurturance among preschool girls.[16] We found such reciprocity among the children we studied in their same-sex interactions. While girls ignore aggressive overtures from boys at age 3, other boys respond to them. Boys' negative initiations are first directed toward both sexes at 3, but by 4 only toward boys. After this, same-sex relations flourish, whereas cross-sex relations fail to develop significantly until adolescence. Jacklin and Maccoby, in their study of 33-month-old children interacting in same-sex and cross-sex dyads, suggest a possible reason for boys' more active involvement with one another in the company of their peers: when a young boy makes a tentative "probe" of another boy, he is more likely to get an exciting reaction than if the probe is directed toward a girl.[17]

In order to evaluate the influence of peer interaction on sex role development, it is necessary to take into account both the social–cognitive factors that provide the unique human flexibility to adapt to change, and the biosocial roots of masculine and feminine development related to our nature as social animals. In this chapter, we will identify commonalities of group social life from an ethological perspective, focusing on sex differences present both in young children's peer groups and in primate societies. Next we present psychological perspectives which address the unique factors that characterize *human* sex role development: the role of the *father* in his child's masculine or feminine development, and the important *cognitive* factors in the development of children's gender identity and sex role attitudes. The sociological perspectives that follow describe the influence of gender on the integration of the child into society through membership in two groups—the family and the peer group. We conclude the chapter with a discussion of the social implications of the sex differences we have identified in peer group organization and same-sex friendships.

ETHOLOGICAL PERSPECTIVES

Throughout childhood, human peer groups are characterized by same-sex friendships, which generally exclude any close association with the opposite sex. The preference for same-sex playmates is present through all of early and middle childhood, reaching a peak in pre-adolescence.[18] This segregation of social groups by sex is common to human and nonhuman primates, and is widely recognized in the play groups of the young as well as among adults.[19] Because the sex cleavage and its attendant power relations in children's peer groups are similar in structure to those in primate societies, an examination of social relations among nonhuman primates is particularly relevant to our focus on sex roles and peer relations. To make this comparison, we draw upon ethological studies of juvenile peer groups. Ethology is a specialized discipline within biology concerned with the direct observation of naturally occurring behaviors and the comparison of behavior across species. Ethologists examine human evolutionary history to determine the influence of biological factors in social life.[20]

Dominance Relations between and within the Sexes

In all social groups, including groups of primates and children, members are integrated into an organization of social relationships particular to their species (and in humans, particular to their culture as well). The integration of infants into a society places important constraints on their individual behavior. Group existence requires a degree of interdependence and cooperation which limits the expression of certain kinds of behavior, particularly aggression. Aggression within groups is regulated through dominance relations that structure conflict to control interpersonal behavior. Social conflict is contained and controlled when a stable dominance hierarchy forms and is maintained among the group's members. This structure of status relations allocates prerogatives allowing each individual to anticipate and avoid the adverse consequences of severe and continued aggression.[21]

Since males are generally more aggressive than females, their dominance relations tend to be more complex, and thus necessarily undergo more negotiation than those in female groups. Separate hierarchies are present among males and females in all primate societies, including human societies, and thus dominance has a clearer meaning within one sex.[22] Males and females are not equal in any animal society in the sense that status is never independent of sex.[23] The literature on primate social life indicates that males generally rank higher than females in the total group hierarchy and that a well-developed hierarchical structure is more common among males than females in primate societies. This is true of children's peer groups as well. The sex cleavage that develops as children are integrated into the peer group is associated with separate hierarchies among boys and girls.

There are clear-cut and important differences between male and female dominance relations and status. Female dominance is primarily based on individual relationships; male dominance is related to the individual's ability to enlist the aid of other males in coalitions. These coalitions require relatively strict hierarchical relationships, more characteristic of males than females. Social rank for the female primate is primarily dependent on kinship relations: the rank of the mother is one of the most prominent determinants of the social position of a female. Other factors in some species include age, birth order, and, for estrous and pregnant females, the dominance rank of her consort. None of these determinants of dominance in females depends upon the physical or behavioral characteristics of the individual. The male primate, by contrast, can establish a social rank through personal traits such as strength, ability to form alliances, and fighting ability. The influence of the mother's social rank is important for the young male as well as the young female, however, and in many cases its effect continues throughout his life.[24]

The ordering of dominance relationships results from social learning; individual recognition is the basis of hierarchical organization. Latent learning of hierarchies begins in primate infants of both sexes through observation of the mother's social encounters. Mothers tend to support their young against other infants in play situations, and it is this aspect of maternal behavior that is responsible for the transmission of social rank.[25] The adult female rank order has the function of establishing the ordered structure of the group without much agonistic activity. This order can be modified in later life, to a larger degree for males than females.

In peer play the experiences of the sexes begin to diverge. The period of juvenile play for females is brief. Observational learning of troop hierarchies suffices, for their rank is inherited and remains relatively stable. Juvenile males, on the other hand, are literally pushed to the periphery of the group and engage in a long period of play with peers. Play teaches the young primate about his strengths in relation to those of his peers. Males actively learn expectations for social interaction in the prediction of outcomes of agonistic encounters. Thus segregated from the rest of the social network, young males are in a sense stripped of status derived from their mother (to a greater or lesser extent, depending upon the species), and must determine their own rank vis-a-vis their male cohorts.

Primate societies are enormously complex; there are significant differences in the social organization of various species, particularly in the separate roles that males and females play. Despite this variety among primate groups, there seem to be certain common elements in the development of males and females. In the general primate pattern, immature females stay near the center of the group, whereas immature males move to the periphery, where they congregate in sizable "peer" groups. The juvenile males on the periphery, no longer dependent on their mothers and not yet a part of the adult male hierarchy, must adapt to a peer culture rather than one structured by adults. Male power structures, which are significantly more distinct than those of females, enable them to band together in large groups, actively participating in the formation of hierarchies that structure conflict resolution and lend stability and expectancy to the social environment. Females, who remain in dyads or small groups, recognize male dominance hierarchies but do not form their own as readily, at least not along dimensions of strength or toughness.

The pattern of sex differences we found among preschool boys and girls at play is consistent with research and theory that explore the development of peer group relations from an evolutionary perspective. A researcher who approaches child development from an ethological perspective describes the role of dominance in children's peer groups:

> Power relations in children, as in other primates, are not chaotic, but are typically organized in terms of a group dominance hierarchy. The concept of "dominance" provides a good bridge linking ethological and psychological considerations. Dominance is a structural model for a group that describes agonistic relationships observed for all dyads in the group. Its meaning is only in relation to the group, and it is best viewed as an "emergent property" at the structural level of analysis. . . . It is not a property of individuals. While psychologists have tended to focus on "aggression," and have used the term as an individual descriptor or as a trait concept, ethologists have more characteristically bypassed this focus and have been more concerned with the function and organization of conflict interactions within and for the group.
>
> Dominance essentially involves asymmetrical social relationships. Dyadic dominance describes the relative balance of social power between any two members of a social group, while a dominance hierarchy summarizes the organization of such power relations among all possible dyads within the stable group. In dyadic dominance, the hierarchy is governed by a linear rule, such that if A dominates B, and B dominates C, then A is dominant to both B and C.[26]

A group of researchers have found that the first dimension along which status is differentiated among human peers (as well as among nonhuman primates) is that of "toughness," the equivalent of what primatologists mean by "dominance," i.e., being strong, being good at fighting, and being able to get what is wanted.[27] Omark and Edelman studied the rank order of aggressiveness in three different hierarchies.[28] They measured the agreement on toughness within the separate male and female rank orders as well as between the same-sex groups. The pattern of sex differences they identified is predictable from the primate dominance pattern—and from our study, to the limited extent one can infer group relationships from our dyadic data, which trace general patterns of same-sex contacts only, not specific same-sex friendships.

Measuring how much children agree on who is "toughest," Omark and Edelman found a developmental shift between kindergarten and first grade (ages 5 to 6), when hierarchies become relatively stable. This is the same age at which we found a decrease in negative contacts in children's free play, particularly in boys' negative initiations. Thus, although hierarchies are present in all children's groups,[29] it is not until the end of the preschool years, when children begin to use perceived dominance interactions to form conclusions about the outcomes of aggressive encounters among other children, that they can perceive consistent hierarchical relationships.

In addition, Omark and Edelman found that highest agreement on children's dominance interactions was reached on the boy–girl hierarchy, where the boy was ranked higher and thus considered tougher. Rank-ordered relations seem to be more clearly defined between rather than within the sexes. As among nonhuman primates, males dominate females.

The agreement on who is toughest was significantly higher in boy–boy dyads than in girl–girl dyads. The boys' dominance hierarchies were more distinct and linear than the girls' hierarchies. Stevens has reported that one girl was quite explicit about the fact that toughness is not an organizing principle for girls' activities: "When she wants to be rough, then she plays with boys and is rough. When she wants to be a girl, then she is gentle and plays with girls."[30] In spite of the sex difference in the strength of their respective hierarchies, boys and girls do not differ in their ability to perceive the dominance relations of the whole peer group accurately. The children's direction of attention included the opposite sex, so that, despite the apparent lack of contact between the sexes during play periods, each sex could accurately perceive the hierarchy created by the opposite sex.

Although there apparently is no sex difference in the accuracy of perceiving hierarchical relationships, the sexes have different modes of learning about the group structure. Boys overrate their own hierarchical positions as compared with how others rate them. Omark and Edelman found this result consistent with the literature showing that boys are more competitive than girls, at least in endeavors that require "toughness." This demonstrates the emotional involvement of boys when they are asked to compare themselves with others; emotional involvement appears to interfere with boys' judgement of hierarchies more than it does for girls. Overrating one's status in the hierarchy is more characteristic of younger than older children and more common among boys than girls. The egocentric preschool child tends to overrate his position in order to ignore defeats and maximize winnings.[31] This perceptual adaptation enables the child to confront his peer group. The tendency of older boys to overrate themselves suggests that confrontation with the peer group remains an active issue for boys even after children's hierarchies have stabilized at age 5.

Parker compared mixed-sex and single-sex classrooms on toughness hierarchies in grades one through three.[32] He found that boys in sex-segregated classes had significantly less agreement on "toughness" hierarchies than did boys in mixed-sex classes, whereas girls' scores were the same in both kinds of classes. Girls in single-sex classes, however, overrated themselves significantly more than girls in coed classes, whereas the boys were the same under both conditions. Parker's interpretation is that "it would seem that the lack of the opposite sex in the classroom increases the emotional salience of toughness for the girls, while for the boys it decreases the stability or clarity of the hierarchy." He concludes that the opposite-sex audience was important in "calling out" sex-related behaviors. Thus it seems that girls become more aware of dominance relations among themselves when boys are not around, yet their interactions remain dyadic and do not become as rigidly hierarchical in structure as the boys' interactions do. For boys, power positions remain emotionally important whether or not girls are around, but their positions are less well defined in all-male groups. These findings suggest that the benefits of coed and single-sex education differ for boys and girls, since same-sex peer groups work out dominance differently than do heterosexual groups.

One of Omark and Edelman's most interesting findings, reported often in the literature on children's peer relations, is that boys begin to band together in large groups at about 5 years of age, whereas girls remain in dyads or small groups. The greater disposition of males than females to associate in groups has also been reported for 10-year-olds[33] and for adults.[34] Beatrice Whiting reports that large groups breed aggression, furthering the links among males, hierarchies, and aggression.[35] When more than six children are together, the rate of aggressive behavior increases. This increase results from attempts of children to influence the behavior of age-mates with a comparable level of complexity who frustrate them. When other children refuse to comply with their wishes, frustrated children employ a series of techniques of persuasion to achieve their ends, and these styles become increasingly aggressive if they continue to be thwarted.

Qualitative as well as quantitative differences between boys and girls in aggressive behavior are apparent from the early preschool years. Whiting and Edwards found that boys are more aggressive than girls in six diverse cultures, and suggest that sex differences tend to be a matter of style rather than intent. Girls seek help, boys seek attention; girls justify dominance by appealing to social rules, boys favor straight egoistic dominance.[36] Lubin and Whiting found that when Kenyan children aged 3 to 12 interact with younger targets, there is a marked tendency for girls to use prosocial (adultlike) techniques of persuasion, and for boys to use more aggressive strategies to gain compliance. Girls threaten to summon adult intervention while boys employ direct force or the threat of force with younger children.[37]

Boys' aggression in six cultures undergoes a qualitative change between ages 5 and 7, when their hierarchies become more differentiated than those of girls. Whiting and Edwards found that younger boys (3–6) show more rough-and-tumble play and insulting behaviors than girls, whereas older boys (7–11) are higher than girls in counteraggression and egoistic dominance.[38] This finding implies that boys' originally more overt aggressiveness becomes transformed at about age 5 with the formation of a group hierarchy that controls the expression of aggression. Whiting and Edwards's study also reveals developments in characteristic female behaviors that reflect the impact of socialization pressures on other sex-typed behaviors besides aggression. Younger girls touch and seek help more than boys, and older girls are significantly more nurturant. The authors reason that the significant differences in the younger chidren (male rough-and-tumble play, female touching) are likely to have biophysical roots, whereas the significant differences in the older children (male counteraggression and egoistic dominance, female nurturance) probably result from the influence of sex-differentiated learning environments, which amplify the earlier sex-related tendencies.

Aggression is directly related to dominance; hierarchies structure conflict to minimize, or at least organize, aggression within groups. It is clear that males are more aggressive than females in both animal and human societies. One indirect form in which male aggressiveness is manifest is the rank-ordered nature of their hierarchical peer group. Boys' greater aggressiveness seems to be associated with the formation and maintenance of their more highly developed dominance hierarchies and with their greater emotional investment in these hierarchies. We found that sex differences in nurturance and aggression characterize the sex cleavage by age 5. It seems that nurturance is learned—the sex difference that we found in nurturance became significant only at age 5. Boys' aggression, on the other hand, seems to have biological origins, although its expression is modified during the preschool years. In our study, aggressive initiations are prevalent among boys at ages 3 and 4 but decrease at 5, when same-sex alliances are consolidating and children's hierarchies become relatively stable. Boys' conflict becomes transformed at age 5, more frequent thereafter in response than initiation. Separate hierarchies for boys and girls form within the structure of the group as a whole.

Tiger offers compelling support for our thesis that peer relations are more hierarchical among males and that this structured peer interaction channels their aggression into social power.[39] He argues that the evolution of the human species is related to the dominant hierarchies of bonded males. "Male bonding" is a subtle process associated with political and defensive activity out of which specific individuals recognize others as distinctly related to themselves. The basic structure of society is a stable male hierarchy. Male rivalry is controlled as males inhibit aggression within the group and reassert it as a group. Participation in a bond in which internal aggression is inhibited facilitates aggression against the outside world. According to Tiger's argument, human aggression in a social-organizational sense—the ability to inhibit aggression toward peers and superiors for long-run success in a hierarchical structure—is a propensity of males. Historically, this has indeed been the case, whether or not one agrees with Tiger's belief that male bonding, and thus male dominance, is a biological given and will not be modified by modern social changes.

Sex Differences in the Social Structure of Attention

Rank ordering in dominance hierarchies provides group cohesion in primate social organizations because it ritualizes conflict by assigning roles of dominance and subordination. These roles involve different modes of attention. Chance believes attention to be the basic mechanism of rank-order relationships.[40] Dominance in primate groups relates not primarily to the control of resources or violence but to the amount of deference, by visual attention, paid to leaders by their subordinates. Attention is directed upward in a hierarchy: subordinate primates pay an inordinate amount of attention to those more dominant in status.[41] Rowell reports that high-ranking individuals in groups of primates are better recognized by the behaviors directed toward them by subordinates than they are by their own behavior.[42] She argues that a subordination hierarchy is a more useful concept than a dominance hierarchy, since agonistic interactions are usually determined and often initiated by the subordinate's behavior, and subordination is correlated with physiological changes.

In children's peer groups, attention must be paid to the group's dominance relations even for those of low status who do not participate in aggressive encounters. Indeed, children have more agreement on the ranks of the two toughest children than on the two lowest-ranked children.[43] Onlooking behavior tends to be characteristic of low-ranking children as well as newcomers when they are getting acquainted with the existing group structure. Hold confirms that boys rank higher than girls and that boys' groups are in general more stable than those of girls. She reports that most aggressive behavior in the classroom and playground is shown by upper-midddle-ranking boys against children (in most cases other boys) who have adjacent status and whose relative ranks are being negotiated.[44] Girls, who are generally of lower rank than boys, perceive the dominance relations of the whole peer group even though "toughness" is not emotionally salient for them. Hold observes that subordinate children look significantly more at dominant ones than the reverse, and girls look significantly more than boys. This finding may explain why the 5-year-old girls in our study have significantly more cross-sex peer contacts than do the 5-year-old boys. Since boys are "tougher," the attention of the girls becomes focused on the dominance relations of the boys.

Sex differences are apparent in the way that males and females must pay attention to others with whom they interact. After infancy, the male shifts attention from the matrifocal core to peers, whereas female attention remains focused on established kinship relationships with inherent dependent status. The binding quality of the attention within male cohort groups provides the social cohesion that males lose when they are "peripheralized," i.e., forced as juveniles out of the female-dominated central core in which infants of both sexes begin their life. There they must confront the adult male culture with their age-mates. Among the males, dominant individuals are the focus of attention for those having subordinate status. Male status is relatively unstable, much more dependent than female status on the differing strengths and abilities of the individual group members.

The origins of the differences in male and female experiences with hierarchical social relations lie in the process by which infants are separated from their close relationship with the mother. This weaning, or "detachment" process, lays the foundation for subsequent relationships with peers, and takes a different course for males and females:

> As juveniles of other primate species are weaned from their mothers they move towards their peers. Weaning always extends over a period of time, and the young can be seen moving back and forth between the mother and a "juvenile cluster," but with increasing amounts of time being spent near the other juveniles. This cluster gradually differentiates into like-sexed groups: the males engaging together in rough-and-tumble play, while the young females sit and groom other young females or try to hold the infants who are still associated with adult females (Chance and Jolly, 1970).
>
> With children the formation of peer groups occurs when they are sent to school. The association of children with like-sexed partners appears as early as nursery school—with girls quietly engaging in conversations (and grooming) with other girls, while boys are engaged in rough-and-tumble play with other boys. These analogous behavior patterns are the precursors for entrance into each group's hierarchical structure.[45]

The "detachment" of infants from the mother is more pronounced for males than females among both human and nonhuman primates. A major difference between human beings and their nonhuman cousins is how this detachment comes about. In human development, according to psychoanalytic theory, it is the father's role to "detach" the males and differentiate the sexes. Among nonhuman primates, however, the mother actively separates the males from the core group of females and young. According to Chance, the earlier separation of males from the mother is accomplished by the mother's leaving the infant and not vice versa. The mothers in some primate species promote independence in their offspring by not restraining them and by withdrawing from them; in others they do so by more active rejection—hitting, shoving, pushing, or throwing.[46]

Although the male infant leaves the mother earlier, he is not more "independent" of her. Chance suggests that male dependence upon the mother is of a different type than female dependence. The male infant keeps the mother in view—from a distance—and the mother forces him into a strategy of "looking at":

> What clearly emerges is that the male infant, by being separated from its mother to a significantly greater extent over a period of about three months, is forced to exercise and rely on "looking at" its mother for security, rather than achieving early reduction of alarm through contact. During this period, maturational changes almost inevitably leave their impact on fixing this mechanism, thus evoking its basic form later in life, even if this interval does not span or constitute a critical learning period. So, the young male learns to rely on constantly attending to the whereabouts of possible protective individuals other than its mother. These include, in the early stages, juveniles of its own clan; later the dominant male becomes the most significant in its life.[47]

This phenomenon may be true in humans also, with boys engaging in more contacts (and more "looking at") with other boys, as well as in same-sex contacts involving conflict, which need more vigilance. Girls, as we mentioned, look more at boys than vice versa, but they do not have as much need of this vigilant "looking at" within their own group. Boys more than girls need to attend to other boys in order to define and protect their identities and their status within the peer group.

Chance argues that primate social groups as a whole are brought together, and attention within them is organized, in two distinct modes.[48] "Hedonic" attention is based on the receiver's expectation of reward, "agonistic" attention on his fear of punishment. In the agonistic mode, which tends to underlie male interactions, attention is regulated by conflict and avoidance of attack from dominant individuals. The hedonic mode, based on display as a means of gaining attention, makes possible a far richer and more flexible flow of information than does its agonistic equivalent. Agonistic attention is constricted by its orientation toward a single type of message, that of threat. Attention in the hedonic mode is organized through a different mode of visual attention—"looking around" (scanning the environment) rather than "looking at." Those "looking around" are geared toward responding to others' nonaggressive initiations; those "looking at" are vigilant to others' negative initiations. The agonistic attention mode more characteristic of males tends to terminate active interactions, whereas the hedonic mode, more closely associated with females, tends to promote social intercourse. Hedonic attention is typical of females when they nurture the young and attend to the needs of the old and the sick.

Chance suggests that inherent hedonic and agonistic tendencies are influenced in ontogeny by the sex of the individual, and that this affects gender role development. The great amount of conflict present in the initiations of 3- and 4-year-old boys in our study seems analogous to the threat behavior characteristic of the agonistic mode. As the boys' peer group begins to stabilize at age 5, their aggression becomes ritualized into a variety of dominant and submissive social gestures (e.g., threat or withdrawal) that define their same-sex hierarchies. Girls' aggression is never encouraged; it develops in relatively passive social responses like ignoring, and in less direct means of control than boys' aggressive negative initiations (threats). Girls, more than boys, engage in the hedonic mode of attention getting. They praise and admire other girls, flaunt and attend to personal appearance and dress more than boys (as we noted in Chapter 3, and as Opie and Opie note in examples cited later in this chapter).

SOCIAL-COGNITIVE INTERPRETATIONS OF BOYS' AND GIRLS' PLAY

Sex differences influencing personality develop in young children out of their different cognitive experiences with attentional relations and their different social experiences in play. In recent years there has been a growing interest in the study of social cognition, how social experience contributes to and reflects the child's developing cognitive skills. The study of social cognition, which is the child's capacity to represent others intuitively, represents a contemporary effort to synthesize cognitive and behavioral findings regarding children's social development.[49]

Omark and Edelman propose that the structural similarities of dominance hierarchies among primates and children have important implications for the development of human cognitive capacities.[50] Children must adapt to new complexity in their social environment when they begin to interact with peers. Observation of and interaction with peers generates information that conceptually structures the child's *Umwelt*, the part of the social environment that is perceptually processed and cognitively rendered.[51] The different participation and emotional investment of boys and girls in the formation of dominance or status hierarchies seems to produce sex differences in social cognition.

In the social milieu of the human peer group, attention structures develop with status relationships as children begin to compare and define themselves in terms of others. Dominance relations provide everyday experience that may lead to the development of logic. Children seem to be developing a consistent perception of their dominance relations at the same time as they are developing the logical operations of transitivity, the cognitive principle that controls the rank ordering of objects. Transitivity (if $a > b$ and $b > c$, then $a > c$) underlies both hierarchization, which is the rank ordering of social "objects" such as classmates, and seriation, the ordering of physical objects.

Boys have more overt participation in their social structure, physically interacting with each other more than girls do.[52] Boys seem to develop their logical operations more by participating in the hierarchy than by watching it. Because girls interact less physically, are placed lower in the hierarchy, and are less emotionally involved, they seem more "other"-oriented in their involvement in the hierarchy. Girls develop their ability to reason about the hierarchy through reference to others; they engage in more verbalization than do boys, and much of their time is spent in discussing characteristics of their classmates.[53]

The group patterns of conflict resolution in the recognition of dominance or toughness hierarchies seem to provide experience that contributes to the development of logic, thus relating social activity to cognitive development. If social and cognitive logic are indeed equivalent, then sex differences in the inference of social rank—latent learning through the indirect experience of observation in females, more active learning through direct experience in males—may ultimately influence mature cognitive style. This divergence in social learning may be the source of the active–passive, analytic–intuitive dichotomy in modes of thought traditionally associated with the two sexes. Boys' experiences in perceiving physical encounters ("toughness") and conceptualizing dominance relations with which they are emotionally involved provide a basis for more symbolic means of dominance in the adult world.

Our data on same-sex and cross-sex contacts suggest that girls are dominant at age 3, or at least have some degree of control over boys, probably reflecting the power of the mother for young children, as well as girls' earlier maturation. The significance of the mother for young children, with girls' closer mother-identification and boys' increasing need for distance, seems to account for the 3-year-old girl's advantage in social interactions. Boys initially vie among themselves for power, since they are neither able to enter nor desirous of entering the legitimate female power structure, and they do not yet have access to adult male hierarchies. The greater conflict displayed by 3-year-old boys becomes inhibited within their peer group and channeled outward as the group stabilizes at age 5.

Boys are likely to initiate encounters involving conflict with one another, and in the process teach each other to channel aggressive behaviors, to structure and use them. Vertical hierarchies develop as males seek identities and vie for power. Girls, however, have in the mother a ready model for both affiliative and nonaffiliative behaviors. They, like their mothers, are socialized to use oblique or indirect forms of aggression, such as the reprimand, and to avoid direct fighting. We have mentioned that girls employ less direct means of influencing their peers as same-sex relationships form. Boys threaten, whereas girls persuade more indirectly by nagging or using "feminine wiles." The indirect quality of "typical" female behavior is expressed in Freud's observation that the female sex tends to give precedence to passive aims.[54] At an early age girls adopt culturally-sanctioned affiliative behaviors in same-sex groups; again and again they dramatize the family scene, reenacting personal and social relationships. Their socialization directs them to caring and nurturing behaviors, to "ministering to the needs of others," which has been identified as behavior typical of females cross-culturally.[55]

Traditionally, males assume power over females in organizational spheres, which become increasingly important in adolescence and beyond. There is some evidence in this study that the precursors of this phenomenon are present among preschool boys and girls, reflecting the power of the father in our society, which is still fundamentally patriarchal despite recent gains for women. Perhaps 5-year-old girls are responding to boys with a high frequency of both positive and negative behaviors because the boys are beginning to become the more dominant sex. Active participation in dominant hierarchical processes may represent a functional specialization in males that allows them to enter more formal cultural and institutional hierarchies as adults, while females are channeled into a more "biological" maternal role.

All human and nonhuman primate societies share a threefold division of the larger social world into three primary groups: adult males, females and young, and "peripheralized" juvenile males.[56] These same three "interest groups"—older males, women with children, and younger males—still compete in contemporary human social arenas. In a sense, males are coerced in both their work and play roles to move into a different social world from the one in which they were initially socialized, a world of peers and superiors, rather than that of family and younger children. Van Gennep terms life-cycle changes that involve alteration in status or behavior potential, "rites of passage," with three phases of separation, transition, and incorporation.[57] Our data reflect the beginning of the separation of the males as they segregate themselves into large groups. Their participation in dominance hierarchies may reflect such rites of passage into adult male society. The data also support a psychoanalytic interpretation of emotional development in the sexes at age 5, in which males bond together and internalize social norms while females remain more directly bound to adult society.

PSYCHOLOGICAL PERSPECTIVES

The Role of the Father in the Detachment Process

Freud focused attention on the separate processes through which boys and girls are integrated into the family. He recognized the transition from the primary dyad of mother and child to the triad of the family as an emotional trauma, the "disillusion of the symbiotic ideal."[58] In his theory the father plays a key role in complicating the child's primary identification with the mother, and in differentiating the sexes. The primary social bond satisfies children's dependent needs; it is in their impulses toward independence that they begin to move away from the intense first attachment. Children learn to control dependent needs largely through interaction with the caretaking mother; the father's role, in psychoanalytic theory, is to socialize children's independent social and aggressive tendencies. Many empirical studies, including Evelyn Pitcher's 1957 study, confirm that the father more than the mother differentiates his responses according to the sex of the child. By modulating his style of social interaction, the father offers aggressive stimulation to his son and sexual challenge to his daughter. Because he facilitates gender identification, he directly affects his child's potential for independent social behavior, and particularly for aggression, the most consistently documented sex difference.

In the view of some contemporary psychoanalytic authors, the father's first role is to draw children into the world of things and people.[59] Boys and girls share a common experience in the "attachment" phase of psychological development; Freud himself considered infants "bisexual" at birth. As infants and toddlers, both sexes are "bonded" or attached to the mother. In the next phase of psychological development, the weaning or "detachment" phase, children must go beyond the dependent, symbiotic attachment to the mother and move toward their "individuation." Mahler explains that the father assists his child's developing sense of self by acting as a "necessary support against the threat of re-engulfment of the ego into the whirlpool of the primary undifferentiated symbiotic stage."[60] The father and his difference from the mother initiate the detachment phase, and the child's sex increasingly defines his or her potential social actions. This "detachment" phase spans the preschool years, lasting until the resolution of the Oedipal dilemma and the incorporation of the child into a role-governed society through a same-sex group that includes adults as well as peers.

Mahler provides a developmental theory concerning the successive stages of the infant's detachment or "separation–individuation" from its mother—the "psychological birth" of the infant.[61] Abelin, in discussing Mahler's theory, distinguishes the roles of both parents in the early years of the child's life, and is concerned with qualitative differences between mother–

child and father—child relationships. Abelin studied mother—infant pairs, and later made an intensive longitudinal observational study of a mother, father, and infant.[62] From these studies Abelin made specific theoretical propositions about the timing and nature of the father's role in the development of ego functions.

After forming the first symbiotic relationship with the mother, the child leaves her in stages. In the "practicing" subphase of the separation—individuation process, the mother is a "home base" to fulfill the need for "refueling" through physical contact. Then the "refueling" type of bodily approach is replaced by various forms of verbal and gestural communications, as well as physical separateness, as the infant "employs all kinds of mechanisms in order to resist and undo his actual separateness from his mother."[63] The infant's first physical movements away from the mother widen his experiences of the "other-than-mother" world. The task of the young child is to achieve ego-autonomy through the process of intra-psychic separation from the mother. Abelin postulates that the early tie to the father plays an essential role in the psychological growth and autonomy of the child because the father's male intervention in the mother—infant relationship brings to the infant an example of a primordial difference. The male represents the "first step into the world of novelty, of external reality. . . . When this reality is genuinely achieved in a wide range of non-maternal objects, when the father is firmly established as the 'other,' the 'different' parent, then we need not be too concerned about the development of the toddler toward final individuation and intra-psychic separatism."[64]

For the girl, the task of separation is less straightforward than it is for the boy, since the girl experiences a continuing attachment to the mother. Abelin reports that the infant girls he studied showed different person orientations from those of the infant boys. Girls appear to have more specific ties to both parents, to show more stranger-anxiety with men other than their fathers, and to manifest more coyness and self-consciousness in the presence of males. Abelin speculates about "the symbiotic roots of the world of the father, and of the animate world in general for girls, while in boys the dichotomy between the symbiotic and the non-maternal world would be more clear-cut."[65]

Abelin thus proposes that the infant's specific attachment to the father, which involves the encouragement of exploratory behavior and offers opportunities for identification based on strong positive attachments, plays a decisive role in aiding the processes of differentiation and individuation. Sociologists such as Talcott Parsons hold a similar instrumental view of the father.[66] There have been many studies in the last decade showing that the father—child relationship is as important as the mother—child relationship in shaping the child's personality.[67] Indeed, roles of mother and father are seen as qualitatively different but equally important in contributing to the child's social and sex role development.

Boys approach male adults earlier and in more exploratory ways, but they do not "attach" themselves to fathers as do girls, according to Abelin. In the average nuclear family, the father becomes the first and most familiar of "different" adults. He comes to stand for distant "nonmother" space to which the male child is pushed in his sexual identification. Such an identification may be more with a symbolic representation than with an actual relationship, however, since the boys are not attached to adult males at this early age. In other words, boys respond strongly to male attentions, but they do not seek males out when distressed, turning instead to their mothers. Fathers seem to have a special interaction with their sons that undoubtedly contributes to the attraction toward men felt by young boys, even while they remain more attached to their mothers.

Investigations which attempt to characterize the nature of father–child relationships are few and recent, but quite important. Such studies show that mothers tend to do more routine caretaking and fathers tend to offer more playful stimulation. Mothers engage more in talking, in showing affection, and in verbal and toy stimulation. Fathers are more apt to promote exploratory freedom, especially in boys, and engage in physically active games, such as tossing a ball or bouncing. Lamb sees fathers as twice as active in interactions with sons as are mothers, and as one-half as active in interactions with daughters as with sons.[68] Fathers are more likely to engage their infants in physically arousing, idiosyncratic types of play, whereas mothers tend to engage them in conventional games or play with toys.

Earls and Yogman also see the father–child relationship in young children as qualitatively different from the mother–child relationship.[69] Infants' interactions with fathers tend to be heightened and playful; with mothers, interactions are more smoothly modulated and contained. Mothers vocalized with soft, repetitive, imitative, burst–pause talking (47% of the time) more than fathers (20%), whereas fathers touched their infants with rhythmic tapping patterns (44% of the time) more often than did mothers (28%). They also report that "with fathers, transitions are accentuated from peaks of maximal attention to valleys of minimal attention, while mothers' attentional shifts are more gradual and modulated."[70] Another researcher found that primary caretaker fathers behaved more like mothers, yet they remained just as physical as secondary caretaker fathers. Mothers' verbal play showed the same quality in different kinds of family organizations.[71] We see such differences in the physical contacts of infants with parents as influencing the more active, rough-and-tumble play patterns of boys, compared with the more passive play patterns of girls, described in Chapter 3. Parke speculates, "The fact that male monkeys show the same rough-and-tumble physical style of play as human fathers suggests that we

CHAPTER 4 • THEORETICAL PERSPECTIVES   101

cannot ignore a possible biological component in play styles of fathers and mothers."[72]

Even at 16 months, the majority of boys are said to be more attached to mothers, apparently reflecting the fact that the person of the father remains too elusive for identification, although attraction to him has been well established. As we noted in Chapter 2 in our observations of 2-year-olds, there is a higher incidence of separation problems among boys in nursery school groups, a phenomenon that correlates with the relative vulnerability of the boy's newly emerging self-image. He has begun to split from the mother, yet he lags behind his female counterpart in identification with his same-sex parent. These ideas support Kohlberg's suggestion that, unlike girls, boys identify with same-sex peers before their same-sex parent.[73] The male child is pushed to active and adaptive exploration, turning outward into visual motor space. We have documented his involvement with peers of both sexes, followed by his intensive period of cultivating his masculinity through abundant social encounters in the world of male peers. Girls' experiences are dissimilar in that their reality repeatedly returns them to maternal objects and images, even as they contemplate and attempt to incorporate the reality of the "other" (or male person) into their emerging ego.

Sherman points out the important positive aspect of the father's role in resolving the dependency relationship with the mother for both sexes.[74] Yet she emphasizes that boys are emancipated earlier as a cultural expectation, and postulates that girls tend to experience late dependency conflicts because much of their struggle for independence may be postponed until adolescence or even later. Indeed, this is consistent with Freud's view that the pre-Oedipal or dependent phase of development is more important for women than men, resulting from the observation that the original attachment to the mother is unexpectedly long-lived in many girls, lasting well into the fourth year and often much later.[75] Furthermore, Freud observed that the subsequent attachment to the father and eventual relationship with the husband tended to be a reflection rather than a transformation of the primary relation with the mother. A popular proverb reflects the differing male–female experience: "A son is a son till he gets him a wife, but a daughter's a daughter for all of her life."

The child's detachment from the first intense attachment to the mother differs in timing and quality for boys and for girls, and this is reflected in their sex roles and peer relations. We have noted earlier that a major similarity between human and nonhuman primates is that males are "detached" to a greater extent than females, but that there is a major difference in how this comes about. Among the nonhuman primates, it is the mother who separates the males, whereas among humans, it is the father. Paternity is a uniquely human factor, as Konner indicates:

Male parental investment has increased greatly during the evolution of humans from their primate ancestors, but this has not taken the form of an increase in the amount of interaction between males and their offspring. Rather, it has taken the form of economic investment, which in nonhuman primates is nil (because they eat very little meat). Still, this does represent a greater investment by human males, as would be predicted from the fact that humans are more or less pair bonding.[76]

A common theme in psychoanalytic literature is that the Oedipal complex expresses the power of the father and of patriarchy in our society, since paternal investment in children is still largely economic rather than interactional.[77] The father's intrusion into the original dyadic bond creates a more complex triadic attention structure in the developing child that takes a different form in males and females. The resolution of the Oedipal dilemma represents the incorporation of society's impulse controls and self-regulatory behaviors appropriate for the child's sex. The boy's aggression is ritualized in identification with his father. Male aggression thereby becomes a culturally cooperative process, which is both the product and cause of strong affective ties between men—in Tiger's phrase, "male bonding."[78] By contrast, the girl's aggression is discouraged within her same-sex relationships as well as within her relationship to her parents, beginning in the earliest preschool years.

It is the father's prying loose of the initially similar bond that differentiates the sexes and makes peer relationships possible.[79] The pattern of peer-relationship sex differences that we found in boys and girls at play reflects sex differences in the process of detachment from primary attachment to the mother. Boys are detached to a greater extent than girls; separation–individuation is more complete for them, and they are more influenced by cultural forces, including peers. The father has traditionally been the family's representative of the outside world, and the different status and potential for social action in boys and girls is particularly the consequence of the father–child relationship, which distinguishes sons and daughters.

Male Hostility toward Females

Not only the differing relations with fathers and mothers in the infantile period, but the differing resolutions of the Oedipal crisis for boys and girls are seen to hamper relational possibilities for parenting and other intimate relationships in boys, and to extend such possibilities in girls. Chodorow attributes differing person orientations in the sexes to differing Oedipal crises.[80] She argues that the Oedipal complex is assymmetrical for the sexes. The girl's is "multi-layered, including a continuing symbiotic attachment to the mother, to which triangular, sexualized attachments to mother and then to father are added." Boys, however, are pushed to monitor their emotional tie with their mother, and to develop "a more emphatic individuation and a more defensive firming of experienced ego boundaries." Girls, experiencing themselves as more like their mothers, emerge from this period with "a basis for 'empathy' built into their primary definitions of self, in a way boys do not."[81] Chodorow believes that girls, because of their mothering by women, come to experience themselves as less separate than boys, with more permeable ego boundaries.

The division of psychological capacities in father and mother contributes to the fact that the *person* of the father for the young boy is too elusive for identification. Chodorow notes that "the development of a libidinal relationship to the father and oppositional identifications with him are well in advance of his becoming an internal object. The construction of a mental image of him and internalization of aspects of relationship to him lag well behind those of the mother."[82] Chodorow's reasoning is more subtle than that of many psychologists who consider the father's lack of salience to be the major problem a boy faces in identifying with him. A common simplistic conceptualization argues that the boy is seldom, if ever, with his father as he engages in his vocation, although both boys and girls are often with the mother (or a female caretaker) as she engages in her household activities. Lynn compares the father's role as a model for the boy with "a map showing the major outline but lacking most details, whereas the mother as model for the girl might be thought of as a detailed map."[83] It is true, indeed, that the concept of fathering is to a large degree missing in contemporary culture. The fact that little girls will someday become parents is almost implicit in their cultural upbringing, in a way that is not true for young boys.[84]

Under the circumstances of our present organization of parenting, the availability of the mother and the relative invisibility of the father may mean an earlier entry of the boy into the Oedipal situation than is the case with girls. The mother is sexually attractive; the boy wants to possess her, but cannot have her. He becomes his father's rival, wanting the power he will achieve "when I grow up and become. . .". But as we have seen, the ideal is hard to achieve. The mother tends to be real, whereas the boy's fantasied and abstracted relationship to his father presents difficulties for masculine identification. Not really knowing what a male is, young boys do not know what to expect from one another in initiation, and their initiating behaviors in particular show much conflict. Identification is thus a complicated process for boys, since a boy's bond with his mother must be radically broken at an early age as he separates himself from relational issues. He is prompted to take risks in both physical and cognitive domains in his search for power and identification, even as he must learn to reject all that is feminine in himself and to devalue femininity in general to make possible his masculine self-differentiation.

There has been recent speculation that the male's Oedipal crisis represents merely a sociocultural by-product of a cultural tradition in which fathers are relatively detached from routine, daily caretaking of infants and children.[85] But we do not yet have evidence of paternal investment in early child care. Chodorow writes:

> As a result of being parented by a woman, both sexes are looking for a return to this emotional and physical union. A man achieves this directly through the heterosexual bond which replicates for him emotionally the early mother-infant exclusivity which he seeks to recreate. He is supported in this endeavor by women, who, through their own development, have remained open to relational needs, have retained an ongoing inner affective life, and have learned to deny the limitations of masculine lovers for both psychological and practical reasons.[86]

Chodorow sees that "women as mothers and men as non-mothers produce sons whose nurturant capacities and needs have been systematically curtailed and repressed. This prepares men for their less affective family role, and for primary participation in the impersonal extra-familial world of work and public life."[87]

The girl's early bond with her mother need not be broken. Although theoretically she wishes to possess her father as a love object, evidence suggests that the young female engages early in coquettish overtures to her father (and to other males) and shares an early sexual alliance without needing to displace her mother.[88] Contrary to the experience of males, it is the love–power relationship that is complicated for girls, not the issue of identification. We have seen in the reports of role playing in Chapter 3 girls' early expressions of interest in love and marriage toward unresponsive boys, and the emergence of "penis envy" (power envy), as they reach out at age 5 in efforts of indirect control over boys. We have witnessed girls' strong emotional feelings about babies and children; we have evidence of strong emotional dyadic relationships with other girls who become "best" friends, yet lack identification with same-sex peers as a group. The female's emotional task is exercised through her life-span: to capture the male–father in love, to repudiate yet identify with the "castrating" mother who is deprived of penis-power, and at the same time to keep room for the inevitable emotional bonding with infants.

The masculine personality emerges as one which tends to deny relation and connection (and to deny aspects of femininity within itself). The boy, in reflecting his feminine identification and in trying to feel masculine, tends to devalue and degrade feminine activities and stress the superiority of masculine over feminine roles. Freud, in a number of his disparaging references to women, provides interesting examples of masculine resentment of women.[89] He sees women as secretive, insincere, envious, lacking a sense of justice and honor, masochistic, deprived, and mutilated. Maleness seems to be described as the norm, and femaleness as an incomplete or deficient aspect of it. Klein suggests that many males harbor a fear of dependency on a woman, whose power they cannot duplicate; she sees men motivated to dominate women in order to cope with their own dependency needs.[90] Schlegel's anthropological study of the Hopi Indians indicates that beneath the Hopi view that women are the prized source of life runs an undercurrent of resentment toward them.[91] It has been suggested that a woman's power is awesome and that men are averse to the absolute power of the mother in early life.[92] Our data revealed that young girls as well as boys were likely to insult and disparage the oppposite sex; in psychoanalytic theory, penis envy is a pervasive female point of view, although women do not persist in a rejection and devaluation of men. The feminist vision of Utopia is not of a society in which women dominate men, but of one in which egalitarian relations exist between the sexes. Apparently, women do not need dominance to support their feminine identities.

We noted in Chapter 3 how boys' interactions, particularly in teasing and rough-and-tumble play, involve specific references to male genitalia. This type of play does not commonly occur among girls. We speculate about why such play would be more characteristic of boys than of girls. Clearly, male genitals are physically much more obvious than those of the female. Possibly phallic interest and pride in a boy is a secondary manifestation developed as a reaction to and defense against aspects of his relationship to his mother. The young boy tends to flaunt his sexuality, assert his penis possession—"see my ding-a-ling!" The boy achieves liberation from mother's omnipotence through his possession of a penis. We have also noted in Chapter 3 how boys' behaviors frequently involve competitive issues over property or possessions. Again we speculate that such concerns are related to the male's relation to his mother, where there tends to be an early focus on the possession of phallic sexual oppositeness.

The senior author found in her 1957 study that fathers strongly discourage sex-inappropriate tendencies in their sons.[93] Boys are altogether less likely to accept, choose, or prefer toys already sex-stereotyped as "feminine." Wolf attempted to vary the preferences of children aged 5−9 for sex-typed toys (a doll and a fire engine).[94] The manipulation worked better for girls than for boys. Indeed, the cross-sex experience sometimes produced even stronger male preferences in boys. Maccoby and Jacklin speculate that the more stringent socialization demands for boys may reflect a "realistic parental appraisal of the fact that homosexuality is considerably more common among males than females."[95] Udry, as we reported in Chapter 3, believes that the continuation beyond the childhood years of the phenomena of rough-and-tumble play in males represents a strong taboo against homosexuality:

> There are no direct ways of expressing friendship and affection among males. . . . Emotions can be expressed indirectly through "horseplay," "horsing around," a kind of fake aggression in the form of bopping, tripping, wrestling, and other minor physical abuse. The verbal form for the same expression is insultive kidding in which friendly males trade insults which would bring forth immediate violence from a non-friend."[96]

The core of male hostility toward women is viewed as promoting the sex objectification of women, making women in many instances appear to be not human beings but objects to be possessed and used sexually. Udry reports the high interest in sex in preadolescent male (but not female) subcultures.[97] These preadolescent boys are carrying on with types of language and interests similar to those which we reported for 4- and 5-year-old boys, who are beginning to band in groups to exchange "forbidden" words for sexual acts, eliminations, and anatomy. Girls, in their preadolescent subcultures, do not compare and discuss heterosexual encounters. They focus more on considering the male as a potential marriage partner. The male peer group, however, engages in exchanging sexual information and vying for actual or fictitious heterosexual prowess.

Stockard believes that men reinforce their masculine gender identity by treating women as sex objects: "If a woman is a 'cunt,' a 'piece,' a 'skirt,' or if one looks at women as assemblages of 'asses,' 'tits,' and 'beavers,' then the male is in control of them." Even in male prisons, "fucking" another male is a symbol of dominating him. In female prisons, on the contrary, Lesbian relationships between a "stud" and "femme" are usually patterned after traditional marriages. Partners call each other "mommy," "poppy," "my old lady," "my old man."[98] A study of sex differences in romantic attachments postulates that perhaps a "greater degree of control for women in the domain of their own emotions is a necessary adaptation to their lesser degree of power and control in other domains."[99] Men are seen as deficient in sexual interpersonal relations with women. Males, more than females, are likely to view the opposite sex as "sex objects."

A father in our earlier research study declared that "Femininity can't be divorced in my mind from a certain amount of sexuality." Parents reported that their sons developed an early opposition to the female sex. Fathers' comments included the following observations: "He's not interested in dolls. He's not interested in playing with girls. He stays away from them completely—they're no fun to play with." "He likes men more than women." "Drawn to men, not to women." "Hates dolls, loves cowboys, spacemen. No playing house." Mothers commented that their sons' interests in dolls arose from their desire to tease girls, and that boys dislike girls: "He has a passionate devotion to little boys. He liked Emmy Lou until he found out that she was a little girl." "He doesn't care about dolls except to annoy his sister. Doesn't love a doll or play with it." "He asked me to change the doll's diaper, but he never played with the doll. No tea parties." There was no comparable reporting of girls' rejecting boys' toys.[100]

Lynn views masculine role identification as containing hazards not found in feminine role identification. The boy is told what not to do rather than what to do, and demands are enforced with punishment.[101] Boys are therefore seen as more anxious than females with regard to their sex role identifications. The punishments they receive lead not only to dislike for girlish activities, but also to feelings of hostility toward females who engage in those activities. There is less pressure on girls than on boys to avoid opposite-sex activities since mother-identification is an easier and surer process than masculine role identification.

Thus we witness in children a differential overlearning of sex role antagonisms among boys, resulting in the culturally stereotyped and reinforced "I hate girls" phenomenon. The situation evolves as the male's primary sense of gendered self is reactive and defensive in its masculine role adoption. In the Oedipal crisis, the boy must renounce his early identifications with and sexual attractions to his mother, and therefore tends to renounce all feminine interests and processes. Males, more than females, continue throughout their lives to be involved in different ways and on different levels with a gender identity problem. Females, more secure in their gender identity, tend to experience more individual identity problems.

In a sense all females inherit only one image of the mother. A helpful metaphor is to think of the girl as a "twin" to the mother, whereas the boy is a "brother" to a father image that is multidimensional. Girls, with their early similarities in identification, know early what to expect from one another. Their relations with one another tend to prompt positive behaviors and foster personal interests. A boy's earliest experience of self is one in which he is forced, in the relationship with his mother, to realize himself as different. There is more conflict in boys' relations with one another; they do not know what to expect from one another, lacking a similar early figure for identification and often needing to adopt fantasy figures as power symbols of masculine attributes they must achieve. Thus boys and girls have quite different beginnings, and quite different subsequent tasks and outcomes in their social development.

Cognitive-Developmental Theory

Two Transitions in Preschool Social-Cognitive Development: All human societies are clearly distinguished from any animal society by the existence of gender.[102] Sex roles develop parallel with children's awareness of their gender identities in a complex social learning process. Peer social relationships, as well as sex roles, develop with children's social and cognitive abilities during play. Kohlberg focuses on the cognitive aspects of children's sex role socialization, and describes how the development of a stable gender identity facilitates their sex role learning. He discounts Freud's notions of definite and instinctively patterned sexual stages, but notes that "in modified forms the notion that an experience at a critical period in the unfolding of instinctive patterns can affect subsequent attitudes and behaviors has received considerable support from animal and clinical research."[103] This research provides evidence suggesting that there is "something like sexual imprinting in humans" since the development of normal adult sexual behavior is contingent on having been *socially* assigned to a given sex before the age of 3 or 4.

In contrast to Freud, Kohlberg shows how the development of gender identity is part of the general development of cognitive skills, with the distinguishable elements of sexual identity emerging in a developmental sequence instead of all at once. Gender self-labeling, the first step of gender identity development, acts as a filter through which other sex-related aspects of behavior and identity are assimilated. Kohlberg argues that gender self-labeling is present by age 2 or 3. This gender identity results from a basic simple cognitive judgment made early in development. Although verbal self-labeling of gender begins along with other classifications made by 2- to 3-year-old children, a complete understanding of gender— gender constancy, the concept that an individual's sex is a permanent attribute of the person, regardless of changes in the person's hair, clothing, or activities—is not achieved until about age 5 or 6, when children no longer confuse gender and age differences.

These specific changes in gender identification in Kohlberg's theory reflect general trends in cognitive development described by Piaget.[104] Piaget recognized qualitative differences between the child's thought and the adult's. He described radical transformations in children's thought as they actively structure their experience with gradually maturing cognitive skills. Piaget proposed that children's abilities to think about their social world, like their conceptualizations of physical objects, show culturally-universal developmental shifts. In his theory there are major transitions in cognitive development at the beginning and the end of early childhood, which are related to the two changes in gender identity development that Kohlberg has identified.

First, in the second year of life infants begin to grasp the rudimentary concept of object permanence, the recognition that objects continue to exist after they disappear from sight. Piaget claims that the first permanent objects (the first mental representation of a nonpresent object) are usually the parents rather than physical objects. There seems to be something in the richness of social interaction that leads to the earlier emergence of human identity concepts. Research indicating that a significantly greater number of children perceived object permanence with persons earlier than with physical objects confirms Piaget's hypothesis.[105] Kohlberg associates gender self-labeling and object permanence: "Children develop a conception of themselves as having an unchangeable sexual identity at the same age and through the same processes that they develop conceptions of the invariable identity of physical objects."[106]

The increase in social skill and knowledge at age 3, so apparent in our data, occurs at the same time that language is rapidly developing, supporting Kohlberg's claim that skill in gender labeling is acquired at this time. One research team reports that the simple act of labeling infants with gender-typed first names prompted 3-year-olds to sex stereotyping.[107] The children ascribed personal attributes to the infants on the basis of gender-based social categories, which they had already learned to associate with different name labels.

A second transition in cognitive development begins at about age 5 at the end of the preschool years. The preoperational child is egocentric, unable to take another person's perspective. A girl would be unable to think that another person (a boy) would be thinking of her differently than she thinks of herself. Piaget describes the intellectual revolution that occurs in human development as thought becomes "operational," or logical, and the young child acquires the capacity to think abstractly. Kohlberg's gender constancy, identified by the correct application of gender labels to men and women outside the family, is correlated with the child's performance on Piagetian conservation tasks and with other kinds of classification development. Kohlberg regards gender constancy as part of the general process of children's conceptual growth, parallel to conceptual constancies involving conservation of an object's quantity along some dimension.

White studied the conspicuous cognitive change at the end of the preschool era, which he terms the "5-to-7 cognitive shift." He argues that maturation of the brain aligns with personality and cognitive development. Cortical association areas mature at this time, facilitating intersensory transfer and accessibility to memory.[108] At the same time, the child begins to coordinate three dimensions on Piagetian conservation tasks. Logical principles such as transitivity, hierarchization, and seriation become "operative," or usable, although they are still tied to concrete situations. As we have mentioned, hierarchies in children's peer groups become relatively stable at this time. Children's understanding of cognitive principles that underlie the presence of hierarchies at age 5 coincides with the consolidation of social hierarchies in their peer groups. The resolution of the Oedipal dilemma, resulting from parental identification and superego formation, also coincides with the sociological and cognitive processes of organization that are based principles of hierarchy. The Oedipal resolution introduces hierarchy into children's emotional make-up. The superego (the internalized parent function) forms to provide self-regulation in the child's ego, balancing the socialized superego against the unsocialized id.

These two transitions in cognitive development coincide with two phases in psychological development recognized in contemporary psychoanalytic theory. Greenacre observes that there are two periods of "exhilaration" in children's relationship with the father as they separate from the mother, at 18 months and between the fourth and fifth year.[109] Other psychoanalysts find an early and a later "triangulation" at these same points—18 months and 4–5 years. Triangulation is the mechanism, described by the French "stucturalists," which allows the mental organization to pass from the level of relationship (acted, sensorimotor) to images (represented, symbolic).[110] The first triangulation occurs with children's ability to form simultaneous symbolic images of themselves and their objects, which is necessarily preceded by the sensorimotor schema of the permanent object. The second triangulation at about age 5 constitutes an even more elaborate step—the simultaneous representation of the image of the self and both parents, which seems to represent the formal element of the Oedipal complex.[111]

During the preschool years, when there is minimal sexual dimorphism, sex roles assumed in fantasy play are what differentiate boys and girls. Pretense or fantasy play undergoes transformations along with other aspects of social-cognitive development. The parallels are particularly clear when pretense is considered within Piaget's theory of play.[112] According to Piaget, symbolic play appears as imaginative make-believe at the end of the sensorimotor or infancy period when the child is about 18 months old. In symbolic play, interest shifts from the object's actual properties to its potential, imagined ones. The symbolic function renders a "transformation in intelligence itself" when the representation of internalized schemes, or images, becomes possible. Make-believe, which is play in its unadapted, distorting form of pure assimilation, wanes from 4 to 7, along with other manifestations of egocentrism in Piaget's theory. Play conforms to reality and becomes organized and collective in his third type of play, games with rules. The child accommodates to reality at this time, gaining perspective that enables him to juggle his thoughts; his intellectual capabilities are transformed at the end of the preschool era as dramatically as they were at the beginning.

A number of parallels exist between the development of pretense and that of peer social interaction. Both skills emerge in the second year and are initially deeply embedded in the object world. Pretense depends on concrete "pivots," and interaction among 2-year-olds centers on object disputes. Pretense emerges when behavior is detached from real-life contexts and symbols rely less and less on perceivable objects, becoming increasingly distinct from that which they represent. The elaboration of language between ages 2 and 3 stimulates development in make-believe and in peer relations. Language becomes the predominant form of imaginative, sociodramatic play in the third year, when verbal symbols become more conventional and less egocentric.

Vygotsky's metaphor of play as a pivot from the real to the imagined points to a different use of imagination in boys compared to girls.[113] The boys in our study assume a greater variety of roles than do girls, often depending on props such as the fireman's hat or the doctor's stethoscope to pivot from a reality they do not fully understand to a future containing a variety of fantasized options. Boys' role models are not only fantastic, they are more active, adventuresome, and aggressive than those of girls. Although boys occasionally adopt the roles of father or baby in the house areas, they are not attracted by domestic roles. Girls, on the other hand, usually adopt domestic roles, pivoting from a concrete reality to a future not far removed from the visible reality of their daily lives. For girls in our observations, in contrast to boys, mother is the favorite role to adopt, then sister, baby, or nurse. Sometimes girls are fathers, brothers, or firemen, but these roles are fleeting, seldom developed. The girls really know the specifics and subleties of the mother role. They cook all kinds of food, clean the house, care for the babies. The mother is authoritative and powerful. She gives directions for cleaning the house, maintains calm and quiet, stops quarrels—"no fighting because mother says so." Curiously, neither sex knows how to develop the father role.

In a sense, we see girls assigned to their status, whereas boys create theirs. In sociological terms, boys earn an "achieved" status, while girls learn an "ascribed" status. Lynn finds that boys and girls have separate methods of learning about their sex roles: boys solve a problem, exploring a situation and finding a goal, while girls learn a lesson, memorizing and imitating, with selective reinforcement from their mothers.[114] Female behaviors increasingly bind girls intimately to one another in a kind of domestic ghetto (the doll corner used as a house), whereas male behaviors allow a sharing of interests that are at once similar and highly differentiated, behaviors that are aggressive, property- and object-oriented, and suited to the work world.

In Piaget's theory of play, sociodramatic play disappears only a few years after its emergence, becoming transformed into games with rules. Fantasy does not actually disappear from children's lives, of course, but it does become less central to role learning at the end of the preschool years. The cognitive growth that begins at age 5 marks the decline of pretense (at least in Piaget's theory) and the consolidation of peer relations in stable same-sex groups. At this point, sex role development seems no longer centered in pretend play, as fantasized sex role behaviors begin to be applied in wider contexts. For example, we witness a great deal of nurturance in girls' pretend play (particularly in the doll corner) at ages 3, 4, and 5, but it is only at 5 that girls begin to show more actual nurturance than boys in their general social interactions. It seems that sex roles become "games people play" at 5, and children begin to apply their fantasied sex roles in games with rules and in real situations. The rules and organization of older children's play are quite different among boys and girls, equipping them for traditional adult sex roles.[115]

The Rigidity of Preschool Sex Role Attitudes: Gender identity in Kohlberg's theory is central to the development of other aspects of sex role attitudes because basic self-categorizations determine basic values, the meaning imposed by the culture on the two sex categories. The clear sex differences found by researchers in specific values and interests as early as age 2, in such areas as toy preferences, activity rate, aggressiveness, and fearfulness, eventually become generalized into masculine and feminine concepts and values.[116] Kohlberg observes that studies show more clear-cut stereotyping of parental and sex roles in young children (5−8) than in older children or adults. Although age-developmental trends in childhood are toward high same-sex typing, trends in adolescence are toward a broadening of sex role attitudes. The inflexible sex stereotyping of preschoolers results from the process through which the label "boy" or "girl" is translated into the individual's general thought patterns.

Kohlberg stresses the role of general competence motivation in identification attitudes. In his theory, motivation for gender identity development stems from a general human tendency to balance the self-concept with value judgments. Children tend to equate what is good with the self and the self with what is good, and they tend to perceive conformity to conventional roles as morally right and deviance from it as morally wrong. The egocentric young child "usually does not make a distinction between the value he places upon objects; that is, he does not recognize that the value of an object differs for different people . . . hence he [the child] assimilates the 'objective' social values of others into his own egocentric value perspectives."[117]

At ages 4 and 5, children's extreme positive evaluation of the same-sex or the sex-typed seems to reflect an egocentric, absolutist evaluation of whatever is like the self. At this egocentric level, however, children value the masculine or feminine as it is identified with themselves; they do not value the masculine or feminine as an absolute stereotype, standard, or category. By ages 5 to 6, however, children become more objective about sex roles and make role-appropriate choices of sex-typed objects and activities. The choice is defined by a role-appropriate preference rather than by the imagined absolute value of the toy or by the child's own preference.

The evolution of children's reasoning as they cope with understanding the social expectations associated with being female or male is illustrated in work by Damon.[118] Damon analyzed the successive levels of reasoning used by children aged 4 through 9 as they first accept, then reject, the validity of conventions. He studied the extent to which children think that sex role attributes are "musts," whether people are forced to change such things as manners or style of dress to conform to conventional male and female roles. Children Damon studied were told a story about a little boy, George, who liked to play with dolls. Although his parents told him he shouldn't play with dolls, he still wanted to play with them. The children were asked whether he was right or wrong. Consider the answer of Alvin, age 4 years, 8 months:

"Why do you think people keep telling George not to play with dolls?"
"He can play with them if he wants."
"Why is that?"
"He can play with anything he wants to."
"So you think George will want to play with dolls?"
"Probably not."
"Why not?"
"Because it's too babyish and he doesn't want to be like a little baby."
"So what will he do?"
"Stop playing with them. So that when you play with a lot of other toys, you start playing with the other ones and get to playing with them a lot."
"What will happen if George keeps on playing with dolls? Will his parents get angry?"
"No, because he wants to play with them."
"So nothing would happen to him?"
"Babies would play with him a lot, I guess."
"Is there anything wrong with wearing a dress to school?"
"No, it would look silly, that's all."
"Would he get laughed at?"
"Not if that's what he wanted to wear. Other people wear silly clothes; why can't he?"
"What if a boy wanted to play house?"
"That would be O.K. because I play house and no one laughs at me."
"Could a boy stay home and take care of other kids and wash dishes and stuff while the mother went to work and made money?"
"No."
"Why not?"
"That's a sissy thing."
"Can't boys do sissy things?"
"Well, I don't like to, that's for sure."[119]

Damon assigns the reasoning of children under age 5, like this child, to the most primitive Level 0, a period when the child respects only those social regulations that conform to his or her own desires. Rules, conventions, customs, and personal habits are confused with one another (although sex-stereotyped ideas are clearly influencing the child's thoughts). Social regulations are seen as situation-specific modes of behavior mandated by the self's desire to perform such behavior.

By Level I (ages 5−7), however, most children have come to believe that it is *wrong* for George to play or dress in girlish ways. The child's cognition of sex roles begins to reflect social sanctions that support the sex cleavage. Michael (5 years, 11 months) reveals the increased tendency of older children to determine what is right or wrong through their perceptions of other people's reactions:

"Why do you think people tell George not to play with dolls?"
"Well, he should only play with things that boys play with. The things that he's playing with now is girls' stuff."
"What makes it girls' stuff?"
"Because it's pictures of girls. But the boys' things are boys'."
"Can George play with Barbie dolls if he wants to?"
"No, sir."
"How come?"
"If he doesn't want to play with dolls, then he's right, but if he does want to play with dolls, he's double wrong."
"Why is he double wrong?"
"All the time he's playing with girls' stuff."
"Do you think people are right when they tell George not to play with girls' dolls?"
"Yes."
"Is there a rule that boys shouldn't play with dolls?"
"No."
"What should George do?"
"He should stop playing with the girls' dolls and start playing with the G.I. Joe."
"Does he have to stop playing with the girls' dolls?"
"Yes."
"How come?"
"Because if he doesn't want to play with them, he shouldn't."
"Why shouldn't he?"
"Because dolls are girls' stuff."[120]

Although 4-year-olds think in a more egocentric mode, children by age 5 are becoming uncompromisingly stereotyped in their sex role attitudes and quite forceful in the sex-typing pressure they exact from peers: they are quite ready to ridicule children without mercy for deviations from sex-appropriate behavior, and apparently boys, more than girls, tend to put extra negative pressure on sex-deviant behavior in other boys.[121] They think that "right" and "wrong" in playing with dolls is mainly determined by how other people would react. Indeed, it would be all right for George to play with dolls if no one saw him. Older children, however, become less rigid in sex-typing as their thinking becomes more sophisticated and they begin to distinguish between social conventions and moral laws and duties.

Devaluation of Females: Kohlberg finds that American children associate traditional meanings with sex roles very early (5–6). These universal stereotypes reflect a number of common symbolic, connotative meanings of gender differences that occur across cultures. D'Andrade found that men are connotatively more active, powerful, and aggressive than women in all countries.[122] This consistency in male prestige exists despite the evidence of cultural diversity in sex roles provided by the anthropologist Margaret Mead.[123] She describes societies in which both sexes are passive and gentle, others in which both sexes are aggressive, and yet others in which traditional roles are reversed, with relatively passive men and aggressive women.

Kohlberg claims that children's development of sex role stereotypes is not the product of the direct perception of differences in the behavior of their parents: there is little difference in degree of stereotyping between middle-class and lower-class children, between white and black children, and between children with absent fathers or working mothers and those whose parents hold the traditional roles of housewife and bread-winner. Baruch, who studied own-sex bias, sex role stereotyping, and gender constancy in preschool girls, found no significant relationship between parents' sex role ideology or degree of stereotyping and their daughter's sex role attitudes. "Chauvinism in preschool age girls," she asserts, "does not depend on feminism in their parents!"[124]

According to Kohlberg, cultural universals in sex role attitudes develop from children's cognitive organization of social role concepts around universal physical dimensions, rather than from their biological instincts. He suggests that at early ages (3 and 4) the father is not awarded more prestige than the mother, but that by ages 5 to 6 he is considered stronger and more powerful and competent. Kohlberg shares the assumption of Freud's theory of "penis envy," that there are early and universal tendencies to attribute superior status and power to the male role. Children develop stereotypes of masculine dominance and social power out of a body-stereotyping of size, age, and competence in a sequence of increasing abstraction. They first agree that fathers are bigger and stronger than mothers, then smarter (under 5), and finally (age 6 or older) that they are "boss," having more extra-familial power and status than mothers. Kohlberg attributes the increase in power and competence awarded to the male role to a growing understanding of economic functions and power. Thus, at the end of the preschool years there is a decline in valuing with egocentric self-projective modes in favor of evaluating social rank. This new valuation coincides with the age-related increase in prestige awarded to the male role.

Both sexes seem to award greater value to the male role after age 5. Baruch found that the phenomenon of girls' early own-sex bias is in contrast with their later self-devaluations—which, at least with respect to performance, have been found as early as first grade.[125] Four-year-old girls in her study had a significantly higher level of stereotyping for desirable traits associated with females and undesirable traits associated with males, compared to female-undesirable and male-desirable items. The two most stereotyped items of these girls were *aggressive* (male undesirable) and *nice—gentle* (female desirable); the two least stereotyped items *submissive* (female undesirable) and *independent* (male desirable). Although own-sex bias seems to be a powerful motivation for 4-year-old girls, there is no clear-cut increase in girl's sex-typed preferences after age 4, as there is for boys. For girls, the decline of the egocentric mode of conceiving that what is like the self is best coincides with the growing awareness of the superior cultural prestige of the male role. Girls do not show an increase in preference for same-sex objects and activities from 5 to 8, whereas boys, who identify with the higher status role, do.[126] As with measures of sex-typed preferences of activities and playmates, girls make fewer judgments than boys that their own sex is better, and girls' preferential evaluation of their own sex decreases with age.[127]

Despite the cultural devaluation of the female role, the girl still has reason to develop her feminine identification:

> Although sex role value stereotypes may affect girls' sex-typed preferences, they do not make girls want to give up their gender identity. . . . Furthermore, girls have the option of playing a feminine role in a man's world, whereas boys do not have the option of playing a masculine role in the woman's world. In other words the girl can have opposite-sex interests, and yet maintain her same-sex values more readily than the boy.
>
> More basically, however, adult female stereotypes are positive enough to make femininity attractive to young girls, even though adult females are perceived as less powerful and competent than males. While the stereotype of adult femininity is inferior in power and competence to the male, it is still superior to that of a child of either sex. . . . It should also be noted that stereotypes of femininity rate higher than stereotypes of masculinity in a number of important areas of value or prestige. The fact that the male role is associated with aggression and the female role with nurturance and dependence relations suggests that females are stereotyped as "nicer" than males. Since aggression is a major component of "badness," it is not surprising that almost all girls and most boys of six or seven say boys do

more bad things than girls (Kohlberg, unpublished data). Mothers are said to be "nicer" than fathers by a majority of both boys and girls of 4—7 (Kagan and Lemkin, 1960). "Niceness" is a very important value to school-age American girls, connoting nonaggression, interpersonal conformity, restraint, and nurturance or helpfulness. Another obvious stereotypical distinction between males and females, partly associated with "niceness" stereotypes, has to do with the superior attractiveness of females in the areas of physical beauty, concern with the aesthetic—ornamental in non-body areas, and interpersonal and sexual charm.[128]

In an effort to tap a status dimension important to girls, Omark and Edelman measured how much children agree on who among their peers is "nicest," as well as "toughest."[129] The hierarchy of "niceness" is patterned in the exact inverse order of the "toughness" hierarchy that we described earlier. Among same-sex dyads, boys agree more than girls on toughness, whereas girls agree more than boys on niceness. Among cross-sex peers, although there is more agreement on toughness than there is among same-sex peers, there is less agreement about niceness. The agreement on "nice" for cross-sex pairings is less than if they answered the question randomly. The large difference between the two dimensions among cross-sex peers suggests that both sexes have a similar idea about what "tough" means, but they differ on the meaning of "nice."

Gilligan finds it paradoxical that the very traits that have traditionally defined the "goodness" of women—their care for and sensitivity to the needs of others—are those that mark them as deficient in moral development.[130] An often-cited finding on sex role stereotypes is that the qualities considered necessary for adulthood—autonomy, assertiveness, responsibility—are those associated with masculinity, considered undesirable for women.[131] "These stereotypes reflect a conception of adulthood that is out of balance, favoring the separateness of the individual self over its connection to others and leaning more toward an autonomous life of work than toward the interpendence of love and care," Gilligan asserts.[132] She believes that instead of being seen as a developmental deficiency, the relational bias in women's thinking reflects a different social and moral understanding.

Gilligan charges that the development of boys is taken as the general (and correct) pattern for moral growth, and the autonomy of the individual is regarded above the primacy of relationship.[133] She proposes a dualistic concept of morality to reflect the reality of male and female moral development—the feminine ethic of responsibility and care based on connection and interdependence, and the masculine morality of justice based on separation and equality. She recognizes what we have termed the "domestication" of girls: girls avoid conflict rather than developing rules limiting its extent. Female social interactions proceed through modes of communication that reduce the incidence of violence and obviate the need for systems of rules based on equality. The feminine injunction not to hurt others is the feminine way to insure continuing connection by avoiding conflict with others.

Sequence of Identification with Peers and Parents: Besides showing that children naturally stereotype sex roles along binary paths that reflect male cultural prestige, Kohlberg describes a second cognitive-developmental pattern relevant to our study. Our results are consistent with Kohlberg's thesis that boys identify with their same-sex peers before they do with their fathers, whereas girls identify with their mothers before they do with their same-sex peers.[134] The principle of "homophily"—a boy likes boys because other boys are like him—underlies boys' indentification with their peers. The "homophily," well documented in studies of adolescent and adult friendship development, is facilitated by the tendency to value positively what is like the self and the tendency for similarity to facilitate affiliative relationships. According to Kohlberg:

> These studies indicate a time delay in the affiliative projection of the boy's sex-typed identity; his preference for same-sex peers is established before his preference for same-sex parent figures. The cognitive-developmental theory suggests two reasons for this discrepancy. The first is that the boy's classification of adult males in the common category 'we males' is a more cognitively advanced achievement, and therefore comes later than his classification of other boys in that category. It is not until about ages five–six, when the child begins to sort objects predominantly on the basis of similar attributes, that he forms groupings which include same-sex figures of diverse ages. The second consideration is that the boy's affectional tie to his mother is deep, and it takes time before the boy's self-conceptual or sex-role identity considerations can lead him to subordinate it to the development of a tie to the father.[135]

According to this argument, the boy identifies with his father only when gender constancy is achieved at age 5, after relationships with peers have already been consolidated. The boy's identification with his peers forms at a preconceptual level, dependent on primitive aggressive forces, since no model exists for boys' relationships with one another. His later identification with his father occurs at a more abstract level. This sequence of identification with peer and parent is reversed for the girl. Her identification with her mother is on a primitive, symbiotic level. Her later identification with peers represents a continuation or variation of her relationship with her mother. Thus, the girl's relationship with her mother does not demand the level of abstraction on which the boy engages in identifying with his father, nor does her relationship with other girls demand the level of aggression with which the boy engages his same-sex peers.

The course of same-sex alliances among peers in our observations seems to reflect the progressive identification of children with parents and peers.

Although social contacts developed primarily among same-sex peers in our study, 3-year-old boys and 5-year-old girls increased in cross-sex contacts, contrary to the predominant trend. The increase in cross-sex contacts for the boys at age 3 suggests an initial male difficulty with gender identification. The cross-sex increase of the girls at 5, on the other hand, may indicate an eventual female conflict with love-object choice. This pattern may also reflect the power of the mother for very young children and the increasing power of the father for older children who are entering the larger social world.

The different problems which preschool boys and girls face in developing their gender identities are reflected in the peer relations of their same-sex groups. Both sexes learn to align with their own sex and to complement the opposite sex in a different sequence. Because of female mothering, boys first learn to complement the female role when they achieve gender self-labeling at the beginning of the preschool years. At the end of the preschool years, boys learn to align with all males when they recognize gender constancy. Girls, by contrast, align with their own sex with gender self-labeling, then learn to complement the male role in the Oedipal crisis, when they choose their father as a love-object. The problem, in psychoanalytic terminology, is that boys must switch their gender identification from the mother to the father, whereas girls must switch their love-object from the mother to the father.[136]

Gender identification is simpler for females at the outset. From ages 2 to 3 children's social behavior reflects the impact of gender identity, of which they begin to be aware late in the second year. The "domestication" of the girls occurs as they accept and participate in the well-defined female role. Whereas girls maintain their original orientation to the mother, boys must relinquish close identification with the mother and switch their gender identity to the less visible role of the father. As boys learn that they are "not female," conflict ensues. They invent the male role as they explore the predicament of being males in a female environment. At age 3 boys seem to undergo a period of "detachment," which girls do not. What we see happening at age 3 is akin to the "peripheralization" of the males that occurs in nonhuman primates. Empirical evidence confirms that understanding of personal gender identity is perhaps initially more advanced among girls than among boys. Thompson found that children at 30 months could identify themselves and other children in terms of gender, but boys were significantly poorer at sorting pictures of themselves than were girls.[137] He speculates that boys' knowledge of their own sex classification lags behind that of girls despite the fact that the development of general gender differentiation occurs at the same rate in the two sexes.

At ages 3 and 4 same-sex groups are forming, based on a consciousness of similar sexual identity. Positive interactions with same-sex peers rise dramatically among girls at age 3, and among boys a year later. The battle of the boys emerges from ages 3 to 4 as boys continue to initiate high levels of negative contacts with one another when other negative behaviors are generally declining. By age 4 an "in-group" of authoritarian, maternal girls and an "out-group" of outlaw boys have formed. The battle of the sexes emerges as the groups crystallize at age 5, and the boys assert power through their confident teasing, supplanting the power of the girls, which had peaked at age 3.

The developmental transition at the end of the pre-Oedipal period is simpler for boys than for girls because the boy keeps the same love-object. The girl, however, must change her love-object and learn to love her father. Gender identity in boys is established unequivocally at 5 in the resolution of the Oedipal dilemma, whereas in girls it is made more complicated by the choice of the father as a love-object. Gender constancy is less stressful for boys than girls because the boys' "own sex bias" is supported by the seemingly universal cultural predjudice that puts a higher value, in terms of status and power, on what is masculine; girls' "own sex bias" conflicts with their culture's valuation. The developmental shift from ages 4 to 5 documents the conflict that ensues as the girls become aware of the boys and the boys repudiate the power of the girls in the Oedipal crisis, which resolves more completely for boys.

Thus, although the pre-Oedipal period appears to pose more conflicts for boys than for girls, the post-Oedipal period seems more complicated for girls. Lynn finds that boys have greater difficulty in achieving same-sex identification than do girls, since the demands for sex-typical behavior come at an earlier age for males, when they are least able to understand them.[138] As a consequence, more males fail to make a same-sex identification, and make a cross-sex identification. However, more females show a preference for and adopt aspects of the role of the opposite sex. With increasing age males are relatively more firmly identified with the masculine role because of the male-dominant culture and male privileges. Also, as age increases males develop psychological disturbances at a slower rate than do females. Females show disenchantment with the feminine role, and even other females share their predjudices. Thus, Lynn argues, when there is a discrepancy in an individual's sex role it tends to be a masculine role preference in women and feminine identification in men.

Boys are subordinated as children, girls as adults. Boys fight a feminine biological and early social environment, whereas girls face a masculine cultural environment. The two requirements of gender identity development confront the sexes in an opposite sequence: at age 3 boys must complement or oppose, and girls must become similar to, the female sex role. But at age 5 boys must identify with and girls must complement the male sex role. Boys' "detachment" at 3 resolves into a same-sex identification at 5; girls' same-sex identification at 3 becomes disrupted at 5. The lack of a highly developed same-sex identification for girls as a group creates contradictions in the female role, as lifelong mothering is phased out by modern social changes, and undoubtedly it hampers growth and progress in the status of women in Western society.

SOCIOLOGICAL PERSPECTIVES

The Individual and the Structure of Society

In the psychoanalytic account of psychosexual development, males and females differ radically after age 3. The Oedipal period (ages 3–5) represents a crisis for the child because the infant-mother dyad must broaden to include the father, becoming a triad (at least); the child must assume a properly subordinate child's role in the family. The dilemma of the Oedipal complex—the mother–father–child triangle and its attendant attachments and jealousies—begins to resolve at about age 5 when the child identifies with same-sex adults and acquires a stable sexual identity. This step initiates sex role development in children, and enables them to enter the larger social world of peers, which is becoming increasingly important as Western society develops in complexity.

Psychoanalytic theory provides insight into sex role development by describing how social forms and child-rearing practices affect the individual. The sociologist Talcott Parsons expands the psychoanalytic view with an analysis of the changes in the growing child's role in the family. He focuses on Freud's theory of object-relations, which "is essentially an analysis of the relations of the individual to the structure of the society in which he lives."[139] Parsons describes Freudian theory as a "primary meeting ground" of psychology and sociology, of personality development and sex role development, because it links the individual to the social system. Freud's point of view in analyzing this relation was that of the individual; Parsons's is that of the structure of the social systems in which the individual is embedded.

Parsons describes Freud as "clear and insistent about the existence of what he calls constitutional bisexuality, and hence about the fact that the motivational structure of sex role is importantly influenced by object-relations in the course of the person's life history."[140] The psychoanalytic theory of object relations emphasizes the importance of social objects in the child's psychological development, and is an important link between social and cognitive development. Object relations theory offers an important perspective on the way in which the child's history of social relations molds a masculine or feminine personality.[141] The child's experience of relationships produces a psychic structure unique to his or her history of identifications. Boys and girls experience different patterns of identifications because the same-sex parents with whom they learn to identify play very different functions in their socialization.

It is during the period of the child's separation from the mother that the child begins to learn roles and gain some predictive knowledge regarding the nature of the social system. Parsons argues that to assume status in the nuclear family, children undergo a new phase in the process of identification, after primary identification with the mother is achieved in infancy and toddlerhood. The problem of independence training—"detachment"— becomes the focal problem of the pre-Oedipal, preschool period. Parsons suggests the critical significance of the "detachment" period for the differentiation of personalities by sex role. "Detachment" involves identifications with the family as a collectivity, in terms of sex, and by generation or age:

> Two of the subsidiary identifications within the family, by sex and by generation, are to become structurally constitutive for his status in a wider society, and these are cross-cutting. It is essential to the understanding of the differential impact of the Oedipal situation on the sexes that for the boy the tie to his mother—the original object of identification and of subsequent object-cathexis—is not included in either of these new identifications; whereas for the girl the tie to the mother is included in the identification by sex.
>
> Hence the girl can, in relation to her mother, repeat on a higher level the infantile identification, and can to a degree take over the mother's role as an apprentice in the household and in doll-play. She is, however, precluded from taking over the mother's role in relation to the father by her categorization as belonging to the child generation.
>
> The boy, on the other hand, must break radically with his earlier pattern; he cannot turn an object-cathexis into an identification except on the familial level, which has to be shared with the other members. He is blocked by the importance of the sex categorization from identifying with the mother in intrafamilial function, and he is blocked by the generation categorization from taking a role like the father's in relation to her. Moreover, the father is a more difficult object of identification, because so much of his role is played outside the household.[142]

With the resolution of the Oedipal crisis, the child develops a conscience, representing the voice of the father, through which values of the culture are transmitted. This detachment of the child marks the transition from the dyadic system (mother—child) to the quadratic system of the nuclear family. The mother relinquishes to the father her instrumental role and her relationship with the child becomes primarily expressive. Parsons and Bales's well-known instrumental—expressive distinction reflects an essential differentiation of function found in all group life.[143] The *instrumental* function, characteristic of the male role, relates the family system to the outside world through work roles. The *expressive* function, characteristic of the female role, reflects concern with the internal affairs of the family system and maintenance of harmonious relations among the members. Parsons's distinction is supported by cross-cultural research: Zelditch found the father's role characterized by a preponderance of relative instrumentalism in seventy-five primitive societies.[144]

Parsons observes that one important outcome of the detachment phase is the internalization of sex roles. The young child must accomplish a difficult transition during the preschool years, moving from a dependent relationship within the family to an independent status within the peer group. The dynamics of family interaction result in extension of the child's reference system outside the family into the greater society. After children are brought into the total family on a responsible level and categorized by sex, they are motivated to adopt a whole pattern of behavior appropriate to their gender. This serves to bring the child for the first time into equivalence with persons outside the family, with boys and girls of their age level. School activities further accentuate this experience.

Parsons finds it striking that even "in the United States with its tradition of coeducation in the schoolroom, . . . in the latency period the peer group is overwhelmingly a *one*-sex peer group. The child is here 'practicing' his sex role in isolation from the opposite sex."[145] He indicates that the one-sex peer group is the "primary heir of the earlier security-base in the family of orientation" for the latency child.[146] The middle-childhood period differs from the preschool period in that the significant object for identification is not an individual but a collectivity, the same-sex peer group. For the first time the pattern of relationships with which children must deal are not ascribed in advance, since age and sex status are identical for children within their same-sex peer group. A child is "exposed, within the limits permitted in the community, to open competition with his age-peers, from which a significant structuring of the social groups will emerge, independent of the structure of the families from which the competitors come."[147] In this context children learn to assume "roles of leadership and followership and of primarily task-oriented or primarily integrative roles in relation to their peers," and boys are exposed to this peer socialization more than girls.

The Dyad and the Triad: Boys' and Girls' Same-Sex Relationships

Girls' relations are dyadic and individual; relations among boys tend to be more triadic, i.e., their friendships are influenced by each individual's position within and relationship to the group as a whole. Sex differences in peer relations reflect the different power relations that are required by groups and dyads. Schecter indicates that the higher-level interpersonal world is triangular, without the sense of exclusiveness and the "dual unity" that characterizes the dyad.[148] The "disillusion of the symbiotic ideal" that accompanies the boy's passage from infancy into early childhood constitutes the ground for moving into a social group and valuing one's peers. Boys tend to value peers more, and girls value adults. Furthermore, although preschool girls have more extensive peer relations and preschool boys have more intensive peer relations, in elementary school this pattern reverses: boys subsequently have more numerous peer relationships, whereas girls have closer peer relationships.[149]

The earlier growth of positive behaviors with same-sex peers among girls, probably a result of their earlier biological maturation[150] as well as cultural conditioning, suggests that they are more susceptible to adult social pressures than are boys. Boys tend to resist adult authority, but thereby become more liable to influence from their age-mates. Dweck and Bush cite evidence that boys are more peer-oriented than girls in all cultures, and that to gain the approval of peers it might be necessary for boys to violate adult standards of socially desirable behavior.[151] For example, Hollander and Marcia found that leadership and popularity in the fifth grade were associated with independence from adult authority for boys, and with cooperation with adult authority for girls.[152] Dweck and Bush conclude that "girls can gain the approval of both adults and peers by conforming to one standard of behavior. Boys, however, are confronted with a choice between conflicting behavior—that approved by peers and that approved by adults. The evidence indicates that over time boys become increasingly likely to choose in favor of the peer."[153]

Dweck and Bush's study examines the sex difference in "learned helplessness," the attribution of failure to uncontrollable factors. Previous research has suggested that as a result of differential rearing, and with autonomously determined motivations, boys develop internal standards of excellence which allow them to become relatively independent of evaluative feedback from others. Girls, viewed as other-directed, rely more on external social evaluation. Dweck and Bush have refined this simplistic view, finding that girls tended to attribute their failures to lack of ability with *adult* agents of evaluation and not peers, while boys tended to do so with *peer* agents and not with adults. It appears that as a result of different histories with peers and adults, evaluative feedback has different interpretations for boys and girls, and affects their performance differently, depending upon whether it is delivered by an adult or a peer.

We see at age 5 the beginning of play patterns that develop over the course of childhood, i.e., the sex cleavage with teasing boys playing in groups that are larger and more structured than the girls' groups. Rubin comments that "the boys need group support in order to break the rules of adult society. Such rebellion seems to be less common and less overt among girls."[154] The sexes display a different stance toward authority: boys are a "band of rebels," girls are "intimate confidantes."

Although girls' dyadic relationships nurture their sensitivity to personal relations, the dyad relationships pose problems for females. Simmel sees a predictable limitation in dyad relationships:

> The difference between the dyad and the larger groups consists in the fact that the dyad has a different relation to each of its two elements than have larger groups to their members. Although, for the outsider, the group consisting of two may function as an autonomous super-individual unit, it usually does not do so for its participants. Rather, each of the two feels himself confronted only by the other, not by a collectivity above him. The social structure here rests immediately on the one and on the other of the two and the secession of either would destroy the whole. The dyad, therefore, does not attain that super-personal life which the individual feels to be independent of himself. As soon, however, as there is a sociation of three, a group continues to exist even in case one of the members drops out.[155]

Girls, in their dyad relationships, engage in behaviors which are relevant for romance or marriage but not for organizational life or group cohesiveness. The early dyad relationships among girls, in which girls often reject one another totally, is seen as shaping women's ways of relating in adult life. Bardwick states, "Many girls will have experienced or anticipate a pattern of being chosen as a special friend, followed by rejection, and this establishes a core sense of mistrust which has a powerful impact on women's relationships with each other. Divisiveness within the women's movement is enhanced when historically powerless people mistrust each other and especially those with power."[156]

Lever's study of elementary-school-age children accords a major role to children's play-time activities in sex-typed socialization.[157] Observations of 181 children aged 10 and 11 revealed play patterns which Lever sees as calculated to equip boys with the social skills needed for occupational careers, while equipping girls with the social skills suited for family careers. Boys' games continued for a longer period of time:

> Because boys could resolve their disputes more effectively . . . boys were seen quarreling all the time . . . . Boys seemed to enjoy the legal debates every bit as much as the game itself . . . . The moral lessons inherent in girls' play are fewer since there are almost no areas of ambiguity comparable to a player sliding into first base . . . . Traditional girls' games like jumprope and hopscotch are *turn-taking* games, where the nature of the competition is *indirect*. . . . These turn-taking games do not contain contingent rules of strategy as in sport games; rather they are regulated by

invariable rules of procedure. Given the structure of girls' games, disputes are not likely to occur. Thus girls gain little experience in the judicial process.[158]

We recognize in Lever's study an excellent presentation of the differing kinds of games played by boys and girls, and tend to give a broad interpretation to the data. Boys' group games of baseball and football lead to cooperation and leadership skills and experience in the judicial process. Such games, as contrasted with the more intimate dyadic games preferred by girls, seem to organize masculine conflict and power struggles in the boys' rank-ordered peer group, which is more detached from the adult power structure than the girls' group. The boys' games are, in a sense, benign warfare. We tend to emphasize that male relationships in such games are devoid of personal intimacy. It seems, indeed, that it is in the area of intimacy, or the avoidance thereof, that the games children play in middle childhood testify to salient sex differences. Lever does point out that girls in middle childhood avoid group games and prefer play "mimicking primary human relationships." Such play tends to occur in small, intimate groups or dyads. Girls tend to develop intimate awareness of one another in the same way we witnessed their development of an early intimate awareness of their mothers. Boys and girls play different games, and their different social relations are manifested in opposite modes of communication as they play. These sex differences in social attention produce different psychological orientations to life that are reflected in boys' and girls' dyadic interactions, in their same-sex relationships, and in the power structure of the two same-sex groups.

Opie and Opie collected 340 essays from elementary-school-age children in which they described their friends and why they liked them.[159] The essays reveal that during the first four years of grade school, children are engaged in elaborating their basic sex identities. These essays also show the differing personal orientations of the girls and boys. Girls are eager to describe their friends' appearance, dress, and personality:

"I have two friends called Carol and Brenda. I like Brenda because she is very funny and very small. I also like Carol because when she has any sweets she always gives some, and she has lovely curly hair, and she is very nice. Carol, Brenda, and I nearly always go home together. Carol nearly always sends me a birthday present. Brenda has a nice face, and she has straight hair with a fringe"

"My friend Barbara has fair hair and is very pretty and wears a red skirt and a brown sweater, and she has brown eyes and red shoes and white socks."

"I like Hazel because she is a nice girl who always wears a school uniform if possible. She takes great care how she is dressed."

"My best friend is Vera. She always dresses nicely and walks with her shoulders back. Sometimes she wears brown slip-on shoes, a green cardigan and a dress. She wears white ankle socks."[160]

In none of these essays did any *boy* describe the clothes or physical appearance of his friends. They address their friends as "old bean," "old chap," "old sop," "old kiddo," "Hi ya, old horsey," and "Hi chum." Their greatest sign of approbation is to call a person "a good sport" or "sporty." "I like David," remarks a typical 10-year-old, "because he is a good sport and kind to animals. At games he never cheats, and he sits out if he is out." The characteristic they most want in a friend is that he should like playing the same games that they do:

> *"My best friend is John Corbett, and the reason I like him is that he is so nice to me and we both draw space ships, and what's more he plays with me nearly every time in the playground. Another thing about John is that he is sensible and nice. Whenever we are playing rocket ships he never starts laughing when we get to an awkward point."*[161]

A friend is colloquially referred to as "my bud" or "buddy," "chum," "crony," "mate," "my monkey," "partner," or "pal." They identify a friend as one who always plays with them in the playground, who "knocks" for them at 8:45 to go to school, and who goes home with them after school. A friend is also "a member of one's gang."

Similar sociobehavioral traits seem to be the basis of friendship choice in girls, whereas complementary qualities seem to be more salient in the friendship patterns of boys. One study found that girls choose friends who are congruent on variables measuring adaptable, outgoing social behavior (e.g., reputed interest in having a good time, being fun, and being a best friend).[162] Boys, however, choose friends who have complementary qualities on a measure of peer reputation. For example, a high proportion of boys who were reputed to be "attention-seeking" interacted with other boys who, conversely, were willing to share the limelight. Boys' same-sex relations, therefore, seem based on complementarity and functional difference, which supports agonistic, rank-ordered relations. Girls, on the other hand, respond to "displays" rather than "threats" when forming friendships.

There is a suggestion in our data on peer interaction that the male role develops as a skill in initiation, while the female role develops as a skill in responsiveness, reflecting different attentional demands placed upon the sexes. Male dominance is associated with male initiative in the form of threats, since "dominance provides the ultimate sanction by which one animal or human enforces his prerogative to take the initative to another." Leaders of groups, who are typically male rather than female, combine "dominance and initiative in judicious amounts," using dominance to make sure that the group they are leading responds to their initiative.[163] Girls' interactions, contrasting those of boys, show more conflict in response than in initiation. Whiting and Edwards observe that more social demands are made on girls: other individuals interrupt and try to change the ongoing behavior of girls more than that of boys. They conclude:

> It is this higher rate of interruptions or instigations received that makes the older girls have a slightly lower proportion of self-instigated acts than have the boys. Perhaps this higher rate of attempts to change girls' behavior sets is related to the Western stereotype of feminine "sensitivity" or "responsiveness" and to the reports that girls have greater awareness of their immediate environment than do boys.[164]

We witnessed the beginning of this phenomenon in the 5-year-olds we studied: girls have more cross-sex interactions (particularly in response) than boys, whereas boys have more same-sex interactions. The phenomenon is recognized by many feminists. Polatnick calls attention to the nature of "mothering" responsibilities, which she says militate against sustained commitment to other interests.[165] Not only are long hours involved, but there is the constant strain of being "on call" in women's child-rearing responsibilities. Indeed, nineteenth-century feminists witnessed the degree to which females were accustomed to accept *as natural* interruptions in what they were doing:

> Women are never supposed to have any occupation of sufficient importance not to be interrupted except "suckling their fools," and women themselves have accepted this . . . and trained themselves so as to consider whatever they do as not of such value to the world or to others, but that they can throw it up at the first "claim of social life." They have accustomed themselves to consider intellectual occupation as merely selfish amusement which it is their "duty" to give up for every trifler more selfish than themselves. . . . If a man were to follow up his profession or occupation at odd times, how would he do it? It is acknowledged by women themselves that they are inferior in every occupation to men. Is it wonderful? *They do everything* at "odd times."[166]

The constriction in behavioral choice that rigid sex role typing represents begins in the early childhood years when same-sex peer groups form with different power structures. Attention structures are related to power structures because the allocation and exchange of attention in social interactions is a manifestation, on the dyadic level, of the way in which society is regulated. Recent sociological studies of power suggest how power and attention structures in children's peer groups are related to male and female sex roles:

> Men and women learn to pursue attention differently and expect and accept it in different amounts. In all patriarchal societies, women are typically assigned the attention-giving roles and men the attention-getting

ones. Accordingly, attention-giving becomes defined as a "feminine" skill and responsibility, with men gaining attention as a privilege of their gender.[167]

The same author notes that the roles of men in work and public life differ considerably depending on their social class, but that the roles of most male workers differ considerably from that of female workers because they require attention to machines, objects, or ideas rather than to people.

We have noted earlier in this chapter that boys and girls develop different modes of communication in their play. Females develop skill in giving attention and responding to the needs and demands of others; males develop skill in demanding attention and giving orders to women and men who are subordinate to them. In women's exchange with children, dominance–subordination relationships are inherent in their respective roles, whereas men's exchange with other men of the same social class in formal and informal male groups is potentially equal, i.e., dominance–subordination relations are created as men interact. Maternity is based on dyadic interaction, fraternity on hierarchy. Some men must give attention to other males, but all males can demand attention from females. As children's same-sex groups consolidate at the end of the preschool era, their peer society breaks apart and polarizes. There is little commerce between the sexes in the "latency" years of middle childhood, when the sex cleavage is in full bloom. When the peer group comes together again, to the extent that it does so with the romantic overtures of adolescence, it is differentiated; members are accorded status according to their sex, and girls as a group are subordinated in the "real" world of work.

It seems that gender identity is more complex or triadic for the boy, and that love relations are more complicated for the girl. Triadic love relationships are adaptive for the mature female, who must form close bonds with children as well as with husbands. Mature males, however, have two kinds of relationships with other men, one formal and hierarchical, the other relatively informal and personal. Boys identify with peers before their fathers and peer relations are central to the male role. In contrast, girls' union with their mother precedes and is the basis for their same-sex relations, and motherhood is central to the traditional female sex role. Parenting is less integral to the male sex role and to male play experiences and fantasy life.

At this time of major developmental differentiation in personality structure, gender role identification becomes more of an issue for boys as they identify with positional aspects of the masculine role, whereas feminine identification is predominantly personal. Girls tend to project their own sense of mother-self onto their peer relations and in the process enrich a stereotyped self-awareness; boys strive to discover themselves in peer relationships and in the process become more individuated, more separate and distinct, than do their female counterparts. Girls' associations with peers reinforce fundamental relationships; boys' associations with peers emphasize a denial of intimate, dyadic relationships.

We are suggesting the sexes exercise not only different patterns of socialization but different cognitive strategies as well, one intimately influencing the other. Boys' wider range of conflict situations and of role explorations and activities, and their less intimate emotional involvements with one another, predispose them to more varied curiosities, experiences, and eventual solidarity, which can be marshaled to aggressions against society at large or to internal aggressions with one another. Girls, on the other hand, are more likely to invest thought and energy in relationships. Pitcher writes, "The female is more likely to be interested in the man running the locomotive than in the structure of its parts, or in the creation of another locomotive."[168] Such differences are influenced by the female's identification with and attachment to her mother, and attraction to home and children, and by the male's identification with fantasy power figures, and his discovery of and allegiance to other males in active power struggles.

Girls, primarily focusing on the maternal function for a long period, have not by late adolescence had the same preparation for finding their identities as boys, who have focused on the performance of function in the wider society. Girls tend to avoid coping with questions of determining relationships in the larger societal context when approaching adulthood, and instead pay attention to their potential relationship to one man. The male, vulnerable to erotic seduction, can join in the relationship the female craves, and in doing so can satisfy his own basic need to return to the female—mother. Often he is held in this relationship by well-developed techniques of nurturing and appeals to appropriate rules of conduct. Nurturance and reprimand will later be summoned by the female in her control of her children and passed on as fundamental modes of behavior to her daughters. Males, meanwhile, continue their power struggles and develop their hierarchies in work, games, clubs, politics, and warfare. We have identified in children at age 5 the result of a developmental process involving conflict that has brought them to a sex cleavage that foreshadows the predicament of their adult years.

When children are 5 years old, we see boys beginning to band together in large groups in which females have no important role to play. At the same time girls, remaining for the most part in dyads, are attracted to males and try unsuccessfully to engage in their rough-and-tumble play and group endeavors; but they must acknowledge that male "bonding" does not include them. Through the talent identified and copied early from their mothers—the reprimand, the invocation to propriety and rules of appropriate behavior—girls try to control the male, but do not appear to gain popularity or acceptance with boys by doing so. Eventually they will learn to capture the male through erotic and nurturing behaviors. For the female, in contrast with the male, the achievement of Erikson's psychosocial stage of identity has as much to do with connection as with separation.

Both men and women suffer from traditional sex role socialization in which girls' peer relationships do not become independently organized and boys' are radically detached from intimate dyadic relationships. Girls, in a sense, miss the rites of passage between the dyadic world of attachments and the triadic group realm, which is characterized by peer relations and complementary roles. Girls seldom reach the same developmental level in peer relations, and they suffer consequent degradation as potential status in the adult world is taken away, and their range of action narrows.[169] Girls suffer a devaluation in the power of their peer group; boys' eligibility in the nurturing mode of social interaction is curtailed. Whereas the degradation of women leads to a greater rate of depression and neurosis among adult women,[170] the rank-ordered attention structure common to males contributes to a sense of alienation common to contemporary work life.

As children move into middle childhood, attention structures develop differently in the two same-sex groups. Boys attend to one another in interlocking dyads or groups that devalue girls. Girls attend to best friends in dyads and to boys in power relationships. When boys begin to organize in power relationships (building and destroying structures, playing "rockets"), their exciting play is carried on primarily without the participation of girls. We have documented how girls learn that boys are tougher, beginning at age 3. At 5, girls are subject to denigrating remarks from boys that are more personally humilating than girls' insults to boys. Girls show, by their many cross-sex contacts, that boys' play tends to attract their attention. Girls, in learning that boys are tougher, accept a subordinate position in the larger social world, which in Western society has a rank-ordered power structure. In the preschool years, two different "societies" form: the boys', bounded by the power of strong, intrusive negative behavior; and the girls', bounded—and limited—by the initiation of socially approved behaviors of nurturance and domestic guardianship. We witness a battle of the boys, beginning at age 3, develop into a battle of the sexes at age 5, as hierarchies form that anticipate the social structure of adult culture.

Chapter 5 Changing Sex Roles

INEQUALITIES IN SEX ROLES AND RECOMMENDATIONS FOR CHANGE

In earlier chapters we set forth the manner in which social influences from the family and from peers affect the child's personality in sex-typed ways. Until the present time, most cultures have preferred to maximize the sex differences from such origins and influences, rather than reduce them. Increasingly, however, there has been insistence on minimizing the polarization of the sexes and on redefining sex role behaviors to foster greater human equality. Although those who request sex-change operations, so far at least, are nearly all males who want to become females, the push for equality in the sexes has been, to date, primarily a female movement. Indeed, males have used such terms as "castrator" and "bitch" to label women who seek to move from their restricted roles. Male scholars who assert that in their insistence upon equality women are disregarding fundamental characteristics of womanhood, are frequently labeled "chauvinistic."

The reaction to *Women in the Kibbutz* illustrates these points.[1] In the early years of the kibbutz movement, women entered roles previously reserved for men. But a second generation regressed to traditional roles, resisting recruitment to a higher level of commercial and political leadership. The authors state:

> [The women of Israel] have voted against the principles of their socialization and ideology, against the wishes of men in their communities, against the economic interest of the kibbutzim, in order to be able to devote time and energy to private maternal activities rather than to economic and public ones. . . . They are seeking an association with their offspring which reflects a species-wide attraction between mothers and their young. . . . If the predisposition of workers to be with their offspring

is a positive attraction, not a negative retreat, it is because of our mammalian and primate origins and the long formative hunting-gathering period of our evolutionary past.[2]

Not only in this publication, but also in *Men in Groups*, Tiger's thesis centers on male–female differences that are believed to be deeply rooted in our nature as primates. Such differences, according to this line of reasoning, make them innately suited for different tasks; patterns of male discrimination against females are handed down from our animal ancestry.

Biologically-influenced sex differences are often assumed to be universal, inevitable, and desirable, and have served to justify the social inequality of the sexes. Scientists concerned with feminist issues have criticized ethologists and sociobiologists for assuming that the presumed coincidence between animal and human societies proves that biology dictates the behavior of people as well as of animals.[3] It seems that the biological basis of observed differences between the sexes is an issue, whether explicit or implicit, in any discussion of sex differences. Although Tiger observes that "it becomes important to assess and understand the differences [between males and females] if only to seek accurate predictions about options and constraints in maintaining societies or changing them," he nevertheless concludes that evolutionary patterns that govern the relation between the sexes constrain human behavior potential, including major modifications in sex roles.[4] This view, common to evolutionary social analysis, is limited in its ability to explain human social behavior. The human capacity for thought and creativity can override biologically-influenced behavior. Human culture channels innate sex differences into unique patterns of social functions known as sex roles.

We interpret the ethological evidence presented earlier within a perspective that recognizes that biological or, more precisely, ecological factors are socially malleable. In our view, human behavior is never "instinctually" determined. All behavior is learned and all learning is culturally mediated, even if the aspect of culture that motivates the learning is a legacy of humankind's evolutionary past. Processes and relationships that encourage traditional sex role development, such as peripheralization of young males, and sex differences in dominance–submission and attention structures, are likely to be important—but not necessarily controlling—in human society. The human environment, organized around gender behaviors that evolved in the pretechnical world, is changing. Sex role learning, often regarded as "instinctive," may also change in content during the course of human development. Indeed, technological and cultural progress has created considerable overlap and complexity in modern adult roles.

The physical and temperamental differences between men and women have been amplified by culture into themes of male dominance and the secondary status of women. Such distinctions have been integral parts of a variety of societies for most of recorded time. De Reincourt describes the "great Western cultural distortion" that has origins in Greek thought:

> While Greek thinkers became the pioneers of philosophy and discursive thought, the *psychological* degradation of the female principle (*physiological* creation of new life) led to the debasement of woman's *social* position and status. . . . This cultural distortion—unknown in Eastern civilizations where a somewhat harmonious balance between the two *sexual principles* was maintained—disrupted the Western human ecology by depicting females as inferior or *incomplete* males (biblical Eve, Greek Pandora, and Aristotle's philosophic rationalizations) instead of granting them their *different* specificity, as was done in China or India.[5]

The negative, and often dangerously sexual, image of women is apparent in the Pandora's box myth; in the story of the Greek sirens who lured men to their deaths; in witchcraft; and in the Judaic and Christian religions, in which woman emerges as the mythological embodiment of evil in the style of Eve. The nineteenth-century philosophers Nietzsche and Schopenhauer emphasized the substantial antagonisms between men and women, their subliminal messages implying that what is masculine is somewhat better than what is feminine. As we have elaborated earlier, Freudian theory reflects a patriarchal society which generally depreciates the female role. For centuries the male character has been more or less assumed to reflect "humanity." The cultural products of societies in literature, art, architecture, music, religions, philosophies, and education have conveyed sexual images that mirrored a societal glorification of the aggressive power and supremacy of the male, and the passive, nurturing (yet inferior) power of the female.

Women scholars contend that disproportionate attention has been paid to males in human and other social systems. They show how commonly accepted developmental schedules overwhelmingly emphasize the significance and shape of male behaviors. Activities and perceptions of females tend to be ignored or assigned secondary significance. Gilligan calls attention to a different *quality* in women's development: the importance of attachment, sensitivity to the needs of others, and responsibility for nurturing. She shows how life-cycle theorists, mostly male, have accustomed us to seeing the world through men's eyes; the male child is used as the prototype to explain the development of sex role identity.[6] A woman sociologist argues that the dilemma of women in modern society is a problem of dualism. She contends that feminist discontent derives from the separation of man's sphere from woman's sphere, the public from the private, instrumentality from expressivity, reason from passion, functionality from emotionality. These dualist structures prevent the full human development of both men and women.[7] Marcuse stikes a similar theme, warning that modern technological life tends to develop "one-dimensional men" of either sex.[8]

Although women in the past have experienced varying conditions, history records not a single society in which women have controlled the political and ecomonic lives of men. However, throughout most of history, women have played significant economic and productive roles as well as reproductive ones. Keller points out that "the chief dividing line seems to be the industrial revolution and the physical separation of home and work place, which gradually led to the familiar current division of work by gender."[9] Chodorow describes the significance of Frederick Engels's analysis of the family for modern sex roles.[10] Engels's sociological analysis describes the historical transformation by which the productive world has become organized more and more in nonkinship and market relations.[11] Chodorow notes that both the sexual division that provides the context for women's mothering, and heterosexual marriage, reproduce gender as an unequal status. She concludes that industrial capitalist development in Western society has sharpened the separation of family and work life, which continues to reproduce male dominance:

> The relations of material production, and the extended public and political ties and association—the state, finally—which these relations make possible, dominate and define family relations—the spheres of human reproduction. Many aspects of reproduction are taken over by extrafamilial institutions like schools. Kinship, then, is progressively stripped of its functions and its ability to organize the social world.
> . . . It is apparent, however, that familial and kinship ties and family life remain crucial for women. The organization of these ties is certainly shaped in many ways by industrial capitalist development (though the family retains fundamental precapitalist, preindustrial features—that women mother, for instance). However, as production has moved out of the home, reproduction has become even more immediately defining and circumscribing of women's life activities and of women themselves.[12]

Mothering has traditionally defined the woman's role. The identification of females with mothers continues to a major extent to define both the female role and the female same-sex peer relationships that serve to develop this role. This is happening at a time when women's mothering and kinship relations circumscribe their social power, because in the modern Western world market relations have become more important than kinship relations. Men's social roles have become formally institutionalized in the modern West; women's roles generally have not become organized in the public, materially-productive arena. Earlier societies were centered on kinship relations, which organized production and reproduction in one system. In modern societies production and reproduction have become distinct spheres of life. Bernard finds the isolation of the unemployed housewife a major source of the stress that women experience in contemporary marriages.[13] Women experience a decline in marital happiness during the child-rearing period, followed by a rise after the children leave home. Men don't experience such a decline, and express higher marital satisfaction generally.

Not surprisingly, the female adult has emerged in all cultures as a person with a family (or person) orientation, and has become the human being who is primarily responsible for child rearing and home care. She is endowed with talents associated with ministering to others' needs: empathy, sensitivity, and relative passivity and subservience. She has been called a "compassionate sibyl," but in serving others she has very often neglected to pursue other avocations.[14] Emily James Smith Putnam, the first dean of Barnard College, writes of the female predicament:

> Apart from the crude economic question, the things that most women mean when they speak of "happiness," that is, love and children and the little republic of the home, depend upon the favour of men, and the qualities that win this favour are not in general those that are most useful for other purposes. A girl should not be too intelligent or too good or too highly differentiated in any direction. Like a ready-made garment she should be designed to fit the average man. She should have "just about as much religion as my William likes." The age-long operation of this rule, by which the least strongly individualized women are the most likely to have a chance to transmit their qualities, has given it the air of a natural law.[15]

In 1901, Putnam was promptly dismissed from the presidency of Barnard when she informed the board of trustees that she was pregnant. Eighty years later, in 1981, her latest successor, Ellen V. Futter, the youngest president of a major U.S. college, became the first Barnard dean to give birth while in office. This support by a women's college of women's simultaneous working and mothering should not surprise us in the 1980s, but such support has not become widespread. The recent failure of the Equal Rights Amendment and current conservative policies that are cutting back the already meager support for adequate day-care threaten the real, albeit partial, gains women made in the 1960s and 1970s.

Once they become divorced or widowed, men and women who are socialized to conform to traditional, polarized sex roles lose important supports that their socialization has led them to expect. Divorced or widowed housewives tend to lack opportunities to support themselves economically, and single men often lack the resources to support themselves socially and emotionally. A recent, popular novel whose main character is a recently divorced (and bitter) woman, contains passages reflecting strong hostility toward men. She feels subjugated by men and regards a "man" as "he who screws and kills . . . [and] makes money." "Women," she says, "are trying hard these days to get out from under the images that have been imposed on them. The difficulty is there is just enough truth in the images that to repudiate them often involves repudiating also part of what you really are. Maybe men are in the same boat, but I don't think so. I think they rather like their images, find them serviceable."[16] Van Gelder scrutinizes what she calls "a new American syndrome"—the unmarried man—whose dilemma is different from that of the divorced housewife, but equally distressing. She talks about the large number of current movies, television specials, and books about the effects of divorce, all told from the point of view of the husband:

> These men, by their own admission, were emotionally on different planets from their wives. How can you miss someone you never knew? I wonder, to borrow from the theories of Dorothy Dinnerstein, whether many adult males suffer an extra dimension of psychic pain when they are left by women—the child's fear of abandonment by the mother.[17]

Most people see the equalization of the sexes as a task that involves both men and women. This is in a sense inevitable, since sex roles are reciprocal in any society. Changes taking place among the members of one sex inevitably affect the other, involving a redefinition of masculinity as well as of femininity in both adults and children. A controversial point keeps re-emerging: should women share the same roles as men, or should what women do be different, yet complementary, to what men do?

There is a growing literature among social scientists who examine the male role. Articles in popular journals deal with a wide range of male roles and male experience, including discussions of sexism, racism, heterosexual behavior, homophobia, and fathering. Unquestionably such publications attempt to promote understanding of conscious and progressive changes in men. Some contend not surprisingly that men, who are incumbents in power, do not usually see the need for change as forcefully as women, who are aspirants for power. Others believe, moreover, that if men should *choose* to change, the way would be easier for them than it is for women. Block contends that there appear to be differential effects of socialization for men and women, which make it easier for men to adopt nurturing traits than for women to adopt assertive ones.[18] She believes that socialization for women tends to reinforce nurturant, submissive, conservative behaviors; for males socialization tends to enhance experiential options and encourage more androgynous sex role definitions. Females tend toward approaches that are conservative rather than creative, while males tend toward strategies that foster innovation.

There are those who feel that even if society does encourage broader sex role possibilities for males, the average contemporary man is poorly equipped to cope with personal insights or nurturing emotional relationships. This view is clearly unfair to many contemporary men, but the portrait does fit the extreme manifestation of the male role. Some feminists feel that men need to express their feelings more, to shed their "machismo."[19] Men in the work world are not noted for nurturing individual sensitivities. There is, however, a solidarity group for adult males in work, a place where they meet challenges, engage in battles, find self-definition as males in relationships reminiscent of the male peer contacts of childhood. The world of work involves "togetherness" in aggressive games and conflict: getting a job and going higher in an upward-mobility syndrome is quite different from what is expected from women in their roles as wives and mothers. While a sensitive response to the needs of others is held up as the ideal for women, men ritualize their relationships in competitive games, which are mirror images of their activities in industry, in politics, and on the battlefield.

Miller identifies issues that each sex must face as men and women strive for growth.[20] She agrees with those who see the male as relatively deficient in interpersonal relationships. Miller views the male as handicapped in his early alienation from the care of children, and in the

> . . . close and direct emotional engagement with another human being who is different—and female. The boy is encouraged to turn to the world of men, where processes are structured to limit direct emotional involvement with anybody, male or female. What is rare is a man who has incorporated an image of himself as a person who takes care of his equals—both men and women—who who feels this identification as a critical part of his inner sense of self, equal to or more important than other inner images, like that of being superior to his equals, for example.[21]

Miller considers women's potential growth to be related to her ability to achieve a sense of worthwhile identity. There is a general acceptance of women's functioning in expressive roles—women serve others not only in home and family but in other fields relating to human needs—but there is no universal acknowledgment of women's excellent functioning in instrumental roles. Indeed, women themselves have feared to acknowledge their executive and organizational abilities. "Recognition of effectiveness or valid achievement provokes in women frightening visions of destruction."[22] Women have a fear that if they acknowledge their "instrumental" abilities they may lose their accepted "feminine" place in society. Horner found that bright women exhibit a "fear of success" unrelated to their abilities.[23]

As women are urged to develop a new sense of "self," they are encouraged to do so through a productive use of *conflict*. Miller draws on her own professional practice as well as the clinical evidence of others to formulate new directions which male–female relationships should take. "Women do not come from a background of membership in a group which believed it needed subordinates. . . . Most women are not practiced in the forms and conventions by which men have been geared for rivalries since childhood," she explains.[24] Miller sees the "crucible of conflict" as a potential for change. She sees women traditionally unwilling to initiate conflict, but feels that they must do so to become self-directed and create their own personhood, instead of accepting the form and content prescribed by the dominant group.

Conflict need not result in the formation of dominance hierarchies, although conflict resolution among men often does involve subordination of other men. Miller challenges women to engage in conflict that enables them to develop new conceptions of themselves by breaking down internal barriers that result from early socialization practices. New conceptions will prompt new desires, and new actions will come from these new desires as women cultivate identities that are competent and strong. Miller utilizes case histories to show how various women have made use of conflict to discover themselves and to free themselves from dependence. She urges women to discover inner resources of creativity and leadership, and hints that the way is already apparent in the achievement of groups of women. Miller sees that women are capable of replacing feelings of individual meaninglessness with feelings of group strength and belonging. Already, "a new sense of connection between knowledge, work, and personal life" has begun to evolve among women.[25]

Organized groups of women have inherent problems, however. In politics, women are seen to lack solidarity, to identify more with their families than with their sex, and, unlike other "minorities," to lack loyalty toward their own sex.[26] Hammer believes that women are not yet ready to profit from involvement in a collective, nurturing group.[27] She sees trouble when some individuals in the group become assertive, or achieve more success that others; women in such groups tend to equate egalitarianism with anonymity. Women, unlike men (she believes), do not form hierarchies.

Although women may not form hierarchies like those of men, a compilation of studies of the process of hierarchical formation in human and animal communities reveals that females do indeed organize behaviors along hierarchical lines.[28] Women tend to form lattice structures which are more flexibly organized than those of males. They tend to move in and out of hierarchical structures depending on the nature of the task to be performed. The female lattice structure is more effective in solving social problems when a rapidly changing environment requires that new information be processed and acted upon quickly, bypassing hierarchical (male) levels that require less interpersonal trust and skills. Tiger and Shepher see difficulties, however: female hierarchies have problems of discipline, reluctance to accept authority, and further strained relations among the workers.[29] Hammer identifies problems similar to those mentioned by Tiger and Shepher: "There is conflict between the nurturing mode and the individual achieving mode: between our desire to relate and our desire to act. Can we find room for competition and nurturing, for individual power and achievement and egalitarianism?"[30] It seems, indeed, that even as women are being encouraged to use conflict in freeing themselves from positions of subordination, and in working productively with one another, there is an acknowledgment that women will need to learn to use conflict in ways that are compatible with their basic orientation toward nurturing and being nurtured.

In one African society male and female roles are institutionalized in formal groups that retain distinct social functions. In the women's religious Sande society among the Mende of Sierra Leone, initiation rites are held for women at adolescence. This ceremony represents a rite of passage that teaches girls to bring the biological events of their lives under cultural control.[31] Initiates are instructed during weeks or months of seclusion, following which the girls are reincorporated into society with the status of adults (as is usual with the much more common male initiation rites). In each local chapter, senior adult members in a hierarchy of offices provide leadership, and the organization renews itself when a class of initiates is ritually "born" into the corporation, which exists in perpetuity. Sande, which links corporate groups exclusively composed of women, provides a transformation into responsible womanhood.

Poro is the male equivalent of Sande, concerned with socialization of adolescent males in such areas as religious belief and adeptness in manly skills. Poro and Sande complement rather than oppose each other, respecting each other's separate domain of social control. Poro is more overtly political than Sande, functioning at the local level to counterbalance the largely secular power of chiefs, who may be men or women. Sande women, as individuals or as officials of their organization, also enter the political arena, exerting significant direct political force on the larger society. Sande "gives women a solid base of conceptual thought, practical experience and social cohesion from which to launch out farther into the cultural domain of thought and technology, the stuff of national development. . . . In this institutional setting, women dramatically pass on a strong, positive self-image to other women."[32] Although our society is much more complex than that of the Mende, Sande does suggest that the female role can be institutionally and culturally supported without threatening the separate identities of male and female social functions.

There is an avalanche of publications by women who see their sex as powerless and who try to correct the perceived sexist oppression in American society. Weitz sees that women have had a primary relationship to men rather than to work.[33] She sees the critical question for adolescent boys as, "What is my work?"; for girls it is, "Who is my husband?" She notes that men stand basically firm in their position in the sex role system, since work confers an identity on the male, but not on the female who remains in the home. Since women have their primary identification with the home and child care, no real revolution in the sex role system can occur without fundamental changes in these spheres.

Current contradictions in traditional sex role socialization are being amplified by women's new work role. Masnick and Bane distinguish three aspects of women's paid work outside the home: participation, attachments to careers, and contributions to family income.[34] Of the three, only women's participation has changed dramatically across the age groups in the three adult generations studied. They believe "a second revolution is just under way in attachment, particularly among the women of the younger generation, born after 1940, who are also revolutionizing family structure."[35] As evidence of this revolution, in which more women are working full time more continuously, they identify recent trends toward year-round, full-time, and continuous work, especially among younger women. Greater attachment will in turn raise women's contributions to family income (although the gap in male and female wages shows no signs of closing yet). Changes in family structure are also occurring. Masnick and Bane project that by 1990 there will be "a very diverse world of households, families, and individual life histories." Households will be smaller and change more often, and there will be "more two-worker households and more households of men and women living alone than husband–wife households with one worker." These new kinds of households are likely to "create unprecedented challenges for the economy, for the community, and for the government—challenges that the society must prepare to meet."[36]

Historically, interest in sex differences has always been high when women's roles are in rapid transition.[37] With the recent entrance of large numbers of women (many with preschool children) into the work force, and with the availability of modern contraceptive techniques, the complexion of male–female social roles has been changing. Maccoby cites a study of women's life cycles by an Italian demographer who compared the situation of women prior to the mid-1880s with that of contemporary Europe.[38] Women's life expectancy in that time has more than doubled, and the number of children borne by most women during their lifetime has drastically declined. Maccoby wonders whether the major demographic change in the proportion of her adult life that a woman spends in procreation and child care represents "a profound conflict between what is biologically given in human nature and the conditions of life we now encounter."[39] Thompson poses the same dilemma in social rather than sociobiological terms:

To be sure, there have always been women who, by their cleverness or special circumstances, have been able to circumvent this position, but in general the girl child has been trained from childhood to fit herself for her inferior role; and as long as compensations were adequate, women have been relatively content. . . . Our problem with women today is not simply that they are caught in a patriarchal culture, but that they are living in a culture in which the positive gains for women are failing.[40]

Women are now demanding changes in their social roles, not primarily because the sexes have traditionally performed different functions, but because of the enormous gap in political and economic power between males and females. The pertinent issue for human equality is not that sex differences exist in style and social functions, but rather that Western women have been excluded from the decision-making process that governs contemporary society and from the professions that support it. At the same time, polarization of sex roles tends to alienate men from women and to alienate men from aspects of femininity within themselves, as well as alienating women from aspects of masculinity within themselves.

There has been a movement among women, primarily in Western culture, to re-examine their role in the family, which many tend to view as an indoctrination center or prison of the female spirit. Traditionally women had viewed themselves wholly in the center of the family; feminism told them to view themselves totally outside of that context. There has been a strong reaction against the wife–mother–housekeeper role. Previously women had been taught to ask, "What do others want?"; feminism urges them to ask "What do *I* want?". Betty Friedan, who started the National Organization for Women (NOW) and wrote *The Feminine Mystique*, emerged in the 1960s and 1970s as a voice for millions of American women seeking increased status and respect.[41] In *The Second Stage*, Friedan contends that women, like men, need both family and work to be happy.[42] Unlike those who view the family as a "leaden jail," she believes that most women need men to love, be loved by, to nurture, be nurtured by, and to help make the "second stage" of their liberation happen. She apparently has reached the conviction that it is acceptable to be a feminist and need a family too; yet she sees a necessary revolution in the concept of family. She wants to strengthen women's place in that family with day-care, expanded maternity and paternity leaves, and a more flexible workplace. Indeed, she wants to extend the concept of home to include communal arrangements that become house-extended families.

Gersin, however, has voiced a caveat that support of family life may also encourage sex role differentiation and further the retreat of women from public affairs.[43] Unlike Tiger and Shepher, who see biological foundations for sex differences, he sees social foundations for sex differences in the subtle discriminations against women in the kibbutz, and in the economic dependence of child and parent relationships.[44] He believes that traditional sex role differentiations can only be altered if political steps are taken to integrate men into the service branches of society, and women into positions of management and leadership in its productive branches.

Keller's review of the current female role in the United States reveals a host of stereotypes. She states that although women are by now engaged in virtually every occupational category, few of them manage to get to the top.[45] High occupational achievement, accompanied by a high salary, reflects the masculine role. The benefits of the female role include economic and emotional security (via men), a cult of beauty and nurturance, and a lack of pressure to achieve. The costs include a lesser autonomy, (except in family and erotic power), ignorance and lack of training, and categorical subordination to men. Keller perceives a cause of woman's position to be the discontinuity of authority figures in her life: women need to replace the powerful mother of childhood with powerful males in adult life.

Rossi echoes the same theme: "By the time they reach adulthood, women are well socialized to seek and find gratification in an intimate dependence on men, and in responsible authority over children."[46] She sees a problem in the economic demand that men work at persistent levels of high efficiency and creativity, while women serve as "shock-absorbing hand maidens" of the occupational system. Professional women, suggests Rossi, need a wife! A new model, she proposes, would involve greater changes in men than in women: family and community play would be valued on a par with politics and work.

The mother-daughter relationship is one calculated to restrict rather than enhance female growth, when females view the mother's role as subordinate and demeaning—which is indeed the prevailing reality. Miller writes that "Without a full assessment of the devaluation of women, we cannot grasp the nature of these and other conflicts specific to the girl."[47] She sees problems in the emotional ties and inequalities of the present nuclear family, and Mitchell maintains that the family as it exists may be incompatible with the equality of the sexes.[48] Komarovsky is among those who believe that women's involvement in child care will keep male power intact unless some way is found for men to assume equal responsibility for rearing children.[49] Chodorow also looks for changes in the present organization of parenting, in favor of a system in which men and women have equal responsibility in working for the family:

> Children could be dependent from the outset on people of both genders and establish an individualized sense of self in relating to both. In this way, masculinity would not become tied to denial of dependence and devaluation of women. Feminine personality would be less preoccupied with individuation, and children would not develop fears of *maternal* omnipotence and expectations of *women's* self-sacrificing qualities. This would reduce men's needs to guard their masculinity and their control of special

and cultural spheres which treat and define women as secondary and powerless, and would help women to develop the autonomy which too much embeddedness in relationship has often taken from them."[50]

Ortner sees woman's nearly universal and unquestioning acceptance of her own devaluation as related to culture's "arguments that her body and its functions seem to place her closer to nature, and to put her in social roles, as opposed to men, whose physiology frees them more for the projects of culture. Whereas men create relatively lasting, external objects, women create only perishable objects—human beings." Ortner believes that the way out of the circle is to have men and women equally involved in "projects of creativity and transcendence. . . . Only then will women easily be seen as aligned with culture in culture's ongoing dialectic with nature."[51]

Abernethy sees value for both sexes when women acquire social power in a professional setting: "Women are able to empathize in a new way with men who have always had this power and responsibility," she writes. In marriage, both partners "are allowed a full range of human expression— from competence and rationality to passivity and boldness. Both men and women are, in turns, tough and soft."[52] Abernethy identifies a need for men to find strength and independence in their wives, and for women to accept weakness and self-doubt in their husbands.

Bem emerges as an eloquent proponent of androgeny.[53] A number of agreed-upon qualities have been identified as typically more male than female. Bem believes, however, that it is possible in principle for a person to be both masculine and feminine, depending upon situational appropriateness. Men and women should both retain the traits they prize and adopt cross-sex attributes, and thus move beyond sex role limitations. The integration and interdependence of both masculine and feminine traits within an individual are essential for the development of androgynous individuals who will be free from culturally-imposed definitions of masculinity and femininity. Bem views human behavior as uniquely flexible—human beings are makers of their own culture.

The present generation has addressed sexual inequalities in a number of ways—in the increased education of women and in their increasing involvement in the labor force, the economy, and the polity. A recent government report reveals that women, more than men, said they were given a "special advantage" because of their sex.[54] There are efforts to do away with cultural symbols and language usages that tend to foster a secondary status for women. Men have been encouraged to undertake roles of expressiveness and nurturance instead of competitive striving. Many fathers involve themselves in the birth process; fathers obtain custody of children. There are a number of innovations in fathering, with fathers having paternity leave when infants are born, and otherwise sharing roles.[55]

If people went on behaving like children, it is possible that men and women might never mix, feeling at home amid the familiar values and activities of their different worlds. But there is an increase in mixed-sex groups, not only in colleges, clubs, and societies, but also among children in elementary schools. Udry reports that there has been considerable cross-sex interaction in elementary schools recently, and predicts this will break up male groups well before adolescence.[56]

Possibly, in time, sex differences will attenuate in younger developmental stages as a trend emerges toward a psychological balance in mature adults between male and female traits, and as men and women learn better ways to know and relate to each other in a true spirit of mutuality. Washburn, viewing all human beings as potentially androgynous, reflects that "one way to become complete in oneself is to make the unconscious conscious, which involves, in part, acknowledging the existence of our opposite sex qualities."[57] In understanding ourselves we are better able to understand and accept our opposite-sex partners. Men and women's exploitative relationships, as they treat one another as money machines or sex objects, may vanish. In such a society we might indeed witness changes in the gender roles and peer relations of young children.

Minimizing sex differences may not be in the best interests of human development, however. There would be pervasive and fundamental difficulties in *eliminating* sex differences. Katz engaged a group of students in a discussion which challenged them to construct a hypothetical environment with a minimum of behavioral sex differences:

> Even with parents fully committed to the ideal, they argued, access to other children, schools, and the media would have to be curtailed; family interactions would have to be stringently controlled; and all the individuals entering the social environment would have to be carefully screened. After discussion of all these problems, many were convinced that such a goal might not even be worthwhile.[58]

Indeed, it is possible that even if major changes in the present system are brought about, human nature may be stubborn, and other differences in gender roles may appear. Our present typology may be more interesting and productive than a society without sex stereotypes. Rosenberg and Sutton-Smith comment, "it could be that though some of today's sex differences may disappear, others may arise, for men and women may invent new techniques for polarization."[59] De Reincourt is even more forceful in his rejection of sex role homogenization:

> The contemporary woman's liberation drive toward a *decrease* in sexual differentiation, to the extent that it is leading toward androgyny and unisexual values, implies a social and cultural death-wish and the end of the civilization that endorses it. The scientific and historical record shows

that all the way from unicellular organisms to human beings, progress in evolution has been stimulated by the *increase in sexual differentiation*. Social engineering and legislative tinkering will not solve the problem. The present dilemma can be overcome only if a profound *cultural* change takes place and an entirely new set of values replaces the traditional values that Western civilization inherited from both biblical and Greek patriarchal sources. These new values will be effective only to the extent that they are based on respect for the different specificities of the sexes and the same reverence for the creation of Life as for the creations of the Mind.[60]

Erikson suggests that women can make better use of their natural talents by applying their "different specificity" to the public realm: "Maybe if women could only gain the determination to represent publicly what they have always stood for privately in evolution and history (realism of householding, responsibility for upbringing, resourcefuness in peace-keeping and devotion to healing) they might add on ethically restraining, because truly supernatural, power to politics in the widest sense."[61] He sees the freedom won by the present generation of women as limited to "career competition, standardized consumership, and strenuous one-family homemaking." Erikson is particularly concerned with the "special dangers" of our nuclear age.

Some women also express adverse criticism of the present direction of the Women's Movement. Berger emerges as a sociologist with strong negative appraisals.[62] After reviewing the status of women in three quite different contemporary societies, she argues that essentially liberation addresses the question of modernity versus tradition, and that the new emphasis on woman as a person primarily opens many more choices of life styles for women. However, the "new" women face issues in sharp conflict with the needs of their children. Berger challenges the notion that success as a woman must necessarily be equated with success in a career. She questions that *work* necessarily endows life with a sense of meaning. She sees the *real* world of private life as the protected sphere in our democracy where personal choice and self-realization best flourish. Berger writes about women that "Eventually they may even have to realize that true liberation and their ultimate identity are to be found in the leaden "jail" of the past: in tradition, marriage, and the family."[63]

Erikson sees the need for men and women to work together, each respecting the unique qualities of the other:

> The study of life histories confirms a far-reaching sameness in men and women insofar as they express the mathematical architecture of the universe, the organization of logical thought, and the structure of language. But such a study also suggests that while boys and girls can think and act and talk alike, they naturally do not experience their bodies and (thus the world) alike. . . . There is a psychobiological difference central to two

great modes of life, the paternal and the maternal modes. The amended Golden Rule suggests that one sex enhances the uniqueness of the other; it also implies that each, to be really unique, depends on a mutuality with an equally unique partner.[64]

INTERVENTIONS IN EARLY CHILDHOOD

Many believe that if major changes in sex roles are in order it would be wise to look at potential interventions in educating children. A task force of the National Organization for Women has made specific recommendations calculated to make stereotypes disappear, particularly in children's literature.[65] Some professionals give specific recommendations for teacher interventions in children's play, interventions calculated to force children from sex role stereotypes before the stereotypes have been internalized. Suggestions include confronting children's acceptance of stereotypes such as "Boys don't cook," or "Only boys go on the rocket," by opening up the issue as a topic for group discussion. One advocate of these interventions admits, however, that teacher actions can contradict their words (a male teacher can be a flirt or a seducer; father-helpers can be excused from "clean-up" time, whereas mother-helpers cannot), and advises that teachers must first reform themselves before they can reform others.[66]

Serbin and her colleagues investigated teacher intervention as a way to minimize the exclusion of opposite-sex peers from play groups.[67] Teachers were asked to attend to cross-sex play contingently and to comment briefly, indicating approval. Although girls responded more strongly to these reinforcement tactics, the treatment had no lasting effects. Cross-sex cooperative play increased when the teacher was present, but returned to its original same-sex groupings once the teacher's attention was no longer involved.

Paley reports her interventions in rearranging "doll corner" space.[68] She tried to respond to mothers' accusations that she was deliberately fostering a sexist institution in providing all the paraphernalia for female domesticity in the doll corner. She took away the doll corner equipment, but after a couple of days she found that "casual housekeeping arrangements were popping up under tables, and breakfast was being served at the sand table. I was witnessing a spontaneous underground movement. Instead of one mother localized in the doll corner, we now had three mothers and a half dozen or more siblings."[69] Bettelheim comments on Paley's report, seeing children's adoption of stereotyped roles in the doll corner as their way of dealing with what preoccupies their minds and feelings. Children engage in "external assertions of what makes their bodies unique."[70] Girls gravitate to nurturing roles that flow from the "inner space" of their bodies; boys gravitate to play that reflects the "intrusive," physically aggressive nature of their bodies. Bettelheim believes that changing the nature of the school environment cannot change children's basic drives.

Various changes in the rearing of young children are advocated. One change that is already under way in a number of families in the United States is the increasing involvement of fathers in child-care practices. We have no firm evidence that young children have a uniquely natural preference for their mothers; research with infants and their parents shows that no clear-cut pattern of preference for the mother emerges in children before 12 months. From 12 months onward, the majority of children show a maternal preference, but a high percentage of children demonstrate equal or paternal preference. The same study reports, however, that among three hundred middle-class families studied in the Boston area, 75% of the fathers did not physically care for their children on a regular day-to-day basis; 43% reported that they never changed diapers.[71] Other studies reveal that in 1976, a man's family work, when his wife was employed outside the home, occupied about 1.6 hours each day; in 1977 a national survey showed that he had increased his family work to 2.6 hours a day.[72] Altogether, the patterning of the husband's household day is reported to be more flexible than that of the wife's. The tasks associated with child care structure the morning and evening activities of employed wives far more than those of husbands who engage in household work.[73]

Suggestions for changes in child rearing come from a cross-cultural study by Whiting and Edwards.[74] They note a differential pressure on girls and boys to be nurturant: "Boys interact less frequently with adults and infants, and proportionately and significantly more with peers, especially male peers." Looking at children in East African societies and in Orchard Town, New England, the study concludes that requiring boys to tend babies and perform domestic chores reduces sex differences in "masculine" and "feminine" behaviors. When less "feminine" work is assigned to girls and where there is less difference in the daily routine of boys and girls, as was true in the New England village, the behavior of boys and girls does not show the great differences found in other societies. Thus, traditional task assignment allows boys more access to play with peers than girls, and this, together with the boys' naturally greater aggressiveness, undoubtedly influences the behavioral tactics that boys and girls learn to use with their peers.

Minuchin, in an earlier study on play, showed that 9-year-old girls from "modern" backgrounds (i.e., where there were relatively open conceptions of sex-appropriate roles) departed most from conventional expectations.[75] Aggressive expression in boys and family orientation in girls were more consistently characteristic of children from traditional backgrounds. Social class and education do seem to be related to the degree of stereotyping.

Yorberg finds that, generally, the higher the social class (except for the upper class, which is more conservative), the greater the likelihood that individuals will adopt modern values like egalitarianism and tolerance, which are associated with greater assertiveness in females and greater expressiveness in males.[76]

Although there are presently a number of changes in parenting, in the work force and in the sexual and familial division of labor, it is far from certain that such changes will in the near future be sufficient to alter present social roles or positions in the hierarchy of gender, so that young children will receive clearly delineated and understandable concepts of equalized gender roles. It is apparent that although there are a number of valuable new studies of the roles of fathers in parenting,[77] we do not yet have any usable information about the effects of having fathers engage in *long-term* sustained care of their children. Many think we never will, believing that men as a group really do not want to rear children, inasmuch as child care is socially devalued. Men can still be assured of substantial child-rearing authority, even when women have the responsibility for child care.[78]

Even when fathers stay home, children do not adopt different sex roles in dramatic play. Paley examined the sex role play of children whose fathers and mothers both worked and engaged in child care.[79] Twenty-four mothers worked at their professions while the fathers worked on graduate degrees and spent much time at home. The thirty children of these parents were in a kindergarten. The roles they chose in dramatic "house" play in school were as traditional as those of children whose mothers stayed home. Girls engaged in mother and baby roles; boys tended to avoid domestic play (as we also witnessed in our observations).

It is apparent from the earlier review of changing sex roles that men and women, singly and together, are being encouraged in various ways to consider new life styles. There is hope that we can transform our present organization of gender, and foster a system in which the sexes have more freedom to engage in behaviors traditionally performed by the opposite sex. Our intensive study of the preschool period persuades us that biological, social, and learning forces, inextricably interwoven, operate from the beginning, so that by 2 to 3 years of age children adopt traditional gender labels. Boys and girls display their learning in the kinds of activities they choose, in how they play and with whom. By 5 to 6 years of age these differences are great and consistent, even though there is minimal sexual dimorphism until adolescence.

Early childhood is a time of rapid, intense learning, and the young child learns in idiosyncratic ways that are different from adult learning. Fundamental and strong emotional components are associated with the child's gender role learning. The concepts of "maleness" and "femaleness" in children tend to be primitive, stereotyped, mutually exclusive, and over-learned. We see a fruitless endeavor implicit in any efforts to alter young children's early *patterns* of learning something so profoundly important for their psychological well-being. We have seen how the peer group operates in the preschool—and even more potently in the elementary school—to transmit messages about gender differences that exist in society. We contend that young children's early identifications and imitations mirror global messages from our adult society, and that their cognitive ability to understand the meanings of gender is dependent upon their developmental ability to understand an abstraction. It is not until children's cognitive development reaches the point beginning with the "5-to-7 cognitive shift," when they no longer think in binary (black-or-white) terms, that more sophisticated notions of what it means to be a male or a female can be assimilated.

As Piaget suggests, egocentric functioning decreases as a result of the child's confrontation with peers who differ in their wishes, perspectives, deeds, and thoughts. Hartup identifies peer *interaction* in general and peer *conflict* in particular as the condition for role-taking to emerge and stabilize.[80] He doubts that "mastery of the complex emotions and behaviors related to aggression could be achieved in the absence of early opportunity to interact with others whose developmental status is similar to one's own."[81] Hartup argues that a constant outcome of aggressive encounters with peers, consistent winning or losing, can be devastating for the child's future social effectiveness and emotional health, and suggests that females suffer from inadequate aggressive experience. For females, traditional socialization develops impulse controls that function to reinforce caution, withdrawal, and compliance—approaches that are conservative rather than aggressive. Hartup comments:

> Peer contacts which never allow for aggressive display or which allow only for successful aggression (never for unsuccessful aggression) may be precursors for malfunctioning in the aggressive system. Clearly, this hypothesis is plausible when applied to boys, although it is more tenuous for girls. Traditional socialization produces women who are ineffectively prepared for exposure to aggressive instigating events (except perhaps for threats to their children). Women are notably more anxious and passive than men when exposed to aggressive instigation, and this sex difference may be greater than is good for the future of the species.[82]

Girls' lack of aggressive experience is reflected in the significant *qualitative* sex differences in rough-and-tumble play when boys and girls have the same opportunities to engage it. Hartup attaches considerable importance to the incidence of rough-and-tumble play:

> Socialization seems to require both rough-and-tumble play and experiences in which rough-and-tumble play escalate into aggression and de-escalate into playful interaction. Field studies suggest that such experi-

ences are readily available to the young in all primate species, including Homo sapiens, although opportunities are greater for males than for females. . . . If women are to assume roles more like those of men, some manipulation of early peer experiences is necessary. Opportunities for early exposure to rough-and-tumble play must be equal for males and for females as opportunities for exposure to other normative behaviors.[83]

We are in agreement with Hartup about the important role the peer group plays in the socialization process that fits children to their culture. As children grow older the winning of peer approval is a central mode of psychological functioning and a primary source of self-esteem. The influence of the peer group enforces conformity to sex role standards at an individual and group level. Peers, like fathers, reward individual and group level sex-appropriate behaviors, and punish those that are inappropriate.[84] We observe that the peer experience is relatively more important for the male role, however, and that parental identification is more influential in female sex role development, since girls are still socialized to be mothers only, and not workers and achievers outside the home as well.

The discouragement of girls in elementary and high schools makes the rewards of early childhood education different for each sex. Researchers recently studied children enrolled in Harlem's Headstart program.[85] Although boys and girls at first showed equal (and substantial) benefits from the program, most of the gains for girls had disappeared fifteen years later, when the young women seemed to be generally no better off than those who had not been in the preschool intervention program. "The competence, assertiveness and questioning skills they had acquired during the intervention experience often conflicted with sex role expectations encountered in subsequent years," the study reports. "Initial gains in self-perception and sense of competence were reversed." The female participants reported that teachers in the upper elementary grades often complained that they were disruptive and aggressive when they expressed curiosity. In addition, about one-third of them became mothers, making college attendance and jobs more difficult.

Social equality between men and women is impeded by crucial differences in male and female peer relations. Male–male extensive peer relations are more highly developed than those among females in competitive strategies supported by the prevailing ideology. Males use relationships with one another to find their identities and establish their positions in a dominance hierarchy in society. Boys in all cultures are more peer-oriented than girls. Peers, not adults, are more likely to sway boys' behavior, but not girls'.[86] Women, readily identifying with the mother role, need not engage in competitive strivings with one another to establish their identities, only to capture husbands. Their intensive peer relations increasingly involve them with a few "best friends," with whom they spend the bulk of their time. In contrast to men, they tend not to engage in activities that involve larger groups of peers. The opportunities for cooperation and competition which are provided more by male than female groups, develop leadership skills that are most relevant to modern organizational life. Male get-togethers are usually outside the home, in sports, clubs, or bars. Women more frequently meet in one another's homes in pairs or small groups.

We believe that relations of male and female children in peer groups reflect the relations of males and females in our adult society. Infants apparently develop different expectations according to sex, and learn different behaviors from each parent; but each also has inherited potentialities for responding to members of his or her own sex. Human beings have characteristics which no society has created and to which all societies must respond. Young children acquire a sexual body from genes, and they develop gender concepts from interaction with the environment. Both are formative influences in the child's becoming a male or female human being.

Establishing gender identity is one of the first and most important accomplishments of the young child; rudimentary beginnings occur in infancy when male and female parents, or care givers, play a major role. Sex differences in parents are signals to infants of differing orientations to the world, differences that are profoundly important for the child's psychological birth as a male or a female. This is both necessary and desirable. What could change, however, are parental influences that operate to form children into adults–parents *exclusively* organized around women's child care–domestic role and men's non-child-care work role. Becoming a parent represents the epitome of sex role identity for most persons. We agree that "most people model the general style of their same-sex parent when they become marital partners and parents, and that the modeling exerts a generally conservative influence on sex role change."[87] Pervasive cultural forces accepting a sex-gender system that supports women's bearing and nurturing children, and men's non-bearing but providing for children, mold the developing child not only through parents, but through siblings, peers, the media, and all the subtle sights, sounds, smells, and touches of the total environment.

Children's relationships with parents prompt differing social contacts with peers, with differential consequences for social skill and personality development. Through play with boys and girls, each child receives and responds to two sets of gender stimuli and codes them either positive (one's own sex) or negative (the other sex). The gender concept takes on value and determines many sex-typed activities and attitudes in children. Cognitive mechanisms for early differentiations and codings are immature, however, and tend toward simplistic stereotyping. In their own special ways of learning, children assimilate messages from the total environment about how males and females are expected to behave and adapt their behaviors to take account of the sex of the children with whom they are interacting in their peer groups.

Our observations of peer relationships in play, our understanding of the child's cognitive processes and our appreciation of the total environment's pervasive social message about sex roles, prompt us to believe that children in the first five years of life learn narrow sex role concepts which conform in general to their culture's stereotyped belief system. Through their play behavior, children steadily incorporate the gender role initiated by their biology, demanded by their psyche, understood by their mind, and supported by their culture. Other investigators have also noted that sex-typing among young children does not appear to change significantly over a span of years. In data collected during a period from 1964 to 1976, behaviors preferred by each sex maintained a remarkable consistency.[88]

Children's first early awareness of gender identity is a cognitive act, probably based on a limited set of features—gender label, hair style, dress, name, and organized rules that they have observed or that have been dictated by adults. Cognitive learning always has social, or feeling, dimensions, since the most powerful concentrations of feelings are those human beings have about themselves. As children and hierarchies develop, children not only learn that there are boys and girls, they learn that they are selves and begin to compare and define themselves in terms of others. When it is no longer necessary to struggle with a binary dilemma, the next step is to start *doing* what you are with same-sex peers, with the inevitable consequence of feelings about what you do. Such feelings ultimately contribute to the same-sex group alliances and opposite-sex rejections and attractions of 5-year-olds. These functional alliances prompt children to regard the same sex with favor and the other sex as different, forming same-sex cultures in which the opposite sex does not feel at home.

Those with a zeal to promote a society with a universal interdependence among equals need not necessarily be discouraged that male and female roles tend to be so discrepant or polarized during early childhood. Nonsexist messages may still be assimilated by children in fragmentary ways, and stored for more mature intellectual processing in elementary school, early adolescence, or young adulthood, when the subtleties of sex roles and the variety of acceptable masculine and feminine behaviors can be better understood. One study concludes that "attempts to reshape attitudes and behavior during the preschool years—for example, to stamp out negative attitudes toward the opposite sex—although perhaps laying valuable groundwork for later attitude change, may not have immediate and/or stable results. In contrast to the usual develomental principle concerning intervention (the-earlier-the-better), the greater cognitive maturity and sensitivity to social influences of older children may make efforts directed toward them more effective."[89]

Although we observed children in schools and organized play groups, we can assume that the differences we have documented will occur in other settings as well. Unless adults or circumstances contrive to arrange things otherwise, boys will prefer to play with boys and girls with girls. Hostilities toward the opposite sex will flourish as same-sex identities need strengthening in the early stages of development. Children will tend to learn and reinforce specific modes of interaction through play with same-sex peers whom they tend to favor because of gender labeling and experienced similarities in behavior. They will increasingly perceive differences, and either denigrate or avoid behaviors in opposite-sex peers if those behaviors are not their own naturally favored or rewarded ways of behaving. Not to do so would be counterproductive to establishing traditional gender identities. By the same token, perception of similarities, and repeated positive experiences with same-sex peers, will encourage sex role behaviors and foster in-group cohesiveness.

Historically, and in a strict sense, peers "are unknown in man's environment of evolutionary adaptedness and in that of his closest relatives."[90] For most of man's history, "peers" have aggregated in mixed-age groups. Konner believes that the mixed-age experience is adaptive and advantageous in that it provides older children with practice in protecting and parenting, and fosters communication and other skills in younger children. Only where competition among young adults is of great importance will individual juveniles accustom themselves and prepare for it by associating with others of the same age who are, as nearly as possible, equal in ability.[91] Such competition has become basic to our age-graded society in which the importance of peers is exaggerated.

The same-age peer group of young children is a relatively modern phenomenon. Before the advent of schools, the socializing import of groups of peers was minimal. Even the concept of *child* is relatively modern. Two centuries ago children were primarily regarded as miniature adults.[92] The change in this attitude has been greater for boys than for girls, as Chodorow points out:

> Aries, in his discussion of the changing concept of childhood in modern capitalist society, makes a distinction that seems to have more general applicability. Boys, he suggests, became "children" while girls remained "little women." "The idea of childhood profited the boys first of all, while the girls persisted much longer in the traditional way of life which confused them with the adults: we shall have cause to notice more than once this delay on the part of women in adopting the visible forms of the essentially masculine civilization of modern times." (p. 61) This took place first in the middle classes, as a situation developed in which boys needed special schooling in order to prepare for their future work and could not begin to do this kind of work in childhood. Girls (and working class boys)

could still learn work more directly from their parents, and could begin to participate in the adult economy at an earlier age. Rapid economic change and development have exacerbated the lack of male generational role continuity. Few fathers now have either the opportunity or the ability to pass on a profession or skill to their sons.

Sex role development of girls in modern society is more complex. On the one hand, they go to school to prepare for life in a technologically and socially complex society. On the other, there is a sense in which this schooling is a pseudo-training. It is not meant to interfere with the much more important training to be "feminine" and a wife and mother, which is embedded in the girl's unconscious development and which her mother teaches her in a family context where she is clearly the salient parent.[93]

One consequence of women's new work role and the diminishing size of families is an increase in the importance of peers in children's socialization. Rapid social change tends to create a hiatus between one generation and the next, increasing the socializing role of age-mates.[94] Eisenstadt argues that peer groups are most likely to develop "in those societies in which the family or kinship unit cannot ensure . . . the attainment of full social status on the part of its members."[95] Today, as more women leave the home to work, exposure to peers is increasing, both for the women at work and their children in preschools. Women's working, which will demand more pre-school and day-care facilities, creates contradictions in the female role, which traditionally de-emphasizes peer relations. The serious discrepancy in girls' socialization, in which they are "overeducated for domesticity and yet insufficiently educated for rewarding work in higher occupational ranks,"[96] is exacerbated by sex differences in children's socialization, in which girls miss valuable peer group experiences.

At present, competition is more conspicuous among men than among women in our patriarchical Western society. The emphasis on the nuclear family and on the heterosexual bond works against group cohesiveness among women. We have described how boys tend to aggregate in competitive groups and girls tend to favor one-to-one friendships in domestic settings. We submit that our data reveal what is happening now, and what is happening appears to show the influence of strong, traditional forces on early sex role development. Yet we acknowledge that sex roles are relative and that they may not be as dependent on biology as has been true in the past. Recent grouping of many children of the same age is not a practice of long standing; groupings of children under age 6 are an even newer phenomenon. Such peer groups are now giving both sexes an opportunity to learn their gender identities in new ways and prepare for a complex society.

Although sex role polarization first develops in the years from 3 to 5, direct intervention in these preschool years is not likely to be effective in changing sex roles because young children's cognitive abilities are immature and egocentric, and because their play, through which they develop sex-appropriate skills and aspirations, is a direct reflection of the adult culture. The present sex role system, in devaluing one sex, limits the development of both. Our study provides challenging evidence that suggests both opportunities and constraints for a culture seeking to develop an equality of behavior potential for both sexes.

APPENDICES

Appendix A
Description of Coding Categories

AFFILIATIVE CONTACTS

1. Sharing ideas or materials

Conversation or activities involving the sharing of ideas or materials with a view to a mutual exploiting and enjoying of their potentialities.

Seeking, offering, or receiving help, information, suggestions, permissions, and invitations, and greetings, verbally or nonverbally.

Facilitating remarks or activities promoting good will (seeking attention).

Help may include getting or sharing supplies, putting materials away, offering substitute materials when ownership is questionable.

Invitations. Compliance or agreement. Willingness to go along with another's suggestions or activities.

> *Initiation: "How I gonna get this water out?"*
> *Response: "Pour it in here."*
> *Initiation: "Hi."*
> *Response: "Hi. You can come to my party some day."*
> *Initiation: "I'm going to work with you."*
> *Response: "Sure."*

2. Bonding of friendship

"In-group" remarks of a friendly nature, which do not come under categories of compliment or awareness of feelings (categories 3 and 6), which are intended to establish or reinforce relationships in which the concept of *friend* is specifically mentioned, or a unity in relationship is implied or reinforced.

> *"We're the only ones that can come into this tent."*
> *"We're the good guys."*
> *"Whoever likes Stacey raise your hand."*
> *"We're friends, right?"*
> *"If you put on your pants I'll be your friend."*
> *"Let's sit close together."*

3. Admiration, compliment, or approval

Verbal remarks or noncontact gestures (such as clapping), intended to express appreciation or admiration of another person's self, apparel, or achievement.

> *"What a pretty ring you have."*
> *"I like your building."* The child smiles and pats it.

4. Nurturance or grooming

Offering, seeking, or receiving food, drink, clothing, medicine (real or pretend), or specific physical care or grooming to a person, an animal, or an object representing a person or an animal.

> *Initiation: "My baby's on fire; I need to get him to the doctor."*
> *Response: "Give him some milk."*
> *"Hey, let me fix your tie."*
> *"Would you like me to make you some coffee?"*
> *"Here's a cookie for you."*
> *"Let me brush your hair."*

5. Physical caress or endearing epithet

Engaging in or offering physical contacts, such as hugging, kissing, stroking, fondling (not mere touching); addressing another as honey, darling, sweetheart, dear.

Initiation: A child kisses and pats another child.
Response: "You're my honey."

6. Awareness of human feelings

Specific expression of affect, such as solicitude, comfort, sympathy, empathy, apology, gratitude. Demonstrated awareness of one's own or another's feelings or concerns. Crying (but not screaming).

Initiation: Denied candy, begins to whimper.
Response: "Don't worry, I'll be your friend."
Initiation: "Is Tucker mad?"
Response: "Don't worry, he won't hurt you."
Initiation: "Did that hurt?"
Response: "No. Thanks."
Initiation: "I know how you feel."
Response: "We're both bored."
Initiation: "Is it okay if he plays with us?"
Response: "If it makes you happy."

7. Rough–and–tumble play, positive teasing, foolish word play

Friendly and heightened physical or verbal activity, often including silliness, giggling, and uproarious laughter.

Initiation: Shoots another child with pretend pistol and giggles.
Response: Falls over, gets up, shoots, and laughs.
Initiation: "You can't catch me. Ha, ha."
Response: Catches first child; they wrestle and laugh.
Initiation: "Look at my ding, a-ling-ling."
Response: "Pink-dink, boo-ba, ka-ka."

NONAFFILIATIVE CONTACTS

1. Assault

Physical violence to a person or property, with or without appropriation of material; destruction of property.

Initiation: One child hits another child.
Response: That child breaks the first child's toy.

2. Molesting, intruding, retention of disputed property

Molesting or bothering gestures or actions interfering with another's ongoing activity, or calculated to annoy; appropriation or retention of disputed property, not involving physical violence. A successful thwarting of another's effort to take over materials.

Initiation: Trudy grabs Anne's paper.
Response: Anne grabs it back.
Initiation: Bob pokes Andy in the face.
Response: Andy pulls at Bob's hair.
Initiation: Tim taps John's head with a stick.
Response: John pokes at Tim's toy.

3. Insult

Offensive, demeaning, or contemptuous speech, demeaning criticism. Blatant statement or action calculated to denigrate another's worth or activity. Name calling, deliberate attempt to exclude another, such as shoving or ordering away, rejecting offer of friendship, or expressing hostility or dislike.

Initiation: "Why are you painting that, stupid?"
Response: "You're yukky."
Initiation: "I don't want to be your friend."
Response: "Get out of my house."
Initiation: "You're a baby."
Response: The child makes a face, saying, "I don't like you."

4. Reprimand, correction, disagreement, or command

Reproof or directive implying insufficient or inappropriate activity on the part of another child, with the implication that there has been misunderstanding and that another course of action is available or preferable.

Refusal to agree or comply, or to participate when invited. Difference in opinion without implication of contempt or insult. Screaming (as a manifes-

tation of disagreement). Authoritarian directive or act expressed in a dominating manner intended to bring action from another; order that entertains
no alternative choice.

Initiation: "You better clean that up now."
Response: "No, I won't."
Initiation: "Get out of my cubby."
Response: "It was my cubby first."
Initiation: "It's not time to eat snacks."
Response: "Well, you ate some first."
Initiation: "That's not how you make a rabbit."
Response: "Yes it is."

5. Bravado

Protestive defense or assertion, denying or competing with another's assertions, in the face of an ego-deflating situation; inflated protestation of one's
worth, accomplishments, or possessions.

Initiation: "I'm five and you're only four."
Response: "So what!"
Initiation: "My building is the best one in the world."
Response: "I have a bigger bed than you."

6. Withdrawal

Willful removal of oneself from a situation, a drawing away, holding back
from responding, turning aside, attending but not responding.

Initiation: "Try to pound the clay, it helps."
Response: The child leaves the clay on the table.
Initiation: "Why are you playing with the clay?"
Response: The child looks away and mutters to self.

7. Ignoring

Attending but not responding. (A neutral response, i.e., one in which the
child was not attending while genuinely absorbed with something else, was
not coded.)

AMBIGUOUS BEHAVIOR

Any behavior whose intent or meaning is so obscure that it cannot be categorized is coded as AMB—ambiguous.

Any category more specifically designated, but including category 1 of the affiliative definitions, will be categorized only by the more specific code number. When two of the more specific categories are included simultaneously in the same initiation or response, the most salient tone of the contact determines the most appropriate category to record.

Appendix B
Reliability

To assess observer reliability, two observers followed the same child for a half-hour period. (Each observer was matched against the observer who had been with the study the longest.) All initiations and responses were recorded individually, in diary form, and records were then compared. Reliabilities based on total number of agreements divided by the combined number of agreements and disagreements were calculated. A disagreement was scored for each time one observer failed to record a contact or the two observers' data differed, such that the same contact was described as discrepant in type or quality. The average reliability obtained across observers was 83%.

Coding reliability was established at 91.6%. Four judges coded four different typed transcriptions of the half-hour observations. Reliability was again calculated by scoring total number of agreements divided by the combined number of agreements and disagreements. Disagreements were scored when any judge scored a contact as a different category than other judges, failed to score a contact, or scored a contact when one did not take place according to the other judges.

Appendix C
Data Analysis

Only the subject's action in each valid peer contact was included in the statistical computer analyses. For each subject of our 255 half-hour observations, we accumulated four sums. The sums represented the total number of that child's peer contacts, distributed into the following four categories:

1. same-sex positive
2. same-sex negative
3. cross-sex positive
4. cross-sex negative

These four variables represented the rate, or the total number of peer contacts per half-hour, categorized by dyadic type (same-sex or cross-sex), by affiliative content (positive or negative), and by sequence type (initiation or response).

Dependent variables were the frequencies (rates per half-hour) of same-sex positive, same-sex negative, cross-sex positive, and cross-sex negative contacts. A data file was created consisting of one record per subject that registered the subjects's sex and age and frequency counts for each dependent variable. We performed a series of three statistical tests, run separately for initiations and responses, on the four dependent variables. The first test we performed (two-way analyses of variance) determined the main and interaction effects associated with the indepen- dent variables of sex and age. The overall sex and age differences which we identified in the first test were further explored with two subsequent series of statistical tests. One series (one-way ANOVAs by sex) measured sex differences at each of the four separate ages we studied (2, 3, 4, 5) to provide details of the overall pattern. Another series (sets of contrasts or t-tests) computed age differences between successive ages (2–3, 3–4, 4–5) separately for boys and girls, in order to identify at which ages the significant developmental changes revealed by the main test actually took place (or whether the change was relatively constant). Although there are slightly more sophisticated multi-variate techniques available,[1] we preferred to avoid the additional complications and restrictions they would have imposed. The more straightforward interpretations possible with the simpler procedures seemed more appropriate for this study.

The results regarding negative contacts seemed more complex than those regarding positive contacts. Negative contacts showed initiation–response differences and other anomalies. To further analyze sex differences in negative, nonaffiliative behaviors with same-sex and cross-sex peers, Kendall rank correlations[2] were performed for the sub-categories of negative contacts.

Appendix D
Statistical Tables

Table D-1. Distribution of Positive and Negative Peer Contacts

Category	Percent	Number
Same-Sex		
Positive	42.1%	3503
Negative	23.3%	1942
Cross-Sex		
Positive	19.6%	1630
Negative	15.0%	1251
Total		
Positive	61.7%	5133
Negative	38.3%	3193
Total	100.0%	8326

Table D-2.   Distribution of Subcategories of Positive and Negative Peer Contacts

	Category	Percent	Number
	Sharing	47.9%	4258
P	Friendship	1.1%	109
O	Admiration	0.5%	43
S			
I	Nurturance	2.2%	179
T			
I	Caressing	1.0%	79
V			
E	Feelings	0.9%	74
	Assault	1.3%	110
N	Molesting	9.0%	707
E			
G	Insult	3.1%	249
A			
T	Disagreement	14.9%	1217
I			
V	Bravado	1.9%	160
E			
	Withdrawal	1.5%	117
	Ignoring	7.8%	633

Table D-3. Summary of Two-Way Analyses of Variance for the Effects of Age and Sex on the Rates of Preschool Children's Peer Contacts

	Source of Variation		
	Age	Sex	Age × Sex
DF:	3	1	3
Categories of Social Contacts	F	F	F
Same-Sex Positive			
Initiation	7.53***	0.01	0.75
Response	6.65***	0.03	1.02
Same-Sex Negative			
Initiation	2.34	8.84**	1.13
Response	2.60	5.11*	1.00
Cross-Sex Positive			
Intiation	2.17	0.84	3.38*
Response	0.82	0.78	2.80*
Cross-Sex Negative			
Initiation	0.76	0.29	5.20**
Response	0.07	8.25**	2.28
Total			
Initiation	5.29***	0.81	0.33
Response	4.28**	0.20	0.96

Note: DF within Groups = 247

* $p < .05$
** $p < .01$
*** $p < .001$

Table D-4.   Mean Rates per Half-Hour of Preschool Children's Peer Contacts

Categories of Social Contacts	Age								Total (n=255)	
	2 (n=33)		3 (n=79)		4 (n=74)		5 (n=69)			
	Boys	Girls	Boys	Girls	Boys	Girls	Boys	Girls	Boys	Girls
Same Sex Positive										
Initiation	2.12	2.69	3.13	5.28	5.89	5.17	6.67	5.70	4.78	5.02
Response	1.18	1.31	2.23	3.35	3.74	3.94	4.75	3.61	3.23	3.39
Total	3.30	4.00	5.36	8.83	9.63	9.11	11.42	9.31	8.01	8.41
Same-Sex Negative										
Intiation	1.18	1.31	2.08	1.10	3.34	1.42	1.53	0.88	2.18	1.16
Response	1.71	1.94	2.18	2.70	3.68	2.39	2.89	1.58	2.75	2.22
Total	2.89	3.25	4.26	3.80	7.02	3.81	4.42	2.46	4.93	3.38
Cross-Sex Positive										
Intiation	0.82	1.38	2.79	2.73	2.37	2.42	1.39	3.52	2.02	2.67
Reponse	0.71	1.19	2.00	1.68	1.13	1.36	0.81	2.12	1.25	1.64
Total	1.53	2.57	4.79	4.41	3.50	3.78	2.20	5.64	3.27	4.31
Cross-Sex Negative										
Initiation	1.00	1.69	1.64	0.60	1.11	0.78	0.83	1.64	1.18	1.06
Response	1.35	2.00	1.49	2.05	1.39	1.78	0.83	2.45	1.26	2.07
Total	2.35	3.69	3.13	2.65	2.50	2.56	1.66	4.09	2.44	3.13
Total										
Initiation	5.12	7.06	9.62	7.65	12.63	9.78	10.31	11.73	10.10	9.26
Response	4.94	6.44	7.85	7.80	9.87	9.69	8.94	9.76	8.36	8.69
Total	10.06	13.50	17.47	15.45	22.50	19.47	19.25	21.49	18.46	17.95

Table D-5.   Standard Deviations for the Rates per Half-Hour of Preschool Children's Peer Contacts

Categories of Social Contacts	Age									
	2 (n=33)		3 (n=79)		4 (n=74)		5 (n=69)		Total (n=255)	
	Boys	Girls	Boys	Girls	Boys	Girls	Boys	Girls	Boys	Girls
Same-Sex Positive										
Initiation	2.36	3.53	3.94	7.18	6.41	5.45	5.41	4.05	5.30	5.58
Response	2.04	1.66	2.81	4.63	4.14	3.98	4.83	3.57	3.96	3.94
Same-Sex Negative										
Intiation	1.55	1.45	4.19	1.91	5.14	2.37	2.16	1.14	3.87	1.83
Response	1.69	1.88	2.17	4.92	4.01	2.56	3.34	2.08	3.15	3.35
Cross-Sex Positive										
Initiation	1.01	2.03	3.19	6.44	2.76	3.06	2.07	5.09	2.65	4.83
Response	1.26	1.22	2.76	3.45	1.70	1.81	1.39	3.81	2.02	2.95
Cross-Sex Negative										
Initiation	1.58	1.82	2.01	1.06	1.33	1.02	1.56	2.09	1.66	1.55
Response	1.62	1.51	1.78	3.55	2.12	1.68	1.16	3.39	1.73	2.56
Total										
Initiation	3.69	5.38	8.59	6.25	10.86	6.99	7.15	7.69	8.74	6.93
Response	3.78	3.81	5.51	5.61	8.12	7.46	7.53	6.19	6.89	6.22

Table D-6.   Sex differences in the Rates per Half-Hour of Preschool Children's Peer Contacts from One-Way Analyses of Variance (by Sex) for Each Age

Categories of Social Contacts	Age			
	2	3	4	5
Same-Sex Positive				
Initiation	g	g	b	b
Response	g	g	g	b
Same-Sex Negative				
Initiation	g	b*	b**	b
Response	g	g	b*	b*
Cross-Sex Positive				
Initiation	g	b	g	g**
Response	g	b	g	g*
Cross-Sex Negative				
Initiation	g	b***	b	g*
Response	g	g	g	g***
Total				
Initiation	g	b	b	g
Response	g	g	b	g

Note: A "b" indicates that the boys' mean ratio was higher than the girls'.

A "g" indicates that the girls' mean rate was higher than the boys'.

   * p < .11
  ** p < .05
*** p < .01

Table D-7.   Age Differences in the Rates per Half-Hour of Preschool Children's Peer Contacts from Contrasts (t-tests) between Successive Ages for Each Sex

Categories of Social Contacts	Ages					
	2–3		3–4		4–5	
	Boys	Girls	Boys	Girls	Boys	Girls
Same-Sex Positive						
Initiation	+	+*	+**	−	+	+
Response	+	+*	+*	+	+	−
Same-Sex Negative						
Initiation	+	−	+	+	−**	−*
Response	+	+	+*	−	−	−*
Cross-Sex Positive						
Initiation	+***	+	−	−	−	+*
Response	+**	+	−*	−	−	+
Cross-Sex Negative						
Initiation	+	−***	−	+	−	+**
Response	+	+	−	−	−	+
Total						
Initiation	+*	+	+	+	−	+
Response	+	+	+	+	−	−

Note: A "+" indicates an increase, and a "−" a decrease, in the mean rate of peer contacts between successive ages.

  * p < .11
 ** p < .05
*** p < .01

Table D-8. Ranks of Negative Peer Contacts Observed among Preschool Boys and Girls with Kendall Rank Correlations at Each Age

Categories of Negative Contacts	Age							
	2		3		4		5	
	Boys	Girls	Boys	Girls	Boys	Girls	Boys	Girls
Assault	5	6	3	7	6	7	7	7
Molesting	1	1	2	3	2	3	2	4
Insult	7	4	4	4	4	4	3	3
Disagreement	2	2	1	1	1	1	1	1
Bravado	6	7	6	6	5	5	5	5
Withdrawal	4	5	7	5	7	6	6	6
Ignoring	3	3	5	2	3	2	4	2
Kendall Rank Correlations S	14*		7 n.s.		14*		16**	
r	.70		.33	.66	.76			

* p < .05
** p < .01

Table D-9. Ranks of Same-Sex Negative Peer Contacts Observed among Preschool Boys and Girls with Kendall Rank Correlations at Each Age

Categories of Negative Contacts	Age							
	2		3		4		5	
	Boys	Girls	Boys	Girls	Boys	Girls	Boys	Girls
Assault	4	6.5	3	7	6	7	7	7
Molesting	1	1	2	3	2	3	2	5
Insult	7	4.5	4.5	4	5	4.5	4.5	3
Disagreement	2	3	1	1	1	1	1	1
Bravado	6	6.5	7	5.5	4	4.5	3	4
Withdrawal	5	4.5	6	5.5	7	6	6	6.5
Ignoring	3	2	4.5	2	3	2	4.5	2
Kendall Rank Correlations S	11 n.s.		9 n.s.		16*		10 n.s.	
r	.58	.47	.80	.50				

* p < .05

Table D-10. Ranks of Cross-Sex Negative Peer Contacts Observed among Preschool Boys and Girls with Kendall Rank Correlations at Each Age

			Age					
Categories of	2		3		4		5	
Negative Contacts	Boys	Girls	Boys	Girls	Boys	Girls	Boys	Girls
Assault	5	4.5	6	7	6	7	6	6.5
Molesting	1	1	2	2	2	3	2	2
Insult	7	4.5	3	4	3	4	3	4
Disagreement	2	2	1	1	1	1	1	1
Bravado	6	5.5	5	6	5	5	6	5
Withdrawal	4	5.5	7	5	7	6	6	6.5
Ignoring	3	3	4	3	4	2	4	3

Kendall Rank Correlations	S	13*		15*		15*		16**
	r	.68		.71	.71	.89		

* $p < .05$
** $p < .01$

Notes

Chapter 1. Peers as Agents of Sex Role Development

1. Eleanor E. Maccoby and Carol Nagy Jacklin, 1974, *The Psychology of Sex Differences.*

2. Marilyn Strathern, 1973, "An Anthropological Perspective."

3. Herbert H. Barry, Margaret K. Bacon, and Irwin L. Child, 1957, "A Cross-Cultural Survey of Some Sex Differences in Socialization."

4. Evelyn Goodenough Pitcher, 1957, "An Interest in Persons as an Aspect of Sex Differences in the Early Years"; 1963, *Children Tell Stories.*

5. Sylvia Feinberg, 1975, "Boys and Girls Drawings of Helping and Fighting."

6. Harriet L. Rheingold and Kaye V. Cook, 1975, "The Content of Boys' and Girls' Rooms as an Index of Parents' Behavior."

7. Gary B. Trudeau, *Boston Sunday Globe*, Nov. 5, 1972.

8. Susan Brownmiller, 1975, *Against Our Will: Men, Women and Rape.*

9. Kate Millett, 1970, *Sexual Politics*, p. 178.

10. Ibid., p. 180.

11. Erica DeJong, 1977, *How To Save Your Own Life.*

12. Walter Mischel, 1970, "Sex Typing and Socialization."

13. Willard W. Hartup, 1970, "Peer Interaction and Social Organization."

14. Robert R. Sears, 1965, "Development of Gender Role."

15. Sigmund Freud, 1938, "Three Contributions to the Theory of Sex."

16. Albert Bandura, 1969, "Social-Learning Theory of Identification Processes"; ed., 1974, *Psychological Modelling.*

17. Lawrence Kohlberg, 1966, "A Cognitive-Developmental Analysis of Children's Sex Role Concepts and Attitudes."

18. Ibid., p. 124.

19. Howard Gardner, 1978, *Developmental Psychology*, p. 223.

20. Ibid., p. 196.

21. Eleanor Maccoby, 1980, *Social Development*, pp. 241–42.

22. Kohlberg, "Cognitive-Developmental Analysis."

23. Stephen J. Suomi and Harry F. Harlow, 1975, "The Role and Reason of Peer Relationships in Rhesus Monkeys."

24. Harry F. Harlow, 1965, "Sexual Behavior in the Rhesus Monkey."

25. John Money and Anke Ehrhardt, 1972, *Man and Woman, Boy and Girl.*

26. Jeffry Z. Rubin, Frank J. Provenzano, and Zella Luria, 1974, "The Eye of the Beholder: Parents' Views on Sex of Newborns"; Peter K. Smith and Linda Daglish, 1977, "Sex Differences in Parent and Infant Behavior in the Home."

27. Erik Erikson, 1951, "Sex Differences in the Play Configurations of Pre-adolescents."

28. Thomas H. Middleton, 1980, "Boys and Girls Together," p. 26.

29. Maccoby and Jacklin, *Psychology of Sex Differences;* Ruth Hubbard and Marion Lowe, 1979, *Genes and Gender II.*

30. Willard W. Hartup, 1978, "Peer Interaction and the Behavioral Development of the Individual Child," p. 270.

Chapter 2. The Formation of Same-Sex Relations

1. Willard W. Hartup, 1970, "Peer Interaction and Social Organization."

2. Nicholas Blurton-Jones, 1972, "Categories of Child–Child Interaction."

3. Barbara Tizard, Janet Philips, and Ian Plewis, 1976, "Play in Pre-school Centres—I. Play Measures and Their Relativism to Age, Sex, and I.Q."

4. Judith H. Langlois, Nathan W. Gottfried, and Bill Seay, 1973, "The Influence of Sex of Peer on the Social Behavior of Preschool Children."

5. Carol Nagy Jacklin and Eleanor E. Maccoby, 1978, "Social Behavior at Thirty-Three Months in Same-Sex and Mixed-Sex Dyads."

6. Eleanor E. Maccoby and Carol Nagy Jacklin, 1974, *The Psychology of Sex Differences.*

7. Zick Rubin, 1980, *Children's Friendships.*

8. Lawrence Kohlberg, 1966, "A Cognitive-Developmental Analysis of Children's Sex Role Concepts and Attitudes."

9. Rubin, *Children's Friendships.*

10. Helen Faigin, 1958, "Social Behavior of Young Children in the Kibbutz."

Chapter 3. Sex Differences in the Style of Boys' and Girls' Play

1. Beatrice B. Whiting and Carolyn Pope Edwards, 1973, "A Cross-Cultural Analysis of Sex Differences in the Behavior of Children Aged 3 through 11."

2. Eleanor E. Maccoby and Carol Nagy Jacklin, 1974, *The Psychology of Sex Differences.*

3. "Dennis the Menace," by Hank Ketcham, in Phyllis Taube MacEwan, 1972, *Experiences in Day Care Centers, Play Groups, and Free Schools.*

4. Crosby N. Bonsall, 1973, *Mine's the Best.*

5. Catherine Garvey, 1977, *Play.*

6. Spencer K. Thompson, 1975, "Gender Labels and Early Sex Role Development."

7. J. Richard Udry, 1971, *The Social Context of Marriage*, p. 81.

8. Adelaide Haas, 1981, "Partner Influence on Sex-Associated Spoken Language of Children."

9. Jean Stockard and Miriam Johnson, 1980, *Sex Inequality and Sex Role Development*, p. 243.

10. Esther Blank Grief, 1976, "Sex Role Playing in Preschool Children."

11. Bruno Bettelheim, 1975, "Some Further Thoughts on the Doll Corner," p. 368.

12. Evelyn Goodenough Pitcher, 1957, "An Interest in Persons as an Aspect of Sex Differences in the Early Years."

13. Nancy Chodorow, 1978, *The Reproduction of Mothering;* Jean Baker Miller, ed., 1973, *Psychoanalysis and Women.*

Chapter 4. Theoretical Perspectives on Sex Roles and Peer Relations

1. Robert Hinde, 1975, "On Describing Relationships"; 1976, "Interactions, Relationships and Social Structure."

2. Jeffry Z. Rubin, Frank J. Provenzano, and Zella Luria, 1974, "The Eye of the Beholder: Parents' Views on Sex of Newborns."

3. Howard A. Moss, 1974, "Early Sex Difference in Mother–Infant Interaction."

4. John Condry and Sandra Condry, 1976, "Sex Differences: A Study of the Eye of the Beholder."

5. Eleanor E. Maccoby and Carolyn N. Jacklin, 1974, *The Psychology of Sex Differences.*

6. Louise Cherry and Michael Lewis, 1976, "Mothers and Two-Year-Olds: A Study of Sex-Differentiated Aspects of Verbal Interaction."

7. Willard W. Hartup, 1978, "Peer Relations and the Growth of Social Competence"; Stephen J. Suomi, 1978, "Peers, Play, and Primary Prevention."

8. Hartup, "Peer Relations," p. 159.

9. Shmuel Noah Eisenstadt, 1956, *From Generation to Generation.*

10. Robert R. Sears, 1965, "Development of Gender Role."

11. Willard W. Hartup, 1976, "Peer Interaction and the Behavioral Development of the Individual Child"; idem, "Peer Relations."

12. Suomi, "Peers, Play, and Primary Prevention."

13. Ibid., p. 134.

14. Ibid.

15. Rosalind Charlesworth and Willard W. Hartup, 1967, "Positive Reinforcement in the Nursery School Peer Group."

16. Mary Ann Einenger and John P. Hill, 1969, "Instrumental and Affectional Dependency and Nurturance in Preschool Children."

17. Carolyn N. Jacklin and Eleanor E. Maccoby, 1978, "Social Behavior at Thirty-Three Months in Same-Sex and Mixed-Sex Dyads."

18. Willard W. Hartup, 1970, "Peer Interaction and Social Organization."

19. Stephen J. Suomi and Harry F. Harlow, 1975, "The Role and Reason of Peer Relationships in Rhesus Monkeys."

20. Robin Fox, 1977, "Primate Kin and Human Kinship."

21. Floyd F. Strayer, 1980, "Child Ethology and the Study of Preschool Social Relations."

22. Ernst Caspari, 1978, "The Biological Basis of Female Hierarchies."

23. Ibid.

24. Ibid.

25. Caspari, "Biological Basis."

26. Strayer, "Child Ethology."

27. Floyd F. Strayer, et al, 1977, "Ethological Perspectives on Preschool Organization."

28. Murray S. Edelman and Donald R. Omark, 1973, "Dominance Hierarchies in Young Children"; Donald R. Omark and Murray S. Edelman, 1976, "The Development of Attention Structures in Young Children"; Idem, 1975, "A Comparison of Status Hierarchies in Young Children: An Ethological Approach"; Donald R. Omark, Murray S. Edelman, and Monica U. Edelman, 1975, "Formation of Dominance Hierarchies in Young Children."

29. Hartup, "Peer Interaction and Social Organization."

30. C. Stevens, 1971, "Peer Relations and Sex-Based Social Structures," unpublished manuscript, cited in Omark and Edelman, "Development of Attention Structures in Young Children."

31. Omark and Edelman, "Attention Structures in Children."

32. Richard E. Parker, 1975, "Social Hierarchies and Same Sex Peer Groups."

33. Janet Lever, 1976, "Sex Differences in the Games Children Play."

34. Lionel Tiger, 1969, Men in Groups.

35. Beatrice B. Whiting and John W. N. Whiting, 1975, Children of Six Cultures.

36. Beatrice B. Whiting and Carolyn Pope Edwards, 1973, "A Cross-Cultural Analysis of Sex Differences in the Behavior of Children Aged 3 through 11."

37. David A. Lubin and Beatrice B. Whiting, 1978, "Techniques of Persuasion in Peer Interaction."

38. Whiting and Edwards, "A Cross-Cultural Analysis."

39. Tiger, Men in Groups.

40. Michael R. A. Chance, 1975, "Social Cohesion and the Structure of Attention; Idem, 1976, "Social Attention: Society and Mentality"; Idem, 1978, "Sex Differences in the Structure of Attention."

41. Michael R. A. Chance and Alison Jolly, 1970, *Social Groups of Monkeys, Apes and Men*.

42. Thelma E. Rowells, 1974, "The Concept of Social Dominance."

43. Barbara C. L. Hold, 1976, "Attention Structure and Rank Specific Behavior in Preschool Children."

44. Ibid.

45. Omark and Edelman, "Attention Structures in Children."

46. Chance, "Sex Differences in the Structure of Attention."

47. Ibid., p. 153.

48. Ibid., "Social Attention."

49. Carolyn Shantz, 1975, "The Development of Social Cognition."

50. Omark and Edelman, "Attention Structures in Children."

51. J. von Uexkull, 1957, "A Stroll through the Worlds of Animals and Man."

52. Omark and Edelman, "Attention Structures in Children."

53. Ibid.

54. Sigmund Freud, 1933, "Femininity."

55. Herbert H. Barry, Margaret K. Bacon, and Irvin L. Child, 1957, "A Cross-Cultural Survey of Some Sex Differences in Socialization."

56. Chance and Jolly, *Monkeys, Apes and Men*.

57. Arnold Van Gennep, 1960, *The Rites of Passage*.

58. David E. Schecter, 1968, "The Oedipal Complex: Considerations on Ego Growth and Parental Interaction."

59. Ernest L. Abelin, 1971, "The Role of the Father in the Separation–Individuation Process."

60. Ibid., p. 231.

61. Margaret S. Mahler, Fred Pine, and Anni Bergman, 1975, *The Psychological Birth of the Infant*.

62. Abelin, "Role of the Father"; Idem, 1975, "Some Further Observations and Comments on the Earlier Role of the Father."

63. Ibid., "Role of the Father," p. 249.

64. Ibid., "Further Observations."

65. Ibid., "Role of the Father," p. 247.

66. Talcott Parsons, 1958, "The Interpenetration of Two Levels—Social Structure and the Development of Personality."

67. K. Alison Clarke-Stewart, 1980, "The Father's Contribution to Cognitive and Social Development in Early Childhood."

68. Michael E. Lamb, 1978, "The Father's Role in the Infant's Social World."

69. Felton Earls and Michael Yogman, 1979, "The Father–Infant Relationship."

70. Ibid., p. 222.

71. Tiffany Field, 1978, "Interaction Behaviors of Primary versus Secondary Caretaker Fathers."

72. Ross D. Parke, 1981, *Fathers*, p. 42.

73. Lawrence Kohlberg, 1966, "A Cognitive-Developmental Analysis of Children's Sex Role Concepts and Attitudes."

74. Julia Sherman, 1971, *On the Psychology of Women.*

75. Freud, "Femininity."

76. Melvin Konner, 1975, "Relations among Infants and Juveniles in Comparative Perspective," p. 95.

77. Schecter, "Oedipal Complex"; Nancy Chodorow, 1978, *The Reproduction of Mothering.*

78. Tiger, *Men in Groups.*

79. Schecter, "Oedipal Complex."

80. Chodorow, *Reproduction of Mothering.*

81. Ibid., pp. 166–67.

82. Ibid., p. 71.

83. David Lynn, 1974, *The Father: His Role in Child Development*, p. 146.

84. Myron Brenton, 1972, "The Paradox of the American Father."

85. Felton Earls and Michael Yogman, 1979, "The Father–Infant Relationship."

86. Chodorow, *Reproduction of Mothering*, p. 455.

87. Ibid., p. 7.

88. Evelyn Goodenough Pitcher, 1957, "An Interest in Persons as an Aspect fo Sex Differences in the Early Years."

89. Sigmund Freud, 1957, *A General Selection from the Writings of Sigmund Freud.*

90. Melanie Klein, 1960 (1932), *The Psychoanalysis of Children.*

91. Abie Schlegel, 1979, "Sexual Antagonism among the Sexually Egalitarian Hopi."

92. H. Lerner, 1974, "Early Origins of Envy and Devaluation of Women."

93. Pitcher, "Interest in Persons."

94. Thomas M. Wolf, 1973, "Effects of Live Modeled Sex-Inappropriate Play in a Naturalistic Setting."

95. Maccoby and Jacklin, *Psychology of Sex Differences.*

96. J. Richard Udry, 1971, *The Social Context of Marriage*, p. 81.

97. Ibid.

98. Jean Stockard and Miriam Johnson, 1980, *Sex Inequality and Sex Role Development*, p. 266.

99. Zick Rubin, Letitia Anne Peplau, and Charles T. Hill, 1981, "Loving and Leaving."

100. Pitcher, "Interest in Persons," pp. 309–310.

101. David Lynn, 1969, *Parental and Sex Role Identifications.*

102. Caspari, "Biological Basis."

103. Kohlberg, "Cognitive-Developmental Analysis," p. 86.

104. Jean Piaget, 1952, *The Origins of Intelligence in Children.*

105. Silvia M. Bell, 1970, "The Development of the Concept of Object as Related to Infant–Mother Attachment."

106. Kohlberg, "Cognitive-Developmental Analysis," p. 83.

107. Susan S. Haugh, Charles D. Hoffman, and Gloria Cowan, 1980, "The Eye of the Beholder: Sex-typing of Infants by Young Children."

108. Sheldon H. White, 1970, "Some General Outlines of the Matrix of Developmental Change Between Five and Seven Years."

109. Phyllis Greenacre, 1957, "The Childhood of the Artist," cited in Abelin, "Role of the Father."

110. Abelin, "Role of the Father."

111. Ibid.

112. Jean Piaget, 1962, *Play, Dreams and Imitation.*

113. Lev S. Vygotsky, 1957, "Play and the Role of Mental Development in the Child."

114. Lynn, *Parental and Sex Role Identifications.*

115. Piaget, *Play, Dreams and Imitation.*

116. Kohlberg, "Cognitive-Developmental Analysis."

117. Ibid., p. 114.

118. William Damon, 1977, *The Social World of the Child.*

119. Ibid., p. 280.

120. Ibid., p. 255.

121. Eleanor E. Maccoby, 1980, *Social Development*, pp. 239–42.

122. Roy G. D'Andrade, 1966, "Sex Differences and Cultural Institutions."

123. Margaret Mead, 1935, *Sex and Temperament in Three Primitive Societies.*

124. Grace K. Baruch, 1979, "Own Sex Bias, Sex-Role Stereotyping and Gender Constancy in Preschool Girls."

125. Ibid.

126. Kohlberg, "Cognitive-Developmental Analysis."

127. Ruth E. Hartley, Francis P. Hardesty, and David S. Gorfein, 1962, "Children's Perception and Expression of Sex Preferences"; Patricia P. Minuchin, 1964, "Children's Sex Role Concepts as a Function of School and Home Environments"; S. Smith, 1939, "Age and Sex Differences in Children's Opinions Concerning Sex Differences."

128. Kohlberg, "Cognitive-Developmental Analysis," p. 121.

129. Omark and Edelman, "Status Hierarchies in Children"; Idem, "Attention Structures in Children."

130. Carol Gilligan, 1982, *In a Different Voice.*

131. Inge K. Broverman, Donald M. Broverman, Frank E. Clarkson, et al, 1970, "Sex-Role Stereotypes and Clinical Judgments of Mental Health."

132. Gilligan, *In a Different Voice*, p. 17.

133. Ibid.

134. Kohlberg, "Cognitive-Developmental Analysis."

135. Ibid., p. 135.

136. Sigmund Freud, 1931, "Female Sexuality."

137. Spencer K. Thompson, 1975, "Gender Labels and Early Sex Role Development."

138. Lynn, *Parental and Sex Role Identifications.*

139. Parsons, "Interpenetration of Two Levels," p. 67.

140. Ibid., p. 64.

141. Chodorow, *Reproduction of Mothering.*

142. Parsons, "Interpenetration of Two Levels," p. 67.

143. Talcott Parsons and Robert F. Bales, 1955, *Family, Socialization and Interaction Process.*

144. Morris Zelditch, Jr., 1955, "Role Differentiation in the Nuclear Family."

145. Parsons, "Interpenetration of Two Levels," p. 64.

146. Ibid., p. 65.

147. Ibid., p. 66.

148. Schecter, "Oedipal Complex."

149. Carol S. Dweck and Ellen S. Bush, 1976, "Sex Differences in Learned Helplessness."

150. John Mourilyan Tanner, 1970, "Physical Growth."

151. Dweck and Bush, "Sex Differences."

152. Edwin P. Hollander and James E. Marcia, 1970, "Parental Determinants of Peer-Orientation and Self-Orientation Among Pre-adolescents."

153. Dweck and Bush, "Sex Differences," p. 149.

154. Zick Rubin, 1980, *Children's Friendships,* p. 107.

155. Georg Simmel, 1950, *The Sociology of Georg Simmel.*

156. Judith Bardwick, 1977, "Some Aspects of Women's Relation with Women," p. 55.

157. Lever, "Sex Differences in Games."

158. Ibid., p. 99.

159. Iona Opie and Peter Opie, 1959, *The Lore and Language of Schoolchildren.*

160. Ibid., p. 67.

161. Ibid., p. 78.

162. Rhea R. Hikevitch, 1960, "Social Interactional Processes."

163. Eliot D. Chapple, 1980, *The Biological Foundations of Individuality and Culture.*

164. Whiting and Edwards, "A Cross-Cultural Analysis," p. 179.

165. Margaret Polantnick, 1973, "Why Men Don't Rear Children."

166. Florence Nightingale, 1859, cited in Ruth Hubbard and Marion Lowe, 1979, *Genesis and Gender II.*

167. Charles Derber, 1979, *The Pursuit of Attention*, pp. 43–44.

168. Pitcher, "Interest in Persons," p. 319.

169. Wynn Schwartz, 1979, "Degradation, Accreditation, and Rites of Passage."

170. Virginia Abernethy, 1976, "Cultural Perspectives on the Import of Women's Changing Roles on Psychiatry."

Chapter 5. Inequalities in Sex Roles and Recommendations for Change

1. Lionel Tiger and Joseph Shepher, 1975, *Women in the Kibbutz*.

2. Ibid., p. 11.

3. Ruth Hubbard and Marion Lowe, 1979, *Genes and Gender II*.

4. Lionel Tiger, 1977, "Introduction," *Female Hierarchies*.

5. Amaury de Riencourt, 1974, *Sex and Power in History*, p. viii.

6. Carol Gilligan, 1982, *In a Different Voice*.

7. Lynda M. Glennon, 1979, *Women and Dualism*, reviewed by Charlotte G. O'Kelly in *Sex Roles* 7(1):79–81, 1981.

8. Herbert Marcuse, 1964, *One-Dimensional Man*.

9. Suzanne Keller, 1974, "The Female Role," p. 418.

10. Nancy Chodorow, 1978, *The Reproduction of Mothering*.

11. Frederick Engels, 1884, *The Origin of the Family, Private Property, and the State*.

12. Chodorow, *Reproduction of Mothering*, pp. 12-13.

13. Jesse Bernard, 1975, *The Future of Motherhood*.

14. Margaret Adams, 1971, "The Compassionate Trap."

15. Emily James Putnam, 1910, *The Lady*, p. 70.

16. Marilyn French, 1977, *The Woman's Room*, p. 197.

17. L. Van Gelder, 1979, "An Unmarried Man," p. 72.

18. Jeanne H. Block, 1973, "Conceptions of Sex-Role."

19. Margaret Polantnick, 1973, "Why Men Don't Rear Children."

20. Jean Baker Miller, ed., 1973, *Psychoanalysis and Women*.

21. Ibid., pp. 253, 386.

22. Ibid., p. 386.

23. Matina S. Horner, 1968, "Sex Differences in Achievement Motivation and Perfomance in Competitive and Noncompetitive Situations."

24. Jean Baker Miller, 1976, *Toward a New Psychology of Women*.

25. Ibid., p. 44.

26. William L. O'Neill, 1978, "Women in Politics."

27. Signe Hammer, 1978, "When Women Have Power Over Women."

28. Lionel Tiger and Heather T. Fowler, 1978, *Female Hierarchies*.

29. Joseph Shepher and Lionel Tiger, 1978, "Female Hierarchies in a Kibbutz Community."

30. Hammer, "Women Over Women," p. 56.

31. Carol P. MacCormack, 1977, "Biological Events and Cultural Control."

32. Ibid., p. 94.

33. Shirley Weitz, 1977, *Sex Roles.*

34. George Masnick and Mary Jo Bane, 1980, *The Nation's Families: 1960–1990.*

35. Ibid., p. 53.

36. Ibid., p. 9.

37. Ruth Hubbard and Marion Lowe, *Genesis and Gender II*, p. 33.

38. Eleanor E. Maccoby, 1980, *Social Development.*

39. Ibid., p. 158.

40. Clara Thompson, 1941, "The Role of Women in This Culture."

41. Betty Friedan, 1963, *The Feminine Mystique.*

42. Ibid., 1981, *The Second Stage.*

43. Menachem Gersin, 1978, *Family, Women and Socialization in the Kibbutz.*

44. Tiger and Shepher, *Women in the Kibbutz.*

45. Keller, "The Female Role."

46. Alice S. Rossi, 1969, "Sex Equality."

47. Miller, ed., *Psychoanalysis and Women*, p. 392.

48. Juliet Mitchell, 1969, "The Longest Revolution."

49. Mirra Komarovsky, 1976, *Dilemmas of Masculinity.*

50. Chodorow, *Reproduction of Mothering*, p. 218.

51. Sherry B. Ortner, 1972, "Is Female to Male as Nature to Culture?", p. 33.

52. Virginia Abernethy, 1976, "Cultural Perspectives on the Impact of Women's Changing Roles on Psychiatry."

53. Sandra L. Bem, 1976, "Probing the Promise of Androgeny."

54. National Center for Education Statistics, Office of the Assistant Secretary for Education, 1976, "National Longitudinal Study."

55. Ross D. Parke, 1981, *Fathers.*

56. J. Richard Udry, 1971, *The Social Context of Marriage.*

57. Susan Washburn, 1981, *Partners.*

58. Phyllis A. Katz, 1979, "The Development of Female Identity," p. 156.

59. Benjamin George Rosenberg and Brian Sutton-Smith, 1972, *Sex and Identity*, p. 90.

60. de Reincourt, *Sex and Power*, pp. vii, x.

61. Eric H. Erikson, 1974, "Womanhood and the Inner Space," p. 334.

62. Brigette Berger, 1979, "What Women Want."

63. Ibid., p. 65.

64. Erikson, "Womanhood and Inner Space."

65. Taskforce of the New Jersey Chapter of the National Organization for Women, 1972, *Dick and Jane as Victims.*

66. Phyllis Taube MacEwan, 1972, *Liberating Young Children from Sex Roles.*

67. Lisa A. Serbin, Illene J. Tonick, and Sarah H. Sternglanz, 1977, "Shaping Cooperative Cross-Sex Play."

68. Vivien Paley, 1973, "Is the Doll Corner a Sexist Institution?"

69. Ibid., p. 572.

70. Bruno Bettelheim, 1975, "Some Further Thoughts on the Doll Corner," p. 365.

71. Milton Kotelchuck, 1976, "The Infant's Relationship to the Father."

72. Joseph H. Pleck, 1978, "Men's Family Work."

73. Karen W. Feinstein, ed., 1979, *Working Women and Families.*

74. Beatrice B. Whiting and Carolyn Pope Edwards, 1973, "A Cross-Cultural Analysis of Sex Differences in the Behavior of Children Aged 3 through 11."

75. Patricia P. Minuchin, 1965, *The Middle Years of Childhood.*

76. Betty Yorberg, 1974, *Sexual Identity.*

77. Michael E. Lamb, 1978, "The Father's Role in the Infant's Social World"; Felton Earls and Michael Yogman, 1979, "The Father–Infant Relationship."

78. Polantnick, "Why Men Don't Rear Children."

79. Paley, "Doll Corner."

80. Willard W. Hartup, 1976, "Peer Interaction and the Behavioral Development of the Individual Child."

81. Ibid., 1978, "Peer Relations and the Growth of Social Competence."

82. Ibid., "Peer Interaction."

83. Ibid.

84. Judith H. Langlois and A. Chris Downs, 1980, "Mothers, Fathers and Peers as Socialization Agents of Sex-Typed Play Behaviors in Young Children."

85. Gene I. Maeroff, 1981, "After 15 Years, a Harlem Experiment Gets a New Look."

86. Urie Bronfenbrenner, 1970, "Reaction to Social Pressure from Adults versus Peers among Soviet Day School and Boarding Pupils in the Perspective of an American Sample."

87. Katz, "Development of Female Identity."

88. Beverly I. Fagot, 1977, "Consequences of Moderate Cross-Gender Behavior in Preschool Children."

89. Grace K. Baruch, 1979, "Own Sex Bias, Sex-Role Stereotyping and Gender Constancy in Preschool Girls."

90. Melvin Konner, 1975, "Relations among Infants and Juveniles in Comparative Perspective."

91. Melvin Konner, 1977, "Evolution of Human Behavior Development."

92. Philippe Aries, 1962, *Centuries of Childhood.*

93. Nancy Chodorow, 1974, "Family Structure and Feminine Personality,"

94. John D. Campbell, 1964, "Peer Relations in Childhood."

95. Shmuel Noah Eisenstadt, 1962, "Archtypal Patterns of Youth," p. 34.

96. Keller, "Female Role." pp. 54–55.

Appendix C

1. Ben James Winer, 1971, *Statistical Principles in Experimental Design*, New York: McGraw–Hill.

2. Sidney Siegel, 1956, *Nonparametric Statistics for the Behavioral Sciences*, New York: McGraw-Hill.

Bibliography

Abelin, E. L. 1971. "The role of the father in the separation–individuation process." In *Separation–individuation: Essays in honor of Margaret S. Mahler*, ed. J. B. McDevitt and C. F. Settlage. New York: International University Press.

———. 1975. "Some further observations and comments on the earlier role of the father." *International Journal of Psychoanalysis* 56:293–302.

Abernethy, V. 1976. "Cultural perspectives on the impact of women's changing roles on psychiatry." *American Journal of Psychiatry* 133(6):657–61.

———. 1978. "Female hierarchy: An evolutionary perspective." In *Female hierarchies*, ed. L. Tiger and H. T. Fowler. Chicago: Beresford.

Adams, M. 1971. "The compassionate trap." *Psychology Today* 11:72.

Aries, P. 1962. *Centuries of childhood: A social history of family life*, trans. Robert Baldick. New York: Alfred A. Knopf.

Bandura, A. 1969. "Social-learning theory of identification pro- cesses." In *Handbook of socialization theory and research*, ed. D. S. Goslin. Chicago: Rand McNally.

———, ed. 1974. *Psychological modelling: Conflicting theories*. New York: Lieber–Athertin.

———, and Walters, R. H. 1963. *Social learning and personality development*. New York: Holt, Rinehart & Winston.

Bardwick, J. 1977. "Some aspects of women's relation with women." Paper presented at Annual Convention of American Psychological Association, 26–30 August, San Francisco. ERIC Reports.

———, ed. 1971. *Psychology of women: A study of bio-cultural conflicts*. New York: Harper & Row.

Barry, H. H.; Bacon, M., and Child, I. L. 1957. "A cross-cultural survey of some sex differences in socialization." *Journal of Abnormal Psychology* 55:327–32.

Baruch, G. K. 1979. "Own sex bias, sex-role stereotyping and gender constancy in preschool girls." (Mimeographed.) Wellesley, Mass.: Wellesley College Center for Research on Women.

Bell, S. M. 1970. "The development of the concept of object as related to infant–mother attachment." *Child Development* 41:291–311.

Bem, S. L. 1976. "Probing the promise of androgeny." In *Beyond sex-role stereotypes*, ed. A. G. Kaplan and J. P. Bean. Boston: Little–Brown.

Benedek, T. 1960. "The organization of the reproductive drive." *International Journal of Psychoanalysis* 41:1–5.

Berger, B. 1979. "What women want." *Commentary*, March, pp. 62–72.

Bernard, J. 1975. *The future of motherhood*. New York: Penguin.

Berne, E. 1964. *Games people play*. New York: Grove Press.

Bettelheim, B. 1975. "Some further thoughts on the doll corner." *School Review* 83:363–68.

Block, J. H. 1973. "Conceptions of sex-role: Some cross-cultural and longitudinal perspectives." *American Psychologist* 28(6):512–26.

———. 1979. "Another look at sex differentiation in the socialization of males and females." In *Psychology of women: Future directions of research*, in press.

Blurton–Jones, N. 1972. "Categories of child–child interaction." In *Ethological studies of child behavior*, ed. N. Blurton–Jones. Cambridge, England: Cambridge University Press.

Bonsall, C. N. 1973. *Mine's the best*. New York: Harper & Row.

Brenton, M. 1972. "The paradox of the American father." In *The future of the family*, ed. L. Harve. New York: Schuster.

Bronfenbrenner, U. 1970. "Reaction to social pressure from adults versus peers among Soviet day school and boarding pupils in the perspective of an American sample." *Journal of Personality and Social Psychology* 15(3):179–89.

Broverman, I. K., Broverman, D. M., Clarkson, F. E., et al. 1970. "Sex-role stereotypes and clinical judgments of mental health." *Journal of Consulting and Clinical Psychology* 34:1–7.

Brownmiller, S. 1975. *Against our will: Men, women and rape*. New York: Simon & Schuster.

Cairns, R. B. 1979. *Social development: The origins and plasticity of interchanges*. San Francisco: W.H. Freeman.

Campbell, J. D. 1964. "Peer relations in childhood." In *Review of child development research*, vol. 1, ed. M. L. Hoffman and L. W. Hoffman. New York: Russell Sage Foundation.

Caspari, E. W. 1978. "The biological basis of female hierarchies." In *Female hierarchies*, ed. L. Tiger and H. T. Fowler. Chicago: Beresford.

Chance, M. R. A. 1974. "Attention structure as the basis of primate rank orders." *Man*, N. S. 2(4):503–18.

———. 1975. "Social cohesion and the structure of attention." In *Biosocial anthropology*, ed. R. Fox. London: Malaby, American Sociological Association Series I.

———. 1976. "Social attention: Society and mentality." In *The structure of social attention*, ed. M. R. A. Chance and R. Larsen. New York: Wiley.

———. 1978. "Sex differences in the structure of attention." In *Female hierarchies*, ed. L. Tiger and H. T. Fowler. Chicago: Beresford.

———, and Jolly, A. 1970. *Social groups of monkeys, apes and men*. London: Jonathan Cape.

Chapple, E. D. 1980. *The biological foundations of individuality and culture*. Huntington, N.Y.: Robert E. Krieger.

Charlesworth, R., and Hartup, W. 1967. "Positive reinforcement in the nursery school peer group." *Child Development* 38:993–1002.

Cherry, L., and Lewis, M. 1976. "Mothers and two-year-olds: A study of sex-differentiated aspects of verbal interaction." *Developmental Psychology* 12(4): 278–82.

Chodorow, N. 1974. "Family structure and feminine personality." In *Women, culture and society*, ed. M. Z. Rosaldo and L. Lamphere. Stanford, Cal.: Stanford University Press.

———. 1978. *The reproduction of mothering: Psychoanalysis and the sociology of gender*. Berkeley: University of California Press.

Clarke–Stewart, K. A. 1980. "The father's contribution to cognitive and social development in early childhood." In *The father–infant relationship: Observational studies in the family setting*, ed. F. A. Pedersen. New York: Praeger.

Condry, J., and Condry, S. 1976. "Sex differences: A study of the eye of the beholder." *Child Development* 47:812–19.

Constantinople, A. 1979. "Sex-role acquisition: In search of the elephant." *Sex Roles* 5(2):121–33.

Council for Interracial Books for Children, Inc., 1841 Broadway, New York, N.Y. 10023.

Damon, W. 1977. *The social world of the child*. San Francisco: Jossey–Boss.

D'Andrade, R. G. 1966. Sex differences and cultural institutions. In *The development of sex differences*, ed. E. E. Maccoby. Stanford, Cal.: Stanford University Press.

DeJong, E. 1977. *How to save your own life*. New York: Holt, Rinehart & Winston.

Derber, C. 1979. *The Pursuit of attention: Power and individualism in everyday life*. Cambridge, Mass.: Schenkman.

de Reincourt, A. 1974. *Sex and power in history*. New York: Dell.

Dweck, C. S., and Bush, E. S. 1976. "Sex differences in learned helplessness: I. Differential debilitation with peer and adult evaluators." *Developmental Psychology* 12(2):147–56.

Earls, F., and Yogman, M. 1979. "The father–infant relationship." In *Modern perspectives in the psychiatry of infancy*, ed. J. G. Howells. New York: Bruner/Mazel.

Eckerman, C. O.; Whatley, J. L., and Kutz, S. L. 1975. "The growth of social play with peers during the second year of life." *Developmental Psychology* 11:42–49.

Edelman, M. S., and Omark, D. R. 1973. "Dominance hierarchies in young children." *Social Sciences Information* 12(1):103–10.

Einenger, M. A., and Hill, J. P. 1969. "Instrumental and affectional dependency and nurturance in preschool children." *Journal of Genetic Psychology* 115:277–284.

Eisenstadt, S. N. 1956. *From generation to generation*. New York: Free Press.

———. 1962. "Archtypal patterns of youth." *Daedalus* Winter:28–46.

Engels, F. 1967 (1884). *The origin of the family, private property, and the state*. New York: International Publishers.

Erikson, E. H. 1951. "Sex differences in the play configurations of pre-adolescents." *American Journal of Ortho-psychiatry* 21:667–92.

——. 1964. *Insight and responsibility*. New York: W.W. Norton.

——. 1974. "Womanhood and the inner space." In *Women and analysis*, ed. J. Strouse. New York: Dell.

Fagot, B. I. 1977. "Consequences of moderate cross-gender behavior in preschool children." *Child Development* 48:902–7.

Faigin, H. 1958. "Social behavior of young children in the kibbutz." *Journal of Abnormal and Social Psychology* 56:117–29.

Feinberg, S. 1977. "Conceptual content and spatial characteristics in boys' and girls' drawings of fighting and helping." *Studies in Art Education* 18(2):63–72.

Feinstein, K. W., ed. 1979. *Working women and families*. Beverly Hills, Cal.: Sage Publications.

Field, T. 1978. "Interaction behaviors of primary versus secondary caretaker fathers." *Developmental Psychology* 14:183–85.

Fishbein, H. D. 1976. *Evolution, development, and children's learning*. Pacific Palisades, Cal.: Goodyear.

Fisher, E. 1979. *Woman's creation: Sexual evolution and the shaping of society*. New York: McGraw–Hill.

Fox, R. 1977. "Primate kin and human kinship." In *Biosocial anthropology*. London: Malaby, American Sociological Association Series I.

French, M. 1977. *The woman's room*. New York: Summit Press.

Freud, S. "Some character types met with in psychoanalytic work" (1915). "Some psychial consequences of the anatomical distinction between the sexes" (1925). In *The standard edition of the complete works of Sigmund Freud*, vol. 19. London: Hogarth, 1950.

——. 1931. "Female sexuality." In *The collected papers of Sigmund Freud*, ed. and trans. J. Strachey. New York: Basic Books.

——. 1965 (1933). "Femininity." In *New introductory lectures in psychoanalysis*, ed. and trans. J. Strachey. New York: Norton.

——. 1938. "Three contributions to the theory of sex." In *The basic writings of Sigmund Freud*, ed. A. A. Brill. New York: Random House.

——. 1948. *An outline of psychoanalysis*. New York: Norton.

——. 1957. *A general selection from the writings of Sigmund Freud*, ed. J. Rickman. Garden City, N.Y.: Doubleday Anchor.

Friedan, B. 1963. *The feminine mystique*. New York: Norton.

——. 1981. *The second stage*. New York: Summit Books.

Gardner, H. 1978. *Developmental psychology*. Boston: Little–Brown.

Garai, J. E. 1970. "Sex differences in mental health." *Genetic Psychology Monographs* 81:123–42.

Garvey, C. 1977. *Play*. Cambridge, Mass.: Harvard University Press.

Gersin, M. 1978. *Family, women and socialization in the kibbutz*. Lexington, Mass.: D.C. Heath.

Gilligan, C. 1978. "Woman's place in man's life cycle." (Mimeographed.) Wellesley, Mass.: Wellesley College Center for Research on Women.

——. 1982. *In a different voice: Psychological theory and women's development*. Cambridge, Mass.: Harvard University Press.

Glennon, L. M. 1979. *Women and dualism: A sociology of knowledge analysis*. New York: Longman.

Goffman, E. 1978. "Gender display." In *Female hierarchies*, ed. L. Tiger and H. T. Fowler. Chicago: Beresford.

Goldberg, P. 1968. "Are women prejudiced against women?" *Trans-action* 5:28–30.

Goldman, J. A. 1981. "Social participation of preschool children in same- versus mixed-age groups." *Child Development* 52(2):644–50.

Greenacre, P. 1957. "The childhood of the artist." *The psychoanalytic study of the child* 12:47–72. New York: International Universities Press.

Grief, E. B. 1977. "Peer interaction in preschool children." In *Social development in childhood: Day care programs and research*, ed. R. A. Webb. Baltimore: The Johns Hopkins University Press.

——. 1976. "Sex role playing in pre-school children," In *Play—its role in development and evolution*, ed. J. S. Bruner, A. Jolly, and K. Sylva. New York: Basic Books.

Haas, A. 1981. "Partner influences on sex-associated spoken language of children." *Sex Roles* 7(9):925-35.

Hall, J. A. 1978. "Gender effects in decoding non-verbal cues." *Psychological Bulletin* 85:845–57.

Hammer, S. 1978. "When women have power over women." *Ms. Magazine*, September.

Harlow, H. F. 1965. "Sexual behavior in the Rhesus monkey." In *Sex and behavior*, ed. Frank Beach. New York: Wiley.

Hartley, R. E.; Hardesty, F. P., and Gorfein, D. S. 1962. "Children's perception and expression of sex preferences." *Child Development* 33:221–27.

Hartup, W. W. 1970. "Peer interaction and social organization." In *Carmichael's manual of child psychology*, vol. 2, ed. P. Mussen. New York: Wiley.

——. 1976. "Peer interaction and the behavioral development of the individual child." In *Readings in developmental psychology*, ed. J. Gardner. Boston: Little–Brown.

——. 1978. "Peer relations and the growth of social competence." In *The primary prevention of psychopathology, vol. 3: Promoting social competence and coping in children*, ed. M. W. Kent and J. E. Rolf. Hanover, Pa.: University Press of New England.

Haugh, S. S.; Hoffman, C. D., and Cowan, G. 1980. "The eye of the beholder: Sex-typing of infants by young children." *Child Development* 51(2):598–600.

Hikevich, R. R. 1960. "Social interactional processes: A quantitative study." *Psychological Reports* 7:195–201.

Hinde, R. A. 1975. "Interactions, relationships and social structure." *Man* 2:1–17.

———. 1976. "On describing relationships." *Journal of Child Psychology and Psychiatry* 17:1–19.

Hoffman, M. L. 1977. "Sex differences in empathy and related behaviors." *Psychological Bulletin* 84:712–44.

Hold, B. C. L. 1976. "Attention structure and rank specific behavior in preschool children." In *The structure of social attention*, ed. M. R. A. Chance and R. Larsen. New York: Wiley.

Hollander, E. P., and Marcia, J. E. 1970. "Parental determinants of peer-orientation and self-orientation among pre-adolescents." *Developmental Psychology* 2:292–302.

Horner, M. S. 1968. "Sex differences in achievement motivation and performance in competitive and noncompetitive situations." Ph.D. dissertation, University of Michigan, Ann Arbor.

———. 1978. "Femininity and successful achievement: A basic inconsistency." In *Feminine personality and conflict*, ed. J. M. Bardwick, E. Douvan, M. S. Horner, and D. Gutman. Belmont, Cal.: Brooks–Cole.

Hubbard, R., and Lowe, M. 1979. *Genes and gender II: Pitfalls in research on sex and gender*. Staten Island, N.Y.: Guardian Press.

Jacklin, C. N., and Maccoby, E. E. 1978. "Social behavior at thirty-three months in same-sex and mixed-sex dyads." *Child Development* 49(3):557–69.

Kagen, J., and Lemkin, J. 1960. "The child's differential perception of parental attributes." *Journal of Abnormal Social Psychology* 61:446–47.

Katz, P. A. 1979. "The development of female identity." *Sex Roles* 5(2):155–75.

Keller, S. 1974. "The female role: Constants and change." In *Women in therapy*, ed. V. Franks and V. Burtle. New York: Bruner/Mazel.

Klein, M. 1960 (1932). *The psychoanalysis of children*. New York: Grove Press.

Kohlberg, L. 1966. "A cognitive-developmental analysis of children's sex-role concepts and attitudes." In *The development of sex differences*, ed. E. E. Maccoby. Stanford, Cal.: Stanford University Press.

———. 1969. "Stage and sequence: The cognitive-developmental approach to socialization." In *Handbook of socialization theory and research*, ed. D. A. Goslin. Chicago: Rand McNally.

Komarovsky, M. 1976. *Dilemmas of masculinity*. New York: Norton.

Konner, M. 1975. "Relations among infants and juveniles in comparative perspective." In *Friendship and peer relations*, ed. M. Lewis and S. Rosenblum. New York: Wiley.

———. 1977. "Evolution of human behavior development." In *Culture and infancy: Variations in human existence*, ed. P. H. Leiderman, S. R. Tulkin, and A. Rosenfeld. New York: Academic Press.

Kotelchuck, M. 1976. "The infant's relationship to the father: Experimental evidence." In *The role of the father in child development*, ed. M. Lamb. New York: Wiley.

Lamb, M. E. 1978. "The father's role in the infant's social world." In *Mother/child father/child relationships*, ed. J. H. Stevens, Jr., and M. Mathews. Washington, D.C.: National Association for the Education of Young Children.

Langlois, J. H., and Downs, A. C. 1980. "Mothers, fathers and peers as socialization agents of sex-typed play behaviors in young children." *Child Development* 51:1217–47.

Langlois, J.; Gottfried, N., and Seay, B. 1973. "The influence of sex of peer on the social behavior of preschool children." *Developmental Psychology* 8(1):93–98.

Lasker, J. 1972. *Mothers can do anything*. Chicago: Albert Whitman.

Lee, L. C. 1975. "Toward a cognitive theory of interpersonal development: Importance of peers." In *Friendship and peer relations*, ed. M. Lewis and S. Rosenblum. New York: Wiley.

Lerner, H. 1974. "Early origins of envy and devaluation of women: Implications for sex-role stereotypes." *Bulletin of the Menninger Clinic* 36:638–53.

Lever, J. 1976. "Sex differences in the games children play." *Social Problems* 32: 478–87.

Lubin, D. A., and Whiting, B. B. 1978. "Techniques of persuasion in peer interaction." Paper presented at the Annual Meeting of the Society for Cross-cultural Research, New Haven, Conn.

Lynn, D. 1964. "The process of learning parental and sex-role identification." *Journal of Marriage and the Family* 28:466–70.

———. 1969. *Parental and sex role identifications*. University of California, Davis: McCutchan Publishing Corp.

———. 1974. *The father: His role in child development*. Belmont, Cal.: Wadsworth.

Maccoby, E. E. 1980. *Social development: Psychological growth of the parent–child relationship*. New York: Harcourt, Brace, Jovanovich.

———, and Jacklin, C. N. 1974. *The psychology of sex differences*. Stanford, Cal.: Stanford University Press.

MacCormack, C. P. 1977. "Biological events and cultural control." *Signs: The Journal of Women in Culture and Society* 3(1):93–100,

MacEwan, P. T. 1972. *Liberating young children from sex roles: Experience in day care centers, play groups, and free schools*. Somerville, Mass.: New England Free Press.

Maeroff, G. I. 1981. "After 15 years, a Harlem experiment gets a new look." *New York Times*, 18 August.

Mahler, M. S.; Pine, F., and Bergman, A. 1975. *The psychological birth of the infant*. New York: Basic Books.

Mailer, N. 1971. *The prisoner of sex*. New York: Signet.

Marcuse, H. 1964. *One-dimensional man*. Boston: Beacon.

Masnick, G., and Bane, M. J. 1980. *The nation's families: 1960–1990*. Boston: Auburn House.

Mead, G. H. 1934. *Mind, self and society*. Chicago: University of Chicago Press.

Mead, M. 1935. *Sex and temperament in three primitive societies*. New York: William Morrow.

Middleton, T. H. 1980. "Boys and girls together." *Saturday Review of Literature*, May.

Miller, J. B. 1976. *Toward a new psychology of women*. Boston: Beacon Press.

——, ed. 1973. *Psychoanalysis and women*. New York: Penguin Books.

Millett, K. 1970. *Sexual politics*. New York: Doubleday.

Minuchin, P. P. 1964. "Children's sex role concepts as a function of school and home environments." Paper presented at the American Orthopsychiatric Association, Chicago, March.

——. 1977. *The middle years of childhood*. Monterey, Cal.: Brooks/Cole.

Mischel, W. 1970. "Sex typing and socialization." In *Carmichael's manual of child psychology*, vol. 2, ed. P. Mussen. New York: Wiley.

Mitchell, J. 1969. "The longest revolution." In *Masculine/feminine: Readings in sexual mythology and the liberation of women*, ed. B. Roszak and T. Roszak. New York: Harper & Row.

Money, J., and Erhardt, A. 1972. *Man and woman, boy and girl*. Baltimore: Johns Hopkins University Press.

Moss, H. A. 1974. "Early sex difference in mother–infant interaction." In *Sex differences in behavior*, ed. R. C. Friedman, R. M. Richart, and R. L. Wande Wiele. New York: Wiley.

National Center for Education Statistics, Office of the Assistant Secretary for Education. 1976. "National longitudinal study: A capsule description of young adults four and one-half years after high school." Washington, D.C.: U.S. Dept. of H.E.W.

National Organization for Women: A Task Force of the New Jersey Chapter. 1972. *Dick and Jane as victims: Sex stereotyping in children's readers*. Princeton, N. J.: Task Force.

Omark, D. R., and Edelman, M. S. 1975. "A comparison of status hierarchies in young children: An ethological approach." *Social Sciences Information* 14(5):87–107.

——. 1976. "The development of attention structures in young children." In *The structure of social attention*, ed. M. R. A. Chance and R. Larsen. New York: Wiley.

——, and Edelman, M. U. 1975. "Formation of dominance hierarchies in young children." In *Psychological anthropology*, ed. T. Williams. The Hague: Mouton.

O'Neill, W. L. 1978. "Women in politics." In *Female hierarchies*, ed. L. Tiger and H. T. Fowler. Chicago: Beresford.

Opie, I., and Opie, P. 1959. *The lore and language of schoolchildren*. London: Oxford University Press.

Ortner, S. B. 1972. "Is female to male as nature to culture?" *Feminist Studies* 1(2):5–32.

Paley, V. 1973. "Is the doll corner a sexist institution?" *School Review* 81(4):569–76.

Parke, R. D. 1981. *Fathers*. Cambridge, Mass.: Harvard University Press, 1981.

Parker, R. E. 1975. "Social hierarchies and same sex peer groups." Paper presented at the biannual meeting of the Society for Research in Child Development, Denver.

Parsons, T. 1958. "The interpenetration of two levels—social structure and the development of personality: Freud's contribution to the integration of psychology and sociology." *Psychiatry* 21:321–40.

——, and Bales, R. F. 1955. *Family, socialization and interaction process.* Glencoe, Ill.: The Free Press.

Piaget, J. 1952. *The origins of intelligence in children.* New York: International Universities Press.

——. 1962. *Play, dreams, and imitation.* New York: Norton.

Pitcher, E. G. 1957. "An interest in persons as an aspect of sex differences in the early years." *Genetic Psychology Monographs* 55:287–323.

——. 1963. "Male and female." *Atlantic Monthly*, March.

——, and Prelinger, E. 1963. *Children tell stories—An analysis of fantasy.* New York: International Universities Press.

Pleck, J. H. 1978. "Men's family work: Three perspectives and some new data." (Mimeographed.) Wellesley, Mass.: Wellesley College Center for Research on Women.

Polantnick, M. 1973. "Why men don't rear children: A power analysis." *Berkeley Journal of Sociology* 18:45–86.

Putnam, E. J. 1970 (1910). *The lady.* Chicago: University of Chicago Press.

Rheingold, H., and Cook, K. 1975. "The content of boys' and girls' rooms as an index of parents' behavior." *Child Development* 46:459–63.

Rosenberg, B. G., and Sutton–Smith, B. 1972. *Sex and identity.* New York: Holt, Rinehart & Winston.

Rossi, A. S. 1969. "Sex equality: The beginnings of ideology." *Humanist*, September–October.

Rowells, T. E. 1974. "The concept of social dominance." *Behavioral Biology* 11: 131–54.

Rubin, J. Z.; Provenzano, F. J., and Luria, Z. 1974. "The eye of the beholder: Parents' views on sex of newborns." *American Journal of Orthopsychiatry* 44:512–19.

Rubin, K.; Terrence, L.; Naimi, L., and Honung, M. 1976. "Free play behaviors in middle and lower class preschoolers: Parten and Piaget revisited." *Child Development* 47:414–19.

Rubin, K. H., and Pepler, D. J. 1980. "The relationship of child's play to social-cognitive growth and development." In *Friendship and social relations in children*, ed. H. C. Foot, A. J. Chapman, and J. R. Smith. New York: Wiley.

Rubin, Z. 1980. *Children's friendships.* Cambridge, Mass.: Harvard University Press.

Rubin, Z.; Peplau, L., and Hill, C. 1981. "Loving and leaving: Sex differences in romantic attachments." *Sex Roles* 7(8):821–35.

Savin–Williams, R. C. 1980. "Social interactions of adolescent females in natural groups." In *Friendship and social relations in children*, ed. H. C. Foot, A. J. Chapman, and J. R. Smith. New York: Wiley.

Schecter, D. E. 1968a. "Identification and individuation." *Journal of American Psychological Association* 16(1):48–80.

———. 1968b. "The oedipal complex: Considerations on ego growth and parental interaction." *Contemporary Psychoanalysis* 4(2):111–37.

Schlegel, A. 1979. "Sexual antagonism among the sexually egalitarian Hopi." *Ethos* 7(2):124–41.

Schroeer, R. S., and Flapan, D. 1971. "Assessing aggressive and friendly behaviors in young children." *Journal of Psychology* 77:93–202.

Schwartz, W. 1979. "Degradation, accreditation, and rites of passage." *Psychiatry* 42:138–46.

Sears, R. R. 1962. "Social behavior and personality development." In *Toward a general theory of action*, ed. T. Parsons and E. A. Shils. New York: Harper & Row.

———. 1965. "Development of gender role." In *Sex and behavior*, ed. Frank A. Beach. New York: Wiley.

Seiden, A. M. 1976. "Overview: Research on the psychology of women. II. Women in families, work and psychotherapy." *American Journal of Psychiatry* 133(10): 1111–23.

Serbin, L. A.; Tonick, I., and Sternglanz, S. H. 1977. "Shaping cooperative cross-sex play." *Child Development* 48:924–29.

Shantz, C. 1975. "The development of social cognition." In *Review of child development research*, vol. 5, ed. E. M. Hetherington. Chicago: University of Chicago Press.

Shepher, J., and Tiger, L. 1978. "Female hierarchies in a Kibbutz community." In *Female hierarchies*, ed. L. Tiger and H. T. Fowler. Chicago: Beresford.

Sherman, J. A. 1971. *On the psychology of women*. Springfield, Ill.: Charles C. Thomas.

Simmel, G. 1950. *The sociology of Georg Simmel*, ed. and trans. K. H. Wolff. New York: Free Press.

Smith, P. R., and Daglish, L. 1977. "Sex differences in parent and infant behavior in the home." *Child Development* 48:1250–54.

Smith, S. 1939. "Age and sex differences in children's opinions concerning sex differences." *Journal of Genetic Psychology* 34:17–25.

Stockard, J., and Johnson, M. 1979. "The social origins of male dominance." *Sex Roles* 5(2):199–218.

———. 1980. *Sex inequality and sex role development*. New Jersey: Prentice–Hall.

Strathern, M. 1976. "An anthropological perspective." In *Exploring sex differences*, ed. B. Lloyd and J. Archer. New York: Academic Press.

Strayer, F. F. 1980. "Child ethology and the study of preschool social relations." In *Friendship and social relations in children*, ed. H. C. Foot, A. J. Chapman, and J. R. Smith. New York: Wiley.

———, and Strayer, J. 1976. "An ethological analysis of social agonism and dominance relations among preschool children." *Child Development* 47:980–89.

———, et al. 1977. "Ethological perspectives on preschool organization." ERIC document no. ED 140 976.

Suomi, S. J. 1978. "Peers, play, and primary prevention." In *The primary prevention of psychopathology, vol. 3: Promoting social competence and coping in children*, ed. M. W. Kent and J. E. Rolf. Hanover, Pa.: University Press of New England.

——, and Harlow, H. F. 1975. "The role and reason of peer relationships in Rhesus monkeys." In *Friendship and peer relations*, ed. M. Lewis and S. Rosenblum. New York: Wiley.

Tanner, J. M. 1970. "Physical growth." In *Carmichael's manual of child psychology*, ed. P. Mussen. New York: Wiley.

Thompson, C. 1974 (1941). "The role of women in this culture." In *Women and analysis: Dialogues on psychoanalytic views of femininity*, ed. J. Strause. New York: Dell.

Thompson, S. K. 1975. "Gender labels and early sex role development." *Child Development* 46:339–47.

Tiger, L. 1969. *Men in groups*. New York: Vintage Books.

Tiger, L., and Shepher, J. 1975. *Women in the kibbutz*. New York: Harcourt Brace Jovanovich.

Tizard, B.; Philips, J., and Plewis, I. 1976. "Play in pre-school centres—I. Play measures and their relativism to age, sex, and I.Q." *Journal of Psychology and Psychiatry* 17:251–64.

Udry, J. R. 1971. *The social context of marriage*, 2d ed. Philadelphia: J.B. Lippincott.

Uexkull, J. von. 1957. "A stroll through the worlds of animals and man." In *Instinctive behavior*, ed. C. Schiller. New York: International Universities Press.

Urberg, K., and Labouvie–Vief, G. 1976. "Conceptualizations of sex roles: A life span developmental study." *Developmental Psychology* 12(1):15–23.

Van Gelder, L. 1979. "An unmarried man." *Ms. Magazine*, November.

Van Gennep, A. 1960. *The rites of passage*. Chicago: University of Chicago Press.

Vygotsky, L. S. 1957. "Play and the role of mental development in the child." *Soviet Psychology* 5:6–18.

Washburn, S. 1981. *Partners: How to have a loving relationship after women's liberation*. New York: Atheneum.

Weitz, S. 1977. *Sex roles*. New York: Oxford University Press.

White, S. H. 1970. "Some general outlines of the matrix of developmental change between five and seven years." *Bulletin of the Orthogenic Society* 20:41–57.

——. 1978. "Competence as an aspect of personal growth." In *The primary prevention of psychopathology, vol. 3: Promoting social competence and coping in children*, ed. M. W. Kent and J. E. Rolf. Hanover, Pa.: University Press of New England.

Whiting, B. B., and Edwards, C. P. 1973. "A cross-cultural analysis of sex differences in the behavior of children aged 3 through 11." *Journal of Social Psychology* 91:171–88.

——, and Whiting, J. W. M. 1975. *Children of six cultures: A psychological analysis*. Cambridge, Mass.: Harvard Unversity Press.

Wolf, T. M. 1973. "Effects of live modeled sex-inappropriate play in a naturalistic setting." *Developmental Psychology* 9(1):120-23.

Yorberg, B. 1974. *Sexual identity: Sex roles and social change*. New York: Wiley.

Zolotow, C. 1972. *William's doll*. New York: Harper & Row.

Zelditch, M., Jr. 1955. "Role differentiation in the nuclear family: A comparative study." In *Family, socialization and interaction processes*, ed. T. Parsons and R. F. Bales. Glencoe, Ill.: The Free Press.

Index

Abelin, E.L., 98–99, 100
Abernethy, Virginia, 144
Admiration, 64, 65, 160
Aggression
  groups and, 90
  inadequate, for females, 150
  sex differences in expressing,
    24–26, 29, 31, 36–38,
    84, 86, 90–91, 95–97,
    102, 115
Agonistic attention, 94–95
Alienation, sex role polarization
  and, 142
Androgeny, 144–45
Assault, 38–40, 56, 161–62
Attention, power and, 92–95,
  128–29

Bales, Robert F., 122
Bandura, Albert, 12
Bane, Mary Jo, 141
Bardwick, Judith, 125
Baruch, Grace K., 115, 116
Bem, Sandra L., 144
Berger, Brigette, 146
Bernard, Jesse, 136
Bettelheim, Bruno, 79, 147–48
Bisexuality, 121
Block, Jeanne H., 137
Bonsall, Crosby N., 179
Boys
  aggregate personality characteristics
    of, 1
  cross-sex identification of, 120
  cross-sex negative contacts of, 24,
    38–40, 58–70
  cross-sex positive contacts of, 22–24,
    58–70
  difficulty of, with gender identity,
    27, 31, 80, 101, 103, 107, 119, 120
  domestic role-playing of, 16, 29, 63,
    111

father's role in separation-
  individuation of, 98–102
five-year-old
  admiration by, 65
  assaults by, 40
  awareness of feelings by, 66
  bravado of, 37–38, 55–56, 120
  building behavior of, 6–7
  disagreement by, 47–50
  friendship of, 68–69
  gender identity of, 114–15
  group formation by, 130–31
  identification with father, 118
  insults by, 51–52
  molesting behavior of, 42–43
  rough-and-tumble play of, 35–36,
    60–62
  same-sex relations of, 31–34
  sex role playing by, 75–78
four-year-old
  admiration by, 64
  assault by, 39–40
  awareness of feelings by, 66
  bravado of, 54–55
  disagreement by, 45–47
  friendship of, 67–68
  gender identity of, 113
  insults by, 51
  molesting behavior of, 41–42
  rough-and-tumble play of, 59–60
  sex role playing by, 74–75
  vying for power by, 30–31
hostility to females, 102–7
humor of, 60–62, 69
physical interaction of, 96
power and, 6–7, 15–16, 30–31,
  49–50
same-sex negative contacts of, 24, 32,
  38–58
same-sex positive contacts of, 22
separation-individuation of, 28,
  98–102, 130

Typography and design by Jeanne Ray Juster
Edited by Jenna Schulman
Printed and bound by Malloy Lithographing, Inc., Ann Arbor, Michigan